hoofprints of the heart

Emma Lou,
May you always walk in God's grace.

Love
Dena Mason

hoofprints of the heart

*How Childhood Gifts of Love
Bestow an Enduring Legacy*

DENA MASON

MEDIA.COM

hoofprints of the heart

Copyright © 2021 by Dena Mason

All rights reserved. No part of this book may be reproduced in any form or by any means—whether electronic, digital, mechanical, or otherwise—without permission in writing from the publisher, except by a reviewer, who may quote brief passages in a review.

The views and opinions expressed in this book are those of the author and do not necessarily reflect the official policy or position of Illumify Media Global.

Unless otherwise specified, all photos are by the author.

Scripture references are taken from the New King James Version®. Copyright © 1982 by Thomas Nelson. Used by permission. All rights reserved.

Published by
Illumify Media Global
www.IllumifyMedia.com
"Let's bring your book to life!"

Library of Congress Control Number: 2021915809

Paperback ISBN: 978-1-955043-10-6
eBook ISBN: 978-1-955043-11-3

Typeset by Art Innovations (http://artinnovations.in/)
Cover design by Debbie Lewis

Printed in the United States of America

Dedication

This book is dedicated to my loving husband and farmer, Randy, who dedicates his life to me and to our three beautiful children: Shayna, Jared, and Maranda.

Contents

Dedication   v

Prologue   xi

1. The Spring of '77 — 1
2. The Drifts of Life — 19
3. For the Gift of Animals — 28
4. Wise as an Owl — 34
5. Gifts Throughout Childhood — 47
6. Harvesting into Fall — 56
7. Kindergarten Experience — 64
8. Halloween Fun and Scares — 77
9. Tidings of Christmas — 81
10. Christmas Joys with Family — 88
11. Winds of Change — 101
12. Report Cards and Closing Sale — 108
13. The Hard Fall — 118
14. Safe Under Grandma's Umbrella — 124
15. Kindergarten Work Ethic — 136
16. The J&J Café — 147
17. Memorial of Summer Memories — 153
18. Fourth of July Blasts — 166
19. A Moment of Change — 173

20.	New Chapter in School	181
21.	Tough Transitions	188
22.	Graduation Ceremony and Wedding Bells	194
23.	When Life Unfolds	203
24.	Life Stumbles	211
25.	Hospital Visitation	219
26.	Death's Sting	227
27.	Growing up Country	240
28.	Scrumptious Homemade Noodles on Track Meet Day!	249
29.	Home on the Range	255
30.	Eckley's Old Settlers	261
31.	Cowgirl Tough	271
32.	From Swimming Suits to Cowboy Boots	275
33.	Painting a Picture of Memories	283
34.	Behind the Summer Smile	295
35.	Into the Unknown	314
36.	Saved by Grace	320
37.	Gifts of the Heart	329
38.	Death: A Part of Life	341
39.	A Moment of Truth	348
	Discussion Guide Questions	364
	About the Author	372

Acknowledgments

My poems and this story come from the depths of my soul, where all experiences and the people who have touched me deeply continue to live. This story was inspired by the many gifts I received as a child and is my way of passing on those gifts to others while being an ambassador for Christ.

I give gratitude to my beloved parents, my sisters, all my beloved aunts and uncles, as well as my cousins on both sides of our families. I also extend my thanks to the many extended family and friends who are too numerous to mention. I love you all.

I would like to thank my in-laws, Merrill and Georgia Mason, who have always encouraged me to write. My love for you is eternal.

So much love goes out to my cousin Julie, who painted the picture for chapter 24. This story wouldn't be if it weren't for her.

I feel my writings are a calling from God. My prayer for this story: May these pages inspire you to leave your hoofprints on the heart of others while leading them to Christ Jesus at the cross of Calvary. Amen!

Prologue

"Yea, though I walk through the valley of the shadow of death, I will fear no evil; for You are with me; Your rod and Your staff, they comfort me." —**Psalm 23:4**

Time travel is possible when you ask someone old enough to understand the true value of a memory. Take a walk through a nursing home where old souls yearn for their younger years. They usually have no problem describing in detail the essence of their childhood. But they may have a hard time telling you what they ate for dinner.

I believe the moments that imprint a memory are the moments that shape us into the people we are and the ones we will become. Throughout our lives, we fall into certain routines that carry us through many weeks and months that lead to years of entrenched habits. But under the surface, there are many changes occurring that ultimately lead us into eternity.

Today is a day filled with such changes. I'm visiting Joyce, my mom's sister, in the nursing home. I'm here with her daughter, Julie, and Julie's husband, Joe. Aunt Joyce is lying on her bed in a fetal position, frail and confused as to why everyone is standing around her.

"I don't know why I'm in here," she says angrily. "Julie and Dena, please take me home. I don't want to be here any longer. Besides all that, I need a cigarette," she pleads, looking up at us with sad eyes and a heavy-hearted expression.

With her memory fading, I'm pleasantly surprised she remembers who we are—especially me, her niece.

"Mom, you'll be fine. You'll be in here for just a couple more days," says Julie. "They won't let you have your cigarettes while you are here. Let me give you some of your soup instead."

"Where are we, anyway?" she asks, confused. "And why can't I go back to the farm?"

"Mom, you haven't lived at the farm in over sixty years!" Julie says, glancing up and smiling at me as we both begin to chuckle.

"Oh, that's right," she says, coming to her senses and giving us a long stare. "But tell me again where I am. And why I am here? Since my husband, Max, died, it's been pretty lonely. Please, just take me back home!" She is begging now, and the desperation in her voice is heartbreaking.

"Mom, you need to lie here and rest for a while. They are taking very good care of you. Joe and I are going out for a bite to eat, and if you want to come, Dena, you're welcome too. We'll be back soon!" Julie says gently but firmly.

"Thanks for the invite, but I think I'll stay here a little longer. Then I need to get home to Randy and the kids," I say apologetically.

"Okay. I'm so glad you came into town today!" Julie replies, folding me into a tight embrace. "I'll call you later. Please tell Randy and the kids hi for us!"

As Julie and Joe walk out of the room, I linger for a moment, glancing around at the pictures of my aunt's grandchildren and great-grandchildren, which have been placed all over the wall. I walk to her bed and take her frail hands in mine, bending down so I'm at her level. "I'll say a prayer for you if you'd like me to," I suggest.

She looks up at me with cloudy, tear-filled eyes. "Oh yes, that would be nice. No one has prayed with me since I've been here," she says excitedly.

Watching her in this state, my mind is racing with the realization that time is everything. As I gaze into her eyes, I get the distinct feeling that she's waiting in the wings for her death. This is the same woman who would hold me upside down so her husband, my uncle Max, could tickle me when I was a child. Now she holds the vague clouds of memories in her eyes and heaven in her heart. A span of an entire lifetime is in the air. Time is slipping faster by the second, counted out by the ticking clock that beats in rhythm with her heart. Patiently, she gazes into the empty space in front of her, waiting for the curtains to open and for her life to melt into the beautiful lights of eternity where she will forever be set free. It's clear to me that some part of her already knows this.

I begin a little shakily, with a choked up-voice: "Dear Heavenly Father, I ask You to take Joyce into Your loving embrace and comfort her. Please take away her worries and let her know it's all right to come home to You. In Christ's name, I pray. Amen!"

"Oh, Dena Bob," she says with pure love, using the affectionate nickname my family gave me when I was a child. "That was a nice prayer. I want to go home as soon as possible! Then you can come to my house, and I will fix you a meal."

Still holding her hands, I reassure her that everything will be fine. "Aunt Joyce," I say, "let me give you a hug, then I need to get home to Randy and the kids."

She smiles up at me and pats my hands. "Get home to Randy and the kids," she repeats. Our embrace lasts about thirty seconds before I pull away.

"I love you," I say as I drop her hands. Then I hurry out the door, knowing I may never see her again.

****

I jump into my car and let my emotions take over as the tears fall down my cheeks. My full intention is to head back home to our farm, where my husband and children will be waiting for me, but an invisible longing pulls persistently on my heartstrings. Instead of turning south, I continue twelve miles east on Highway 34 to the small farming town and community where I grew up: the small town of Eckley, Colorado.

Eckley is a central location for those who commute to the towns of Wray or Yuma, where small businesses, grocery stores, hospitals, and local schools thrive. But sadly, Eckley has become a stranger to me.

In 1979, the only school in Eckley, the elementary school was closed and the town began to shrink down to about three hundred.

PROLOGUE

Most people who live around here are the local farmers and ranchers. The businesses here are the town hall, a post office, and the local bar and grill. There is also a volunteer fire department that most of the men belong to.

In this small farming community, the customs and even the language differ from those in larger cities. Once, my Great-Aunt Olive and Great-Uncle Wallace invited us to their house in Denver to eat dinner with them. When we arrived, no one was there. What we hadn't known at the time was that when they said *dinner*, they really meant *supper*. In Eckley, people eat breakfast in the morning, dinner at noon, and supper in the evenings.

As I drive into my hometown, I'm keenly aware of my childhood surroundings. I drive down Main Street, the only paved road in town, and take the first dirt road heading east. Aunt Joyce's house sits lonely, with her overgrown lawn turning to weeds. I continue slowly around the block to where I grew up. The formerly beautiful yard with a manicured landscape and flowers that my mom once poured her heart into has changed to a dirt yard with no green grass in sight. Driving down the road, it feels like I'm regressing through time, my memories flying past me.

I was born and raised as the youngest grandchild on both sides of my family. My position of being the youngest truly bridges the gap between my generation and the next. On my mom's side, my grandparents were blessed with nineteen grandchildren; on my dad's side, they were blessed with thirteen grandchildren. My mom was the youngest of one boy and five girls, and my dad was the fourth among one girl and four boys.

When I was a child, my sisters and I played alongside our cousins on a regular basis—with children constantly running in and out of our parents' homes. For the most part, my mom's side of the family lived in close proximity, and we saw each other often. My mom grew up on a farm just eight miles north of Eckley.

I continue driving back toward Main Street to where the old yellow stucco church sits with its high steeple and cement banister and stairs. I fondly remember all those church services and Bible school classes that I attended. All of us kids would use the cement banister as a slide and get in trouble for not using the stairs. On hot summer nights, my best friend and I would sit in the middle of Main Street in front of the church with our legs crisscrossed, facing each other to watch out for oncoming traffic, feeling the heat rising from

Eckley Community Church.

the hot summer asphalt and talking about our hair and boys as we wondered who we would marry in our future.

My future happened right here in this church, when I turned twenty-four. My husband, Randy, and I said our wedding vows under that beautiful wooden cross hanging in the sanctuary. I remember coming out of the church while the big bell above us rang, announcing to this community our union as husband and wife. As we walked down those cement stairs hand in hand, I clutched my beautiful, white Bible against my chest. Our extended family and friends threw wheat into our hair that had come straight from Randy's wheat field. At the end of the walkway were two bay Percheron horses (a surprise wedding gift from my dad) and a carriage, waiting to carry us to our wedding reception at the gymnasium.

The gymnasium.

Little did we know that our wedding would be our last big event for everyone to come together before the tragedy of cancer and heart attacks began striking our parents' generation.

I continue driving past the church and head down another dirt road. This time, I come to the place where I attended kindergarten. The two-story red schoolhouse is long gone, and so is the rickety playground equipment of wooden merry-go-rounds, high slides, treacherous swings, and those slam-your-butt-on-the-ground teeter-totters. Everything now has been replaced with colorful plastic safety playground equipment. North of the playground, the yellow stucco gymnasium still stands as a community building. Here, at the site of our lavish wedding reception, we once played on the floor scooters during gym class.

The rickety playground. Photo by Shara Berghuis. Used by permission.

PROLOGUE

I pull into the parking lot and step outside into a beautiful spring evening. I follow the cement walkway, strolling over to the bench swing that sits facing the playground. This swing is engraved with my mother's name, a tribute to her from the funds we received from her funeral.

Sitting next to the swing is my mother's memorial cement block, where my five nephews' handprints and names are beautifully carved. Our oldest daughter was just a newborn and my parents' only granddaughter; her tiny footprint and name are carved perfectly alongside her cousins'. But sadly, there are two missing links, as our two youngest children were not born when we poured the concrete.

As I think about Aunt Joyce, I stop to reflect. When my mom was nearing the end of her life and I was pregnant with our first child, my mom appointed Aunt Joyce to take her place as her grandmother.

Dena's parents' grandkids' handprints.

Years later, Aunt Joyce began to suffer from dementia and ultimately lost her driver's license. I volunteered to take her grocery shopping and out to eat with my kids. But as her health began to decline, I pulled away and stopped coming as often. It was too painful to watch her suffer.

Throughout my life, I've had the beautiful and humbling privilege of sitting next to loved ones as they've approached their dying hour. As morbid as this may sound in foresight, in hindsight I realize I've been given a gift. A person can learn more about life by sitting with someone who is dying than just going through the motions of everyday living. In an odd way, I suspect these experiences have prepared me for my own time of death.

I smile at the evidence of my family in this park, but my heart is heavy.

There's a sense of peace in this quiet, serene environment. But as the present moment clashes with childhood recollections and my knowledge that my aunt is nearing the end of her life, I marvel at how far I have come and wonder what the future holds for my family and me.

CHAPTER 1

The Spring of '77

"While the earth remains, seedtime and harvest, cold and heat, winter and summer, and day and night shall not cease."
— **Genesis: 8:22**

My mind begins to journey back to my childhood days and the impact Aunt Joyce and Uncle Max have had on my life. They gave me the freedom to always be a child and instilled in me my deep love of animals. And like my other family members, they taught me the importance of love and loyalty.

When I was two years old and my older sisters were seven and twelve, my parents decided to move out of the Durango Mountains and back to the Eastern Plains of Colorado, where they grew up and where most of their families were still living. My dad worked for the state and didn't want the stress of clearing off Wolf Creek Pass when it snowed. Our dad made the decision to go into an excavating business with Uncle Neil, who was married to Jean (my mom's sister).

My parents purchased a plot of land from my mom's other sister, Joyce, and her husband, Max, and put in a double-wide trailer. I was blessed to live catty-corner from my aunt and uncle, and only two blocks from my maternal grandmother's house. A path from our backyard led to Uncle Max and Aunt Joyce's backyard. In the center of the path sat a small, red barn. This was where my cousins, Curt and Julie, kept their horses. My oldest sister, Vonie, kept her horse there too. Behind the barn was a vacant plot of land where we would turn our horses out to pasture.

My cousins were considerably older than me—Curt by seventeen years, and Julie by thirteen—but they'd both sparked my early passion for animals.

Uncle Max, their dad, was one of my favorite people—a fun guy who was always teasing and tickling my sister Lori and me and making us laugh. We had silly names for each other. I called him Guy, Weirdo, and Dipstick, and he called me Kid. Nobody knows where the name Dipstick came from, but I think it was from a time when I watched him check the oil in his '57 yellow Chevy pickup. When he pulled out the dipstick, he told me what it was—and for some reason, it stuck.

One of my earliest memories of Aunt Joyce and Uncle Max was from the blizzard of 1977. I was four years old, and the world around us was about to freeze. That year marked one of the biggest blizzards on record. It began with gusty winds and swirling snow, which accumulated in high drifts and buried much of the county's livestock. Weeks later, they were dug out and frozen in place. Overall, it was a storm that devastated this farming community and the whole Eastern Plains, leaving many people in our family and the surrounding area in a state of deep emotional and financial loss.

The local radio and TV stations issued multiple warnings stating that this was not your average winter storm. Extra caution needed to be taken to keep one's family and animals alive. They were recommending that people run a slow, steady stream of water from all the faucets to keep pipes from freezing and breaking; they also encouraged families and neighbors to stay together and use a generator to run the appliances when the electricity inevitably went out.

My dad came home early from work on that cold and snowy day. As he opened the back door, all bundled up in his snow-covered overalls and snow boots, his brow was furrowed with worry. "Everyone, come to the back door and listen to me," he said. "Jan, you need to get bundled up so the two of us can go out to the pasture and help Max and Joyce bring the horses to the barn. This storm is a very serious situation, and our lives could be in danger. We need to do all we can to get some work done as quickly as possible."

Clearly not wanting to worry us, my mother interrupted, "It will be alright, girls. We're going to stay with Grandma for a couple of days. Uncle Max, Aunt Joyce, Curt, and Julie will be there as well. Grandma's floor furnace runs on propane, and it'll keep us warm. I want the three of you to take a brown paper bag and fold two pairs of jeans, a couple of long-sleeved shirts, pajamas, toothbrushes, toothpaste, and underwear. We should be able to wash clothes and shower once we get a generator, so we won't need too many changes. While we're outside, we'll lock the cats up in the shed to keep them safe and warm. And when we come back in, we'll all get ready to go to Grandma's house."

After telling us what to do, my mother bundled herself up tightly and followed Dad outside. The three of us ran and peeked out the window, but all we could see was the ice freezing over the windowsill.

Outside, my parents met up with Uncle Max and Aunt Joyce as they walked out to the pasture to bring in the three horses. With the snow coming down and the wind kicking up, drifts were already forming. The horses saw their humans and came running eagerly toward them. My dad grabbed a scoop shovel next to the barn and dug out the two-foot snow drifts forming quickly against the door. Inside the barn, the horses settled down and walked into their stalls. My mom threw some hay to each horse while Aunt Joyce ran some water in the trough.

"They won't have water by this evening when it freezes," said my uncle.

"I just pray the roof doesn't cave in on them," my dad said, sighing and shaking his head as he looked straight up.

"This is really scary," cried my aunt.

"We're going to get through this, I promise," reassured my mother, who had always been close to her sister. "The horses will be okay in this barn. They can surely go for a couple of days without water, and they may be able to keep the ice broken with their hooves."

"Now that the horses are settled in, we need to get back to the kids and also lock up the cats in the shed. So, we'll see you at Mom's in a little bit," said Mom.

Together, my parents trudged through the drifts while fighting visibility. They wound their way through the path that led back to the little white shed in our yard. Expecting the cats to be in the shed, they were surprised when they were gone.

My dad took my mom's hand, and together they trudged back behind the garage. All seven cats were nestled under the wood pile. When they saw my parents, they immediately meowed and followed them to the shed.

My dad ran back to the house and shouted through the back door. "Lori, pour some dry calf milk into the bucket and mix it with water for the cats, then bring it to me! And you need to hurry!" he hollered, not wanting to track snow into the house.

Lori usually performed all the cat-related chores and was accustomed to making their milk. "Are the cats going to be all right?" she asked anxiously.

"They'll be fine," he reassured her. Lori rushed as fast as she could, trying to ensure that she wouldn't spill the milk as she tiptoed to the door.

Dad took the milk and stomped back to the shed. He poured the milk into a bowl, and the cats quickly slurped it up. Two other bowls sat on the ground close by. Dad poured cat food into them, then left the bag wide open. After making sure the cats were settled, Mom and Dad hurried back into the house.

Scurrying to get everything ready, Mom took out two coolers from the coat closet and began to pack some food for our trip. Then she rushed around the house, packing her and Dad's suitcases, trying to remember everything we might need for the next couple of days. Looking over at us, she asked, "Are you girls ready?"

She then checked the clothes we had packed ourselves and began to carry everything to the door, including the two dog beds and some dog food.

"It's time to go," Dad announced. "Vonie, you need to help Dena get ready."

We began digging through the glove basket to find matching pairs. We finally gave up and put on whatever we could find, recognizing the urgency in the moment.

Vonie tried to help me put on my winter clothes. "Hold out your hand and stretch out all your fingers, like this!" she said, showing me with her own hands how to do it. I stretched out my fingers, and Vonie tried to push each finger into place.

"My two middle fingers are stuck together!" I cried out.

"Dena, you have to stretch out your fingers to get these on right. Now hurry up, we have to leave!" Vonie snapped.

It took a couple of tries for Vonie to finally get one glove over each of my fingers. The third try was a charm, but then it was time for the next glove.

Vonie gave an impatient sigh. "Why do I have to be the one to help you get these things on?" She looked over at Mom. "She could just go outside and be in the vehicle in a second. She'd be okay without them," she griped.

"No!" Mom sternly said. "It's too cold to go out there without gloves. Come here, Dena, so I can help you." In one attempt, Mom had the other glove on. Next, she helped me slip on my snowsuit and boots. Then she zipped Lori's and my coat all the way up to our chins. "Now that you are dressed for the winter weather, Dad and I will load everything into the pickup, including these buckets to store for water. When we have everything loaded, we'll come back for you and the dogs."

Coming back into the house, I noticed my parents' cheeks were bright red, and my mom had snow on her cap. "Okay, Vonie, you take Gidget and I'll take Snapper. Earle, you carry Dena. Lori, you grab my hand, and we'll all run out to the pickup."

As we stepped outside, I was taken aback at how bad the wind was. I buried my head in my dad's chest and closed my eyes, tightly wrapping my tiny arms around his neck. In the next minute, we were both on the ground. I felt stunned and disoriented, and through the wind and snow, I couldn't tell what was actually happening. My dad crawled to me on all fours, "Are you all right?" he shouted, leaning into me so I could hear him above the wind. I began crying. Dad stood up and got his bearings before carrying me to our blue Ford pickup.

I looked out the window to see our entire world turning white. Although I felt safe and sheltered, I was still crying. Lori held my hand and kept repeating that we'd be fine. I wasn't scared, just surprised that we had fallen and that my cheeks were cold and beginning to numb.

My dad's voice was panic-stricken as he began to drive. "I can't even see the road. This reminds me of Wolf Creek Pass."

"At least there's not a thousand-foot drop-off cliff!" Mom replied.

My parents both rolled down their windows as the wind came through, making us shiver. They both navigated the way to my grandma's house, which was only two blocks away.

When we arrived, Uncle Max, Aunt Joyce, Curt, and Julie met us out in the yard. My sisters carried our dogs and my dad carried me, while Mom, my aunt and uncle, and my cousins grabbed the rest of our belongings.

Once inside, we began shedding our winter attire. Mom took our gloves and set them close to the floor furnace. When I first began to crawl, I would get a spanking if I even came close to this furnace. On this day, though, my dad picked me up and stood right on top of it. I could feel the heat from my tiny toes all the way to my ears.

Uncle Max clapped his hands and smiled at me. He closed his three middle fingers against his right hand and stuck out his thumb and pinky. "Here comes the bumble bee to get you, Kid," he said. As his hand tickled me, he took me out of my dad's arms and cradled me in his, giving me a raspberry on my belly. I just giggled and giggled.

Everyone began talking at once about how bad the storm was. My grandma came out from the kitchen and gave my sisters and me a hug. I deeply inhaled the scent of the delicious roast and noodles cooking on the stovetop and the freshly baked bread that had just come out of the oven. Mom and Aunt Joyce went into the kitchen to help set the table for a family blizzard feast.

"It's time to eat dinner," Grandma announced. "I have a special seat just for Dena!"

Uncle Max tossed me into the wooden booster seat, which was decorated with pictures of teddy bears.

"With everyone here, it reminds me of the TV show *The Waltons*," Mom joked as we all gathered around the two tables to eat our delicious homemade roast and noodles.

"Yes, it does!" said my uncle. "Let's make this a game. Everyone pick a character."

"I get to be Elizabeth," Lori insisted.

"No, I'm the youngest, so that makes *me* Elizabeth!" I protested.

"Yes, she is the youngest, so she should be Elizabeth," agreed Dad.

"That's so not fair," whined Lori.

"You can be Erin, Lori. She's really pretty, and she's a great *big* sister. You're a big sister too."

"Oh, all right, I'll be Erin," she said with a sigh.

"I'll be Grandma!" Grandma piped in.

"Curt, you can be Jim Bob," I said.

"No, I want to be John Boy," he responded, crossing his arms.

"I really don't want to play," Mom said. Dad nodded, counting himself out too.

"Okay, then Guy gets to be the dad, John," I said.

"Then I get to be Olivia, the mom," said Aunt Joyce.

It was settled.

"Vonie," I said excitedly, eager for the game to begin, "you can be Mary Ellen."

"I don't want to play!" she said.

I wrinkled my nose at her and promptly moved on. "Okay, Julie, you get to be Mary Ellen."

"Fine," said Julie. "Mary Ellen, I am."

"Who wants to be Jason?" I asked.

"I'll pretend to be Jason, I guess," replied Dad, changing his mind.

"And I'll be Jim Bob," said Mom.

"But you're too old to play the kids, and Jim Bob is a boy, Mom!" I argued, my hands on my hips.

"Ah . . . but this is just pretend," Mom replied with a smile. "It doesn't matter who you pretend to be, boy or girl, especially when there are more boys in that show than girls—and we have more girls here than boys."

"Then why don't you let me be Elizabeth?" Lori quipped.

"Noo!" I screamed. "I'm Elizabeth!"

She grimaced. "Okay, whatever you say. Fine, I'll be Erin."

I smiled victoriously as I slurped up a long noodle.

"Well, since we can be anyone, I'll be Ben," said Vonie. "He's the cutest one on the show."

"Vonie has a boyfriend," Lori started chanting.

"It's not a boyfriend," Mom corrected. "It's called a crush."

"Vonie has a crush!" I picked up the chant.

Vonie's face turned bright red. "Shut up before I hit both of you really hard," she warned, her fist in the air.

"That's enough," Grandma chided us all.

I was ready to keep playing. "Okay, it's time to go to bed. Everyone go to bed now," I ordered in my bossiest tone.

"Why do you want us to go to bed?" Mom asked, looking befuddled.

"Because then we can tell everyone goodnight like they do on the show!"

"But the day's not over, and we won't play if you get bossy, Elizabeth."

"Oh, she plays her character well!" said Grandma with a smile. "After we finish cleaning up our dinner plates, we'll play Go Fish, but remember, in *The Waltons*, everyone takes their plates to the sink to be washed."

"Yeah, and Mary Ellen and Erin get to wash them because they're the biggest," I informed them.

"That's not fair!" Lori frowned and crossed her arms, narrowing her eyes into two small slits displaying her anger.

"But Elizabeth and Ben get to dry them!" offered Grandma.

"I bet the real Ben never has to do dishes," Vonie complained.

All the adults began laughing. "That's not how it works in this household," Mom said.

"Uh . . . but I'm the youngest," I said in my defense.

"Exactly!" replied Mom. "That is why you get to dry them!"

Outside, the wind was howling. My dogs, Snapper and Gidget, were lying under the table with Uncle Max's dog, Toby, and Grandma's dog, Chico. They were waiting for food to "accidentally on purpose" fall to the floor.

Around two in the afternoon, as everyone but me washed and dried the dishes (I always got out of work by being the youngest), we heard a click and realized that we had lost our electricity. Peering outside through the window, we couldn't see past the porch. It was getting a little dark in the house, but the adults encouraged everyone to continue washing and drying the dishes by hand. The one nice thing about Grandma's gas stove was that even though the electricity had gone out, we could still use the stovetop to heat up food and water.

After the dishes were finished, Uncle Max took a couple of pieces of bread and sat down on the floor. He called all four of the dogs to his side. Chico the Chihuahua began growling at all his unwanted four-legged visitors.

"Chico," Grandma yelled, "if you can't be nice, I will lock you in my room where you will sit the rest of the time they are here!"

When Chico continued to growl, Grandma swooped him into her arms and locked him in her bedroom with his own piece of bread.

Toby quietly lay down next to Uncle Max. My uncle threw him a piece of bread as a reward. "Now, you two need to sit," he said to my little gray poodle, Gidget, and my little black Shih Tzu, Snapper.

Gidget sat immediately, while Snapper refused. Vonie had competed in 4-H with Gidget, so she knew tricks, and Snapper didn't. Uncle Max gently pushed down on Snapper's bottom and told him to sit again. As he sat, Uncle Max petted the dogs and spoke gentle words of praise. Finally, both dogs received their own piece of bread.

"This time, it's Elizabeth and Erin's turn," he said with a smile and wink. "Here, each of you take a piece of bread and tell them to sit."

Both Lori and I stood together with a piece of bread in our hands. "Sit!" we both said in unison. This time they listened.

"See," said Uncle Max, "Snapper is learning from Gidget. Make sure you praise them." We gave each dog a giant hug and also petted Toby for being such a good boy.

"We need to have Gidget be the dog, Reckless, from *The Waltons*, and we'll pretend that Snapper is the milk cow, Chance," I said.

"That would be okay, but don't expect Chance to even pretend to let you milk him," advised my dad.

All the adults burst out laughing.

"How about a game of Go Fish, Kid? I mean, Elizabeth," Uncle Max suggested.

Lori and I sat at the table with Uncle Max, Aunt Joyce, Curt, and my mom. "I will shuffle the cards for you, but you have to deal them out," Uncle Max said. "Give one to Jim Bob, John Boy, Mom, Dad, and Erin. Then give yourself one, Kid—I mean, Elizabeth," he corrected himself, smiling. "Now, Kid, you start. Look and see what you have in your pile, then ask me if I have something you want that matches your cards."

"Okay," I responded. "Guy—I mean, Dad—do you have this one?" I asked, showing him one of my cards.

"Dena!" chided Grandma. "You can't show him what you have. Here, I'll sit beside you and help you. We really need to work with you on your numbers. Now, ask him if he has a two."

"Guy—I mean, Dad—do you have a two?"

He grinned at me. "Go fish, Kid—I mean, Elizabeth. Erin, do you have a five?"

She shook her head. "Go fish, Dad!" she playfully said, wrinkling her nose with delight at our Walton play names.

We played Go Fish for what seemed like hours. The trusty furnace was still going strong, and we were staying nice and warm. As the evening came, the snow still hadn't let up, and it began to get dark inside the house. Grandma took some small oil lamps and lit them. She set a few on the table in the living room and one in the kitchen, and soon the rooms of the house began to glow from the firelight, casting dancing shadows on the wall. Lori and I sat in the living room, listening to the wind howling outside. It felt later than it was. Mom and Aunt Joyce made sandwiches from the lunch meat we'd brought from home.

"You and Lori need to put on your pajamas and then come back and listen to me read," suggested Uncle Max.

Grandma took our hands and led us downstairs, holding a small oil lamp. On the floor were three mattresses. On one mattress were the paper sacks we'd packed this morning, full of our clothes. We quickly changed in the darkness, with just a little light shining from the oil lamp my grandma was holding. Grandma gathered up the clothes we'd worn during the day and put them in a basket to be washed later, when the electricity was back on. After we were changed, Grandma lit the way back upstairs for us to listen to the story.

Uncle Max took out a book and sat next to the oil lamp on the table. He began to read aloud from *Little House on the Prairie*. We listened raptly to Laura Ingalls Wilder's saga about life on the prairie in those simpler times. And because of the lack of electricity, I could almost imagine I was right there with Pa as he rode his horse back home with a wolf trailing him the whole way. I breathed a sigh of relief when Uncle Max announced that Pa made it safely home, back to his little log house with his family and a cozy fire.

Lori and I lay down on the floor with pillows and fell asleep while listening to the soothing sound of Uncle Max reading to us. The next thing I knew, I was being carried downstairs by my uncle.

As he gently lay me down on the mattress next to Lori, he whispered, "Good night, Elizabeth and Erin!"

His words woke us up enough to realize that we were still playing *The Waltons*, and I had been waiting for this moment all day. My sister and I began to giggle and shout out, "Goodnight, Mom and Dad! Goodnight, Mary Ellen! Good night, Jim Bob! Good night, Ben! Goodnight, Jason! Goodnight, John Boy and Grandma!"

Everyone played along, hollering back their own goodnight chorus. Lori and I giggled and giggled until my mom yelled, "Dena and Lori, get to sleep *now*!"

The next morning, we woke to a blizzard that showed no signs of dying down. Eager to fall into our pretend Walton family, I raced to the kitchen, where cold cereal was waiting beside a bowl on the counter.

"What kind of cereal do you want to eat this morning, Elizabeth?" asked Mom. "Cheerios or Frosted Flakes?"

"What kind of cereal did Erin eat?" I asked.

"I chose Frosted Flakes," my sister said with a smile on her face.

"Then I want the same," I announced.

Since we'd lost our electricity, we no longer had running water, and the pipes were beginning to break and freeze. Also, we weren't allowed to flush the toilets. Grandma's freezer and refrigerator began to heat up and the frozen meat began to thaw out. Blood seeped out of the freezer and spread across the floor. My mom and Aunt Joyce took some rags to clean up the blood. Uncle Max and Dad pried open the frozen back door to the deck and set out crates of beef and chickens. Before long, the crates were quickly buried in snow.

That day, we followed the same routine as yesterday. We ate together at the table, then washed and dried our dishes with the water Grandma had saved in buckets. After every family meal, we worked with our dogs on new tricks. The focus of the day was teaching them to lie down. They took well to the task at hand and were fast learners. When the dogs needed to go to the bathroom, we put them out in the garage on the dirt floor.

One afternoon, Grandma went downstairs and came back with the game called Aggravation. "Six people can play this game," she said. "And this game will teach Dena—I mean, Elizabeth—how to count!"

"It's the first time I've ever played this game," I said, scratching my head and not knowing quite how to feel about this new challenge.

"Well, you pick out a color you want to be, and all these marbles with that color are your men. You have to roll a one or a six to get out. Then you race around the board to get home, and if anyone lands on you, they can send you back home and you have to start over," explained Mom.

"I'll sit beside you and help you," said Curt.

I quickly learned how the game was played. Rolling the dice for the first time, I got a six and put my blue marble out into the playing field. After a few more rolls, I landed on Uncle Max and sent him home, pointing my finger at him and laughing at him all the while. But as soon as I did, his next marble landed on me. He picked up my marble and sent me home, this time pointing his finger and laughing at me. I promptly went from laughing to crying at the top of my lungs in zero-point-five seconds.

"I think it's time for a nap," Mom said, raising an eyebrow. She carried me to Grandma's bed. "Don't you move, little miss, until you sleep for a little while."

I sniffed, quietly crying myself to sleep. When I woke up, it was getting dark and I felt better. I took my grandma's pink crocheted blanket and wrapped it around myself, walking out to the living room and lying down next to Snapper. I listened to Dad and Uncle Max express their worries.

"This is devastating. I just can't imagine how many animals and people have been lost in this snowstorm. I'm worried that local farms, dairies, and feedlots are losing their entire herds of cattle. It just scares me to death when I think of what we'll find when we get out of here," Dad said nervously.

"Not having phone lines working makes me feel a little nervous. I'm just praying no one needs help out there," Uncle Max quietly commented. "And I feel helpless just sitting in here all day, knowing those horses need water. I sure hope the roof hasn't caved in on them. The wind and the snow look like they're letting up. Maybe by tomorrow we'll be able to shovel our way out and hopefully get back to our homes to see how bad the damage is."

Dad agreed. "Tomorrow, the real work will begin. I'm sure we'll have to thaw out frozen pipes for people too!"

"It'll be a job to even find our vehicles in those fifteen-foot drifts out there," Uncle Max remarked. "Okay, I'm going to get back to reading to the girls early tonight. It'll be a long day tomorrow!"

At the end of the day, Uncle Max read two more chapters from Little House on the Prairie. This time I only pretended to be asleep so he would carry me to bed and tuck me in again. As he gently lay me down, we began giggling through the whole Waltons goodnight routine until my grandma hollered from the top of the stairs, "Dena Jo and Lori Ann, shut up and get to sleep—now!"

Today, while sitting on this park bench as an adult and thinking back to that magical time in my life, I realize that Uncle Max went out of his way to make everything fun for Lori and me.

Chapter 2

The Drifts of Life

"For as the rain comes down, and the snow from heaven, and do not return there, but water the earth, and make it bring forth and bud, that it may give seed to the sower and bread to the eater." —**Isaiah 55:10**

Living on a farm with my husband, I realize how scary and devastating the entire experience was for the surrounding community, who were rapidly losing their livestock.

Early on the fifth morning, I woke to the sound of a tractor in front of the house. The local farmers and ranchers were clearing the roads, and Eckley's maintenance man was running the town's road grader. Even as a four-year-old, it was obvious that this small community came together to help in a big way.

My mom's oldest brother, Keith, and his wife, Dolores, lived out on the farm where my mom and her five siblings grew up. That morning, he began clearing the snow on his farm and digging out the cattle he'd lost, then he began piling the snow into a big hill. When he finished his snow-related chores at the farm, he drove his tractor eight miles into Eckley, clearing a pathway on the road. He also brought in a generator for Grandma's house. Uncle Keith carefully dug out our cars and our neighbor's yard, as well as other vehicles buried under the drifts. He paved a path over to our barn and our shed as he moved huge piles of snow.

Since our electricity was being run by the generator, Uncle Max and Dad dug out the crates of meat, then brought them back to the freezer. Mom and Aunt Joyce took the frozen chickens and set them into a bucket of salt water to unfreeze. We still didn't have running water, so we continued to melt snow on the stovetop.

In the meantime, Dad and Uncle Max finally got their vehicles started by using jumper cables hooked to Uncle Keith's tractor. Then they drove over to our homes and barn. The horses were excited to see their humans. As my dad later told me, they ran outside after their door was opened, but the drifts were too high to go far. They ran back and forth by the barn door, where Uncle Keith had cleared a path for them with his tractor. They kicked up their hooves, excited to be outside.

Uncle Max took an axe and broke the ice while Dad poured the buckets of water, which we'd saved on that first day, into the trough. The horses heard the ice breaking, and greedily came running to take a drink. After the horses were taken care of, the cats were set free and immediately ran out to get a drink of water that my dad poured into a bowl. I was relieved to hear that they had all survived.

Back at Grandma's house, Uncle Keith insisted, "These kids need to get out of the house for a while. Out at the farm, I made a big hill for sledding. The sun is out, and I made sure the road is clear. The tractor has to stay here to run the generator. I need a ride back out to the farm. Why don't you come out with me and go sledding?"

Nobody argued with that. We'd all developed a bit of cabin fever over the last several days. Mom, Aunt Joyce, Julie, Vonie, Lori, and I headed out to the farm for some sledding.

At the farm, Aunt Dolores met us outside with two sleds. The hill was so big and slick that it was hard to climb. My mom helped me, though, taking small steps at a time and setting me up ahead of her as we climbed.

"Hold on to the sled string, Dena," Mom ordered. Then she lifted me up even higher, until we were finally at the top of the hill.

"You can't keep carrying her up there like that," my uncle scolded.

"But she can't make it up here unless I help her," said Mom. "And Lori is having a hard time climbing this hill too."

"I have a solution," said Aunt Dolores. She ran to the front of the house and came back with a snow shovel. She turned the shovel over and shaped the snow into steps, packing it down as she climbed.

Now, both Lori and I could make it to the top of the hill with the steps Aunt Dolores had created. We were also able to pull our sleds behind us. On that cold and sunny day, everyone gleefully took turns sledding down the hill. It was the first time I had ever been sledding like this. My tummy felt like it was being tickled. Vonie and Julie took turns going down, and so did Lori and I. Then my mom and Aunt Joyce jumped on behind us, and we all sledded down together, giggling our troubles away.

When we arrived back into town, Grandma had hot chocolate and marshmallows waiting for us.

"We'll stay at Grandma's for a couple more days," Dad informed us. "The electricity won't be on, and we still need heat. But with the generator, we can make hot meals again."

As the evening fell, it wasn't as dark as usual because of the electricity from the generator. Mom and Aunt Joyce were busily talking and standing over the kitchen sink. They were each holding a butcher knife and cutting up a chicken. Every Sunday, we had our own ritual of fried chicken at our house, and so did Aunt Joyce's family. It began every Saturday morning. First, they'd take a chicken out of the freezer, set it in a bucket of water, and pour a lot of salt over it. In the evening, they would tear off the skin and cut each part into individual pieces. After cutting up the chickens, they placed them back into a fresh bucket of clean water with more salt poured over the top. Then they placed it in the refrigerator, keeping it cool overnight. On Sunday mornings, they rolled each piece into flour, salt, and pepper, then fried it in the hot electric skillet that was filled with Crisco oil, while also preparing the trimmings. "The salt helps thaw out the chicken and also helps draw out the blood," Mom explained. The dogs and cats always ate the remaining skin as a treat.

Tonight, as Mom and Aunt Joyce cut up the chickens, Uncle Max finished reading *Little House on the Prairie*. Even though I was awake, he carried me downstairs and we went through the whole Walton family goodnight ritual.

The next morning, I awoke to the delicious smell of a hot, fried-chicken Sunday meal that immediately stirred me out of my slumber. Walking up the stairs, I could hear the chicken sizzling in the hot skillet. Vonie was peeling potatoes for potatoes and gravy. Grandma was showing Lori how to bake bread. There were fresh canned green beans from Grandma's garden and frozen corn on the cob from Uncle Keith's cornfield. Julie was tearing up lettuce and cutting up some cucumbers for a fresh green salad, while Grandma was also making her homemade macaroni and cheese for us. Sunday dinners were something I took for granted as a child, but these particular meals were by far the best I have ever eaten in my life.

After our delicious dinner was over and the dishes were dried, Vonie and Julie began bundling up to go outside and play in the snow. "You can't come out until we come get you," Vonie ordered us.

"Yes, we are going to make a surprise for you and Lori," said Julie.

While they were outside, Lori and I played with our dolls. We waited impatiently until they came back in to get us. They helped us bundle up tightly before leading us outside. Julie was an artist at heart. She and Vonie had created three snowgirls to represent my sisters and me. They used carrots for the noses and grapes for the eyes and mouth. They put a pair of gloves on twigs, which they used for arms, draped scarves around the necks, and placed snow caps on each of their heads. They even took some of Grandma's yarn and cut it for Vonie's and my blonde hair and Lori's dark hair. Lori and I were so excited. We named them Elizabeth, Erin, and Ben.

As Lori and I stood there admiring the snowgirls, Vonie and Julie grabbed some snow and formed a snowball, throwing it at us. "Got ya!" they both hollered.

Mom formed two more snowballs and handed them to Lori and me. "Get Julie and Vonie back. Throw it hard at them!" she said, laughing. I took off through the yard, where the snow was deep. I fell straight down, giggling. Lori came and lay right beside me.

"If you two start spreading your arms way above your heads and your legs as far apart as they will go, then bring your arms back to your side and close your legs tight over and over again, you'll create snow angels!" suggested Mom.

Both Lori and I stretched out our arms and legs, in and out, over and over. When we grew tired, Mom reached out her hand to help us stand straight up so we wouldn't mess up our snow angels. The snow looked magical, and it really did feel as if two glistening angels were watching over us—even though they were imprinted into the ground.

"That is so pretty!" Lori commented.

"It is!" I replied.

As the sun began to set and the cold swept in, we went inside the house and unbundled our snow clothes by the floor furnace. Aunt Joyce brought us a plate of leftover chicken and sat us down at the card table in the living room. Looking outside, we could see the creations we'd made in the snow and began to fantasize that the angels and snowgirls were alive. We were still giggling and giddy when my mom ran into the bathroom, crying, "No! This can't be happening!"

Aunt Joyce came running behind her. "Jan, wait! Let me at least talk to you!" she called out, her eyes also streaming with tears.

Lori's and my laughter turned to shock and terror. We stopped and stared at each other with our mouths wide open, worried and mystified as to why our mom and Aunt Joyce were crying. I crawled out of my chair to follow them into the bathroom. Tears of confusion and anxiety were beginning to form in my eyes too. "You stay out, Dena," said my dad, shaking a finger at me.

I walked into the kitchen, where Grandma was sitting with her elbows on the table, covering her eyes with her hands. She was crying too. Uncle Max was standing over her and embracing her. "The treatments will work. You will be able to fight this cancer," he said softly.

I didn't understand what was going on or what the word *cancer* meant.

"Let's go downstairs," said Julie and Vonie. "We'll put on a puppet show with Grandma's old-man puppet and with the handheld horse puppet!"

Both Julie and Vonie led us downstairs to the dark and dank corner of the basement, where there was a big crack in the wall between two rooms. Vonie and Julie went to the other side of the wall, while Lori and I stood in the open room. The puppets fit perfectly through the crack, and Lori and I laughed in delight.

"I'm just an old man who wants to ride this here horse," said Julie, wiggling the old man puppet.

"But I won't let you ride me because you're too old to ride a horse," said Vonie as she made a whinnying noise and shook the horse's head. Lori and I giggled uproariously.

Mom came downstairs to see what we were laughing at. She had a happy smile on her face, with fresh makeup and bright red lipstick.

She seemed fine now, so I figured that whatever had been bothering her and my aunt earlier was probably okay now. That night, we fell asleep without even thinking about playing our *Waltons* game.

The blizzard of '77 wrought a lot of damage. My husband is ten years older than me and remembers climbing out of a window in their family's trailer to get outside. My in-laws remember their pregnant heifers being stranded in a herd out in the pasture when the snow began to drift. The snow covered them up until they were frozen in time. My husband and his family had to dig the cattle out of the drifts with their tractors before stacking the carcasses for the animal truck to take and make dog food.

Nevertheless, our family survived. The pretend Walton family shielded us from the seriousness of what was happening, and melted away with the snow until only the memories lingered. To my four-year-old self, it was an adventure I thought would become a winter tradition. It was pure joy to spend those days with my beloved grandmother and our extended family. I had no idea that behind the fun and games, the adults were dealing with their own sorrow with our grandmother being diagnosed with breast cancer. Grandma would be on a long road of battling this devastating disease that lay in front of her.

"Soul of White"

I glisten in the sun
My sparkles shine in beauty
My beauty is breathtaking
Yet
I can be deadly
I come silently
Sometimes loudly
In the wind, I drift high
Soft and sometimes hard
My personality can change in the blink of an eye
Trees bow down in slumber
Children create me
Angels flying in the snow
Snowman smiling
Heart so cold
Skiing, sledding snowball fights
The heart of my soul is frozen
I can bring a peaceful presence
Sit cozy by a warm fire
Watch me turn your world to white
Walk on me, don't slip
Snuggle with your loved ones
On a cold wintery night
Know my power
Be careful. Your fate lies in my soul of white

Chapter 3

For the Gift of Animals

"So let each one give as he purposes in his heart, not grudgingly or of necessity; for God loves a cheerful giver."
—**2 Corinthians 9:7**

Sometimes, when I look back, I learn something new about myself. For example, I recognize that at no point did I feel scared during that blizzard—all I felt was the love of family. I believe the storms of our lives slow us down enough to see in slow motion what truly matters: love.

The snow melted into the earth, giving the farmers good moisture for their summer crops. We settled back into the daily routine of our lives, forgetting all that had been lost. Time moved on and I turned five years old, but I wasn't able to attend kindergarten until I was six.

One day while my sisters were at school, Uncle Keith and Aunt Dolores pulled into our driveway with a horse trailer hooked to the back of their pickup. Keith was the one uncle I was scared of when I got caught doing something wrong—but I also had the most respect for him. When we saw them pull into the driveway, my mom took my hand and we walked outside to greet them.

"We were at the sale barn in Wray today when this cute little pony came through, and I knew Dena would fall in love with him. If no one had bought him, he would have ended up in the kill pen. He sold really cheap. Meet us over at the corrals and we'll unload him," Uncle Keith said.

I jumped up and down, screaming victoriously. I couldn't believe my uncle had bought me this awesome little pony, and I couldn't wait to get him out of the trailer! I had wanted a pony of my own for a very long time. When Santa came to our house the pervious Christmas Eve, riding on the town's fire truck to give us a sack of candy, I informed him that I wanted a pony. But Mom gently broke it to me that Santa couldn't bring me a real-life pony on his little sleigh. I was lucky that I got to ride with Vonie on her horse, Cinnamon, and sometimes with Julie on her quarter pony, Chiefer, and with Curt on his horse, Blaze. But it wasn't the same as riding my own. This news made me feel like a million dollars.

Unfortunately, although I was ecstatic about Uncle Keith's unexpected gift, Mom's brow furrowed.

Uh-oh, I thought to myself.

"Now, wait a minute, what do you mean you bought this pony for Dena?" she asked suspiciously. "You know we can't afford it, so you'll have to take him back. You're going to get me in trouble with Earle. What am I supposed to tell him?"

I immediately began to bawl. "No, Mommy, I want to keep him. I really do. Please let me have him," I begged.

"Just meet us at the corrals and let me unload him," Uncle Keith said. "He even came with a cute little saddle. Why don't we just get Dena on him and let her try him out?"

Clearly outnumbered, Mom let out a sigh and took my hand; together, we walked out to the corrals where Uncle Keith and Aunt Dolores met us to unload the pony. Opening up the trailer, Uncle Keith led out an eleven-hand little red pony with a small white blaze on his muzzle. He looked a lot like Julie's red quarter pony, Chiefer, only smaller. He had a tiny little saddle on him, just for me.

"Oh my gosh!" I screamed, running over to him.

"Slow down, Dena. You need to walk slowly up to him and pet him. Then you can get on him," my uncle instructed me.

Dena and her pony, Little Red.
Photo by Jan Ekberg.

I slowly walked up to the pony and petted his muzzle softly. He was perfect for me.

"His name is Little Red," Uncle Keith said.

"*Big Red?*" Mom and I asked in disbelief, not registering that he'd actually said Little Red.

"Pay attention!" my uncle scolded us.

"*Little Red*, not *Big Red*!" I said, laughing and correcting myself.

"That fits him perfectly," Mom said. I could tell her heart had softened at the cuteness standing before us as she reached out to pet him.

Uncle Keith picked me up and set me in the saddle as he handed me the reins. "Now give a little kick," he told me.

I gave a little kick. Nothing happened. "Use the reins to turn him," he instructed. I turned him to the left, and he did a full circle back to the adults. My mom grabbed the reins and led him around the corral. I was having a great little ride. This time, Mom let go of the reins and I turned him, and he walked completely around the corral.

It was 3 p.m. and Lori was returning home from school. She came out the back door and spotted us at the corrals by the barn.

"Where did he come from?" she asked in disbelief, running out to check the latest addition to our animal family.

"Uncle Keith bought him for me. Isn't he so cute?" I asked.

"He bought him for both you girls," corrected Mom. "Now, Dena, you need to get off and let Lori have a ride."

"Oh, all right," I grumbled.

Uncle Keith lifted me up under my arms and set me down on the ground. Lori jumped up in the saddle and gave a kick. Her legs were longer than the stirrups, but she was happy to be riding. Lori was a better rider than me. She had ridden Cinnamon, in gymkhanas, racing barrels and doing flags, and the last time she'd competed, she'd won a beautiful red trophy with a brass horse that sat on the top. But Little Red had a stubborn pony attitude. He promptly took her to the end of the corral, crow-hopped very fast, and dumped her face-first in the dirt.

My mom gasped and ran over to her. "Lori, are you all right?" she screamed. "Keith, you have to take this pony back with you! I'm not having a pony with that kind of attitude!"

I ran over to my sister, who was dusting herself off and looking sour. "Are you okay, Lori? I'm sorry you fell off!" I wrapped her in a hug.

"I'm okay, but I'm very mad at him," she said.

"I think you need to have a talk with Julie. If she rides Chiefer next to the kids on Little Red, he'll be all right," said Uncle Keith, apparently not too concerned with the pony's attitude.

Mom took the reins and tied the pony up to the corral. Then we walked next door to Aunt Joyce's and Uncle Max's, right into their backyard and through their back door.

"Well, hello," said Aunt Joyce, happy to see us. Her red earrings bobbed a little as she stood over the stove frying hamburgers while Julie sat at the table with an algebra book open. "What are you doing here?"

"Keith bought the girls a pony at the sale barn today. Do you want to come see him? I don't know if we're going to keep him, but he sure is cute," said Mom.

"Sure, I'll be right out," said Julie.

"He threw Lori off, but he likes me!" I chimed in.

"You had better watch it, Dena, or you'll be the next one to fall off of him," warned Mom.

"Julie, I'm thinking if you would pony the kids around on Little Red while you ride Chiefer, he'll do fine. Will you have time to work with them?" asked Uncle Keith.

Julie had a real talent with animals. When she was in junior high, a friend gave her a baby colt that was a quarter pony. Uncle Max and Julie trained him together, and Grandma was the one who came up with the name Chiefer.

"Sure, tomorrow is Saturday. I'll saddle them up in the morning and be over there around eight. We can ride down to the grain elevator where Dad works," suggested Julie.

The grain elevator was where Uncle Max owned and operated his business. Farmers brought their wheat and corn crops there to sell on big semi-trucks. It was right next to the train tracks, where everything could be unloaded and shipped out.

"I don't want to ride in the morning," grumbled Lori, still unhappy with this new pony's attitude.

"Dena, will you be ready by eight?" Julie asked.

"Yes! I can't wait!"

That day was a special one, but it wasn't out of the ordinary. Growing up, Lori and I were constantly around family and farm animals, and being gifted an animal was typical of the generosity in our family.

Chapter 4

Wise as an Owl

"Then God said, 'Let Us make man in Our image, according to Our likeness; let them have dominion over the fish of the sea, over the birds of the air, and over the cattle, over all the earth and over every creeping thing that creeps on the earth."
—Genesis 1:26

Some memories just stick out in my mind. For example, Uncle Max's grain elevator brings back not only the memories but also the smell of the dusty grain and the sound of big semis pulling up to the scales to be weighed.

The next morning, I stood by the bay window in our living room and stretched high onto my tippy-toes. I was watching for any movement down our old, dusty dirt road. My long blonde hair was pulled up into two pigtails. I waited as patiently as any five-year-old could. I had four sugar cubes in my front pockets and two carrots tucked into the back pockets of my blue jeans. A smile stretched broadly across my face. My brown cowboy boots even had spurs tied around them. Today was going to be a great day.

"She's coming, Mom. I see her!" I laugh-screamed. I took off running and jumping to the door, but Mom grabbed my arm and gave me a stern look.

"You have to settle down before you go out there. You know the rules, Little Miss Muffet. You'll scare those ponies, and Julie will be mad at you."

"All right," I said, willing myself to be calmer so that I wouldn't get in trouble or do anything to make her send my pony back. My mother took my hand, and together we walked outside and stood by the two most beautiful ponies in the world. Chiefer and Little Red looked almost identical, both with the same red fur and long manes, but Chiefer was quite a bit taller. Little Red was saddled again, just for me.

"Good morning, Dena," said Julie.

"Hi, Julie!" I said, smiling. Despite our age difference, I loved spending time with Julie. She always gave me rides on Chiefer, and we had so much fun together.

"Hi, Dena! Do you have a treat for Little Red and Chief this morning?"

"I sure do," I replied. I began to dig into my pockets. I pulled out two carrots, one for each of the ponies. The ponies' ears stood straight up and pointed in my direction. Their full attention was on me.

"Here ya goes," I said, smiling. "This one is for Chiefer, and this one is for Little Red." I nervously held out the carrots, which they eagerly snatched from me. I immediately let go and glanced down at my hands to make sure my fingers were still intact. The horses demolished the carrots in record time. I walked between the two of them and patted Little Red on the neck.

"You're a good boy, aren't ya?" As I turned around, I gave the same love pat to Chiefer. "You're a good boy too. I have one more surprise for you guys, but you have to wait until we come back home," I said, giggling.

"Are you ready to go?" Julie asked.

My heart raced with excitement, and I started to exclaim that I was better than ready, but then I saw Mom giving me the glare and I calmed right down. "Yes, I'm ready."

Mom gently picked me up and threw me on top of a tiny kid's saddle. I felt so tall and princess-like sitting atop the tiny pony. Julie held the lead rope, and I held my own reins.

"The first thing you need to learn is to click your tongue to move him. Can you do that?" asked Julie. She began clicking her tongue against the roof of her mouth. I followed suit, but all that came out was air.

"Keep trying," she encouraged. "Now, give a little kick!"

My little legs kicked as hard as I could, and we began to move. Little Red's steady clip-clopping kept the rhythm with Chiefer. I practiced clicking my tongue as we rode along. We were on a cowgirl ride to the grain elevator, and I felt like the happiest girl in the world. Snapper dutifully followed along behind us, wagging his tail like crazy. Eventually, Little Red began trotting. I giggled as I bounced around like popcorn and tried to stay on top of my pony.

The grain elevator. Photo courtesy of the Colorado Genealogical Society.

By the time we reached the elevator, the morning sun was beginning to heat up, and I found myself squinting in the sunlight. The horses' hooves clip-clopped loudly as they hit the cement scales of the elevator.

Aunt Joyce and Uncle Max came running out to greet us with big hugs.

"You weigh 1,600 pounds, Kid. Did you know that?" Uncle Max said with a wink and a smile.

"Tell him uh-uh!" chided Aunt Joyce.

"Uh-uh!" I said, making a mean face up at my uncle.

"That's what the scale says!" he replied insistently, holding up his hands like he had nothing to do with it. I looked at my aunt for help in defending myself.

"Tell him to take the horses off the scale and then weigh only you," said my aunt.

"Yeah, take the horses off the scale and weigh only me," I said, sticking my tongue out at my uncle.

"I'm surprised you're here. Did you learn to fall off your horse yet?" he teased.

"Tell him you're learning to stay on your horse, not fall off your horse," instructed my aunt.

"I'm learning to *stay* on my horse, not *fall* off of him, silly!" I quickly responded, laughing at him.

"If you don't keep that tongue in your mouth, the cat will get it," he offered.

"Uh-uh!" I said, giggling at my uncle's funny expression.

"Well, you'd better come in here and earn yourself a pop. I'm sure you're thirsty, aren't you, Kid?"

"Yes, Guy, I'm thirsty!" I shouted out as he lifted me off the saddle. Aunt Joyce loosened the saddles and tied the ponies next to some hay and water. Then she poured some water for Snapper. We walked into the old, dusty grain elevator. A truck pulled up to the scales, and my aunt weighed the truck.

The scales were a long cement platform where farmers parked their trucks and weighed them upon arriving. Then they would drive around back and unload their wheat or corn before coming back to the scale. The difference between the loaded and unloaded truck told you how much grain was hauled and dumped into the grain bins. Every fifty-six pounds of corn equals one bushel of corn, and every sixty pounds of wheat equals one bushel of wheat.

As the trucker drove out back to unload his corn, my uncle took my hand and led me out to watch. The entire place was cloudy with dust, and I began to sneeze.

The truck driver drove over the pit in the ground; underneath his truck were two small door latches. He slid the latches open, and the corn fell down into the deep, dark pit. In the pit, an elevator leg carried the grain underground to the tall, white grain bins that stood outside by the railroad tracks to be stored until a train came to load the grain and ship it out.

The truck driver eventually came inside to buy a bottle of pop and shoot the breeze with us as he picked up his tickets from the scales. "Looks like everyone is getting their corn in the ground around here. The moisture seems to be pretty good this year." Glancing down at me and giving me a wink, he remarked, "Looks like you have been riding the range on your pony. Is this Jan's youngest daughter?" he asked my aunt.

"Yes, this is Dena," said Aunt Joyce.

It wasn't long before my great-uncle Ed showed up in his '59 yellow El Camino. Uncle Ed was married to my granddad's sister, Cleota. He came in on a regular basis to check out the news around town and talk to my uncle. He parked away from the trucks and walked in with a smile on his face. He always seemed to be in a cheerful mood.

"I came in to supervise and make sure everything is running smoothly, and it looks like you and Julie are ready to round up some cattle on those ponies that are tied outside," he joked.

Peanut shells were scattered all over the wooden floor. "Here, Kid," said Uncle Max as he handed me a broom. "Sweep up a small pile of peanut shells and put them in a dustpan to take to the trash. That ought to be enough work for you to earn a bottle of Pepsi and some peanuts."

I struggled to sweep the shells and push them onto the dustpan. I didn't have to keep working much longer before my uncle was satisfied.

My aunt smiled and walked over to the big gray cash register. I heard the familiar ding as she opened it up and handed me forty-five cents. I ran over to the loud machine and dropped my money into the slot. I opened the door and felt the coolness of the machine on my skin. I pulled the tab for a Pepsi, and my aunt grabbed a bottle. My uncle took a can opener and popped the top. He also grabbed a bag of unshelled peanuts and poured them inside my bottle. The taste was salty, sweet, and very refreshing.

"Hey, Kid, your uncle has a surprise he wants to show you. But you have to be very still and very quiet. If you make even the slightest noise, you won't be able to see what he has," said my aunt.

"Kid, can you be extra quiet?" Uncle Max asked, looking a little doubtful.

"Yes," I whispered.

"Okay, let's step out back and I'll have you stand right here. Now just watch," ordered my aunt.

We walked out back to the area where the wheat and corn were dumped. It was dark and dusty. My uncle stood by the door, where slivers of light shone through. He put on a pair of white gloves and held out a piece of meat.

We waited patiently for what seemed like forever. My uncle blew a whistle. From the corner of my eye, I saw something glide above me. Excitement shot through my body, and I jumped up and down. The bird squawked and flew off, scared by my enthusiasm.

"Dena, you have to be quiet. You said you wouldn't make a noise," scolded my aunt.

My uncle didn't say a word. I hung my head in shame and felt tears forming in my eyes. I was sure that my aunt and uncle were mad at me. My uncle sat in silence for a couple of minutes. Again, he blew the whistle. This time, I watched and waited in wonder. I held my breath, willing myself to remain still and silent.

Uncle Max with his owl.

Inside, I was pleading with the bird to come back. After a while, I heard a screech and a hoot from behind me. A big gray owl landed right on my uncle's hand! I watched in amazement as the owl turned its head nearly 360 degrees. My uncle raised his other hand and gently placed the owl on his shoulder, then placed a piece of meat in front of the owl's beak. The owl eagerly ate out of my uncle's bare hand, gazing at him with his deep, dark eyes.

I just couldn't contain myself any longer. I let go of my aunt's hand and ran toward my uncle. The owl shot off in full flight.

My uncle frowned and said, "I told you to stay still. Now he's gone."

Once again, I hung my head in shame.

"Let's go finish your pop. I think your mom is here," he said.

When we walked back into the elevator, my mom was standing in the doorway. "I see you made it here in one piece," she joked. "Did you see the owl that Uncle Max rescued and raised from the grain bin?"

"Yes, but I scared it away," I said sadly.

"You just got too excited," replied my uncle. "We'll try again. You two had better head back home and unsaddle those ponies. It's getting hot out, and they need some shade."

As we walked out to the ponies, I dug deep into my pockets and found four sugar cubes.

"Make sure you keep your hand straight out so they can't bite you," said my aunt.

"Like this," said Uncle Max. He stretched out his hand to show me, then placed the sugar cubes in the middle of my palm. Then he placed his hand underneath my hand to support it, just in case I got scared and moved it before the ponies could eat their special treat. The ponies eagerly took their treats from my hand, slightly tickling the middle of my palm.

After a final hug, my uncle threw me onto the saddle. Julie and I rode back to the house to unsaddle and brush down our beautiful ponies.

When we arrived back at the barn, Uncle Keith pulled up alongside us. "How was your ride down to the elevator?" he asked.

"It was good! Little Red followed right along," said Julie.

"Yes, it was so fun!" I cooed.

"Before you unsaddle, why don't the two of you ride down to the pig barn? We have a bunch of new babies, and you need to come see them."

At that moment, Mom and Aunt Joyce showed up with Lori. "We'll all go," said Mom. "But this time, Lori gets to ride Little Red."

Mom lifted me off Little Red and threw me on top of Chiefer in the same saddle as Julie.

"He better not crow-hop with me again," warned Lori as she climbed onto the pony.

"Don't worry," Julie reassured my sister. "I have the lead rope, and he's been really good at following alongside Chiefer. You'll be fine."

Together, we rode down the dirt road to the pasture where the pig barn sat. Mom and Aunt Joyce walked behind us, chatting quietly. When we arrived, Uncle Keith was waiting for us. He jumped out of his pickup and lifted me off of Chiefer. Julie and Lori jumped down from the ponies, and Julie tied the ponies to a wooden fence.

"Thanks for not throwing me off," said Lori as she patted Little Red on his neck.

"See, he's fun, isn't he, Lori? I'm so glad Uncle Keith bought him for us!" I said.

Uncle Keith opened up the door to the pig barn. The smell of dusty corn and pigs was very strong, and it was a little dank and dark inside. The barn was long, with farrowing pens running down the sides of the walls. We walked down the center lane on the concrete.

In each pen was a mama with baby piglets on a dirt floor. They had straw for a bed. The piglets were suckling fresh, warm milk from their mamas. Uncle Keith's son, Tony, was feeding the pigs some corn.

"Hi," he greeted us. "Let me hand you a baby piglet." Tony climbed over the pen and picked up two squealing babies. Lori and I jumped back, startled by the loud noise.

"They won't hurt you, I promise," said Tony.

Lori and I gingerly came forward to pet the babies. I wrinkled my nose. Pigs were not soft like baby puppies. These pigs felt rough and coarse; of course, they weren't quiet either. But I had to admit that they were super cute.

As we petted the baby piglets, they eventually began to quiet down. Tony placed each one of them in our arms. We cradled the babies as they took their heads and burrowed themselves into our chests. After they calmed down, my mom asked us to walk outside for a picture. Both Tony and Julie stuck by us like glue in case a slippery piglet escaped out of our hands. Lori and I held on tightly and smiled for a picture.

Walking back into the barn, Tony took the babies and put one in each of his big hands, then climbed back over the pens to reunite them with their mama, who was seeing to six other piglets.

After walking through the pig barn, we said goodbye to Uncle Keith and Tony.

"You can ride Little Red this time, Dena! I'll walk back with Aunt Joyce and Mom," said Lori.

Uncle Keith picked me up and sat me on my pony, then he untied the reins and handed them to me before giving the lead rope to

Julie. Mom, Aunt Joyce, and Lori followed us back to the barn and then went to Aunt Joyce's house for iced tea.

Back at the barn, Julie, took off Chiefer's bridle, and tied him to a tree. Then she led Little Red to another tree. "You need to get off of him," she instructed me. "Take this leg that's in the stirrup and stand with it, then throw your other leg over the saddle."

I was a little scared as I held on for dear life.

"You're right there—just let go," she instructed. I was surprised when I touched the ground so quickly.

Julie quickly unraveled the cinch and took off the saddle and blanket, then returned them to the barn. She came back out with a brush.

"Here you go, Dena. You can brush him down," she said, demonstrating how to do it. "You need to brush *with* his coat, not against." She handed me the brush and watched me for a minute before she returned to Chiefer.

Julie came back and untied Little Red, then gently lifted me up so I was on him bareback. Without the saddle, I could feel every muscle as he moved. "Now hold on to a piece of his mane, and squeeze with your legs to hold on to him," she instructed.

Julie led both ponies out to the pasture, where Cinnamon and Blaze, came running to greet us. Julie lifted me off and set the ponies free. We watched them as they broke into a gallop.

I followed Julie back to the barn while she did the chores. She took some hay with a pitchfork and threw it across the fence and into the hay bunk. Then we checked on the water. In the small tank were eight goldfish. The goldfish lived in the bottom of the tank, where it didn't freeze, during the winter. But they were really hard to see in this murky water. Julie took some flakey fish food and threw it into the tank. The fish swam to the surface to eat, which made me clap my hands in delight. They were orange, very long, fat, and beautiful.

Aunt Joyce and Mom had fishponds in their yards. My mom built her pond from the rocks my cousin Mike and I had collected around town. She dug out an oval-shaped hole in our yard. Then she mixed concrete in our small concrete mixer and poured it inside the hole. Before the cement dried, she stuck all those rocks inside the cement. When it dried, we had a new fishpond. During the summer, some of these fish lived in our front yard, and the others lived in my aunt's backyard.

We kept Little Red for a while. But in life, everything eventually comes to an end.

One morning, I asked my mom if I could ride Little Red. "I hate to tell you this," she said, "but the gate was left open and he ran away. I don't think he will ever come back!"

As a five-year-old, I couldn't understand why he had run away. Did it mean he didn't like me? When I learned the truth, I realized that my mother thought it would be easier to break it to me that way rather than just tell me that they had sold him. But life soon fell into other routines, and while I missed Little Red for some time, he soon became little more than a fond memory. After all, he certainly wasn't the last horse I would ride.

Chapter 5

Gifts Throughout Childhood

"But do not forget to do good and to share, for with such sacrifices God is well pleased." **—Hebrews 13:16**

Growing up was always an adventure. Between being around Uncle Keith's adorable baby pigs and riding down to the grain elevator with Julie on horses, everything about my day-to-day life was carefree, and opportunities to play with beautiful animals never ceased.

That summer before I turned six and was ready to head to my first year of school as a kindergartener, our lives were extremely busy: Baby kittens were being born, cousins came to spend the night, and celebrations in the towns close by kept us busy. And before the summer ended, we went through our harvest routine of freezing corn from Uncle Keith's cornfield to eat during the winter.

One day, we were in Wray visiting our cousins, Mike and Janeil. Out of the blue, Lori asked if she could spend the night with Janeil.

"I suppose it's okay this time. But Dena, you've been sick with strep and need to come home and get some rest, so don't even think about staying here tonight or having Mike spend the night with you. There will always be a next time for the two of you to get together," said Mom.

I was disappointed and in tears as I rode back home in the car with Mom. Being the youngest, I was always left out of the fun. But when we arrived home, the phone rang. It was Curt, and he had a surprise.

"I got something for Dena and Lori today. Can you meet me at the barn?" he asked.

"Oh, what did you get them this time?" Mom asked, curious.

"Come over and see!" he said.

Walking hand in hand, Mom and I walked to the barn and opened the door. Inside stood a two-day-old Holstein heifer calf.

"I was at the dairy today, and they were selling these babies really cheap. I bought one for the girls!"

I couldn't believe my eyes! My disappointment from earlier began to melt away. "I'm so glad that I came home instead of staying with Mike tonight," I said, smiling up at my mom.

I walked into the pen and began petting the calf down her spine. Her long eyelashes fluttered, and she squinted up at me through her deep brown eyes as she held out her neck. Then she started bunting me with her head and almost knocked me down. When I tried to move away from her, she continued to follow me around, basically chasing me.

"She thinks she's hungry," explained Curt. "Baby calves like to suck all the time. And she thinks you're her mama! Here," he said, handing me the calf's bottle from across the fence. The big bottle was filled to the brim with rich and creamy warm milk for the calf.

The calf began to bump into me and demand her bottle. I tipped it up as she drank, and I watched her tail wag. I held on tightly with both of my little hands. She suckled it right down, nudging me as she did so, at times knocking the bottle out of my hands or almost knocking me completely over. I could tell she was very happy to have her milk.

"What are you going to name her?" asked Mom.

"I don't know!" I said, realizing I hadn't even thought about it.

"How about Roast Beef?" teased Curt.

At that age, I didn't fully understand where our food came from, and I thought it sounded like a fun name for a calf. "I like it—Roast Beef it is!" I said, smiling up at Curt.

"You don't want to name her Roast Beef, Dena!" protested my mom. "That's an awful name for a calf."

Since Curt was the one who'd gifted this calf to me, I wanted to stick with the name he had suggested. Curt laughed as my mother frowned. But I liked it, and no one was going to change my mind.

As soon as Roast Beef finished her bottle, I took a step back and handed it to Curt across the feed bunk so she couldn't reach it anymore. But she began to follow me and bunt at me all the same. I laughed, but I was a little worried she would knock me down.

"Let her suck on your fingers!" said Mom. "That way, she'll stop bunting you and settle down so you can pet her."

This worked! In fact, it was the only way I could keep her calm. I held out my right hand and four of my fingers. She put them into her mouth and began suckling. I laughed and cringed at the same time. The sensation was slimy and wet, with a bit of roughness. Her teeth hadn't fully come in yet, so it didn't hurt, but it felt tight as she sucked harder.

All evening, I sat with her, enthralled with this cute and funny creature. As she continued sucking on my fingers, I began to fall in love with her.

"It's getting late, Dena. You need to get home and take a shower and eat some supper. You can play with her tomorrow! And what do you tell Curt for buying this calf for you?" Mom demanded.

"Thank you, Curt," I said, genuinely appreciative but not wanting to leave my calf because I thought she'd feel lonely and scared without me. That night, I tossed and turned in my bed until I fell asleep dreaming of playing with Roast Beef.

The next day, I couldn't wait for Lori to come home. As soon as she walked in the door, I bombarded her with the news. "Come on, Lori, you have to come to the barn with me now! You'll never guess what!" I said, taking her hands and pulling her behind me.

"Dena, I'm coming! Slow down! Are there new kittens in the barn?" she asked.

"No, it's even better. Just wait!" I shouted excitedly, opening the door and leading her into the dark barn. Roast Beef began to bawl as she walked over to us.

"Wow, where did *she* come from?" asked Lori, her eyes wide open.

"Curt gave her to us! Isn't she super cute?"

Lori jumped in the pen and let Roast Beef suck on her fingers.

"Her name is Roast Beef," I informed Lori.

"Why did you name her Roast Beef, Dena?" Lori scoffed.

"Because I like the name!" I replied.

"It's okay, Lori. You weren't here to help name her, so Dena gets to pick the name," said Mom.

I felt as if I had Roast Beef completely trained. She followed us around everywhere, demanding to suck on our fingers. We spent most of the day with her in her little corral. But later, Lori got bored and left us alone. By the end of the day, I began to complain. "Mom, my fingers have blisters on them from where Roast Beef sucked on them all day!"

Mom laughed. "Well, tomorrow you are only allowed to get in with her while feeding her. You can't let her suck on you anymore, not until you get these blisters healed. Now go take a shower. You can play with her again tomorrow."

A couple of days later, Curt came to the barn with his branding iron. "It's time for us to brand Roast Beef," he said to me.

"What does *brand* mean?" I asked innocently.

"This is going to be tough to watch," said Aunt Joyce. "But it's something we have to do. This one is an electric branding iron. When it gets hot, we'll burn this brand into the calf."

I didn't quite understand what she meant by *burn* until I watched Curt put Roast Beef inside a calf chute with bars that held her in place. The branding iron was extremely hot as it burned the fur off of her and made its indentation onto her left hip. There was a horrible smell I'd never smelled before. Roast Beef let out a pitiful cry.

Aunt Joyce put her arms around me as I watched Roast Beef get branded. The smoke rose up and into my eyes, and tears ran down my cheeks.

I fell to the ground and buried my face in my lap while using my hands to cover my ears. "No! Can't you see you're hurting her?"

"I know this seems cruel, but she'll be fine. This is how we identify cattle, Dena. You'll understand when you're older," Aunt Joyce said with a hug.

After Roast Beef was branded, I continued sobbing my heart out and spent the next hour right beside her, petting and giving her my undivided love and attention.

It didn't take long for Roast Beef to heal, and by the next day she was running and bucking out in the pasture with the horses. At night, she would come inside the barn to sleep. She had a friend who also lived in the barn: Aunt Joyce's cat, Sandy.

One evening, Aunt Joyce was watching me give Roast Beef her bottle. She scooped Sandy into her arms and laid her crosswise, cradling her and stroking her soft fur. Sandy began to purr and move her body with my aunt's hand as she stroked her. "When you're finished feeding, come pet Sandy, Dena," my aunt said.

As I walked over to pet the cat, Aunt Joyce turned Sandy in her arms so I could pet her belly.

"Put your hands right here," she instructed. "Do you feel any movement?"

"I do!"

"Those are her babies inside of her belly, moving around and kicking. In a day or two, she'll give birth. Then you'll be able to play with her kittens and help me name them."

Sandy lay there, purring away as we stroked her beautiful coat of fur. I couldn't wait until she had her babies.

The next day, Mom had a surprise for Lori and me. Our older cousin Janet, who was nine, was coming over to spend the night with us. And just as she arrived, Aunt Joyce called us over to the barn because Sandy was ready to have her kittens. I had never seen anything be born before; naturally, I was excited.

We ran over to the barn, where Aunt Joyce met us. She led us to the hay trough, where two tiny kittens lay suckling on their mama. The babies were no bigger than the palm of my hand, and their eyes looked like they were sewn shut. I walked over to pet one.

"No, Dena! You have to stand back and watch. You can't hold them yet! They need to grow up some," Aunt Joyce explained.

"They're still wet and bloody, and if you get your scent on them, the mama might not accept her babies," added Janet, who was four years older than me and had apparently seen a lot more than I had.

"Oh, another baby is about to be born!" shouted Lori.

"I see it coming," said Janet.

I sat and watched, wondering why they were wet and bloody. And then I realized why. Lori and Janet had seen babies being born before, but what I was now witnessing came as a shock. Surely, this wasn't how it was done!

Something is definitely wrong with this cat, I thought to myself. Aunt Joyce, Janet, and Lori were oohing and aahing over this ordeal, while I stood there with hot embarrassment washing over my face.

Aunt Joyce rubbed my back and said comfortingly, "It's okay, Dena, this is how it's done."

I didn't say anything at all. We watched for a while longer, but nothing happened.

"Maybe if we leave her alone for a while, she'll have more," declared Aunt Joyce. "Let's walk back to your mom's, Dena. We can have some tea and then check on her later."

When we walked to my house, Mom asked, "Well, how many babies were there?"

"Three now, unless she has more," said Janet.

"What did you think, Dena?" Mom asked, noticing that I was quiet.

I just looked at her and shook my head, unable to speak.

"You should've seen her back there," said Aunt Joyce. "The look on her face was priceless!"

All of them began to laugh, but I couldn't understand why. I was convinced there had to be something wrong with that mama cat, and I couldn't get over how disgusting the whole ordeal of birth was.

A couple of weeks later, my feelings of disgust melted away. When the kittens' eyes finally opened, I started to play with them. And before long, our own mama cat, Sugar, began showing signs of having babies of her own, which excited me to no end. More adorable kittens!

One morning, our older next-door neighbor, Mr. Spicknel, called Mom and me over to his shed. He could hear newborn kittens meowing above his attic. Sugar had found a safe place to give birth. Mom and I found an old cardboard box and laid some old towels on the bottom to bring the kittens safely over to our shed. Mr. Spicknel climbed a ladder to the attic and reached across some boxes. He began handing baby kittens, one by one, down to Mom, who handed them gently to me to put in the bed we'd created for them. We counted six altogether. Sugar was nervous as she watched us take her kittens away from her. After the kittens were safely in the box, Mr. Spicknel handed us Sugar.

"Can you carry the box of kittens to our house, Dena?" Mom asked. "I'll carry Sugar.

"Yes," I said proudly. I felt so grown up carrying the box of kittens back to our shed as Mom carried Sugar. We set up a place for her with some milk and fresh cat food. I wasn't allowed to play with the kittens for two weeks, when they would begin to open their eyes. But I spent countless hours in the shed petting Sugar while she nursed her babies. She would purr as I scratched and petted her soft fur.

Thankfully, it wasn't long before they were running around outside. I took some string from my mom's crotchet basket and played with them. Their sharp claws would make me bleed if I didn't have an extra-long string. I fell in love with a little black-and-white kitten, who followed me around every place I went. I named him Frisky.

The summer was a busy one, playing with kittens and watching Roast Beef grow. By the end of the summer, she no longer needed her bottle and was eating hay with the horses.

Chapter 6

Harvesting into Fall

"And let us consider one another in order to stir up love and good works." —**Hebrews 10:24**

As the middle of August approached, our families' lives revolved around the county fair. Back then, we watched our cousins run barrels on horseback, and Lori and I spent five dollars that Grandma gave us for cotton candy, snow cones, and carnival rides. Our family traditions seemed to always follow the same routine every year. I understood that once the fair was over, the next week would be all about harvesting sweet corn for our family and getting ready for the new school year. I was excited for school because I would finally be a kindergartner.

A week after the fair, my grandma, mom, sisters, and I, along with many of my cousins and aunts, all piled into Uncle Max's '57 Chevy pickup and headed eight miles north of Eckley to the farm where my mom and her siblings had all grown up. Aunt Jean and all of us kids rode in the back of the pickup. Aunt Jean's son, Mike, was four years older than me, and her daughter, Janeil, was six years older.

When we arrived at the farm, Uncle Keith came out to show us where the sweet corn was planted. We all jumped out of Uncle Max's pickup and hopped straight into Uncle Keith's pickup. Grandma stayed at the house while we went out into the enormous cornfield to pick the corn.

Uncle Keith drove us out to the field and under the irrigation sprinkler, where all of us kids screamed with laughter when we became drenched. We stopped about a quarter mile down, and once we got out, each of us took a five-gallon bucket into the cornfield. We walked through five rows of the tall corn stalks until we reached the stalks that were considerably shorter. This was where the sweet corn lived.

"You have to stay beside me," Mom warned. "If we lose you in here, we'll never find you again." Mom grabbed a piece of corn in the green shuck and twisted it off the stalk. Most of the stalks had two ears of corn attached to them.

"Here, Dena, you need to try this. Just twist it until it breaks off, then put it in the bucket."

It didn't take long for me to get the hang of it. I could hear my sisters and older cousins in the rows next to us, but I couldn't see them.

"When we get our buckets full, we will walk back to the pickup and dump them, then come back for more," explained Mom.

After several trips, we had corn piled high in the pickup bed. When we decided we had enough to freeze for five families, we jumped into the back of the pickup, but this time we sat on the tailgate. Aunt Joyce held on to me tight, making sure I wouldn't fall off while Uncle Keith drove us back to the house. Lori and Janeil decided to walk back instead.

No sooner were we off than I heard a blood-curdling scream, "Snake!"

Janeil and Lori took off running as fast as they could. Lori didn't stop until she got back to the house, but Janeil took a couple of strides, stopped, and turned around to see if the big bull snake was chasing her. It wasn't! So she began laughing and hollering at Lori. "Run fast! The snake is right behind you!"

Lori was too far gone to hear her. Everyone was laughing except for Aunt Joyce and me.

"Oh, good Lord, look at that snake. Oh, I hate them," Aunt Joyce said, shuddering. "I remember when I was little and attending the one-room schoolhouse just west of here, and my friend Shirley was bit by a rattlesnake during our recess. Do all of you remember that?" she asked her sisters.

"Yes, we do remember that," Mom replied.

"Well, I've been so scared of them ever since," admitted Aunt Joyce as we both shuddered at the thought.

When we arrived back at the house, Aunt Dolores came outside with some sharp paring knives. All of the kids joined together to shuck the corn. As we shucked the corn layer by layer, fat, green worms came crawling out of the shucks. Some were eating away at the sweet corn. Mike and I held them and let them climb up and down our arms, tickling our skin. As scared as I was of snakes, worms didn't bother me in the least. My mom and aunts cut the bad parts off the corn, then threw the good corn into cool buckets of water. We then threw the shucks and the bad parts of the corn into a wheelbarrow to later feed the cows and chickens.

Inside, everyone made an assembly line. Aunt Joyce took a scrubbing brush and began scrubbing down the corn to make sure it was clean. Aunt Dolores stood over the boiling pots of water on the stove and timed the corn to boil for six minutes. Then she took it out of the boiling water and tossed it into several buckets of cold water. When it cooled, Mom and Aunt Jean cut the corn off the cob and placed it in a large Tupperware. Aunt Jean took small plastic bags and poured two cups of the cut corn into each bag, adding a twist tie around it. Then she put it in the chest freezer to freeze. All the leftover cobs were placed in several buckets as more treats for the cows.

Mike and I walked out to the corrals with our cousin Tony as he threw the cobs over to the cows. Then we walked to the chicken shed and dumped some over to the chickens. The chickens came to us and began pecking at the corn. They looked so funny with their ruffled feathers as they made squawking noises and fought over their share.

Aunt Dolores saved some corn for dinner, while Uncle Keith fried hamburgers on the charcoal grill. We each took a piece of bread and buttered it, then rolled the hot sweet corn inside our bread for the butter to melt all around the cob. The taste was salty-sweet and delicious.

The weather was hot, and our older cousins took the younger ones out to the stock tank for some swimming. It was a huge cement water tank with underground pipes that sent the water to the smaller tanks for the cattle.

Cousins in the stock tank.
Photo by Dolores Probasco.

Vonie and some of my older cousins had been working on cleaning out the stock tank. They'd spent two full days bucketing out the old, warm, green water and filling it with crystal-clear, cold, clean water. They were tired when they came home on those days. Today, though, their hard work mean the stock tank was finally ready to swim in. (Admittedly, sometimes I would rather swim in the slimy, warm tank than the cold, clean one.)

This stock tank was one of the biggest in the country: it was twenty-six feet around and eight feet in the middle, with a slanted cement bottom. My mom and all her siblings grew up swimming in the tank, and many kids in the area had also learned to swim here, including my sisters and me. Next to the stock tank was a tall tree where my granddad had put up two wooden diving boards when my mom was little. Mom told the story of sitting on her dad's shoulders as he dove off the five-foot-high board to the center of the tank where it was the deepest. She never remembered hitting her head on the cement, but I think it was because she must have had a concussion that put it all out of her memory. This tank would never get approval for safety, but it sure got the award for fun.

Usually, when I swam in this tank, I walked all around the big circle, holding on to the ledge of the tank where it was only two feet deep. I had to be careful because occasional slime on the bottom made it slippery, and my mom and aunts would warn me that I could end up at the bottom of the tank if I wasn't careful. Aunt Dolores always gave me a pink Snoopy float to hang on to. I didn't trust anyone to take me out into the deep part. But today, Julie had yellow rings to put on my arms. I quickly realized I didn't sink when I had them on.

"Come on, Dena, you can jump from the low dive," Julie said. "You might go under, but you'll come right back up. Just hold your breath until you do."

"I'll try it!" I declared. I climbed out of the tank and up to the low dive. "I've never been up here before," I confessed, suddenly feeling hesitant.

"Well, do you want to try the high dive?" Julie asked.

"No!" I said loudly. I stood at the edge of the wooden low dive, but I couldn't make myself jump. I had been shaking from being cold, and now I was shaking because I was scared.

"You've got to jump. You're turning purple from being cold!" shouted Vonie.

"Come on Dena, you can do it!" encouraged Julie. "I'll count to three, and you can close your eyes and mouth, hold your nose, and then jump to me. The rings on your arms will bring you right back up—and if they don't, I will!" said Julie. "Now, one, two, three . . . jump!"

I took a breath, and . . . I didn't jump.

"Let's try again: one, two, three, now jump."

This time I plugged my nose, closed my eyes tight, and jumped. The initial shock hit me hard as I sank down, but the rings around my arms brought me right back up. As I came up, Julie already had me in her arms.

"You did it, Dena!" she applauded.

"I did it!" I yelled, then let out a giggle. "I want to do it again. This time, all by myself. But only on the low dive, not the high dive."

And so it began: my true love of swimming.

I was in the tank so long that my lips chattered and turned purple from the cold water.

"You had better get out before you freeze to death!" said Julie.

The best part about getting out to dry off was that Uncle Keith's teenage sons—Tony, Kenny, and Tim—had put out a waterbed bladder to lie on. It got hot if you didn't lie down on your towel, but it was fun and bouncy, like a trampoline. After we were done swimming, Mike and I began jumping up and down on the waterbed bladder.

Dena on the waterbed bladder when she was two. Photo by Dolores Probasco.

"You had better quit jumping on that before you pop it, Mike and Dena," Uncle Keith hollered from the front porch.

Mike and I stopped in our tracks, looked at each other with our mouths wide open, and promptly got off the waterbed bladder.

After a while, Mom came outside, picked me up, and took me into the bathroom to get dressed before the ride back home. After a long and fun day of freezing corn and swimming in the stock tank, we said goodbye. All of the cousins jumped in the back of the pickup bed to ride back to Eckley. The days on the farm with my cousins, aunts, and uncles stand out as some of the most joyful of my life. I will always remember the experience of pure freedom and discovery, which made the difficult days to come a little easier to bear.

Chapter 7

Kindergarten Experience

"I can do all things through Christ who strengthens me."
—**Philippians 4:13**

Growing up in such a small community, I was blessed to know the kids I'd be attending school with before ever becoming a student at Eckley Elementary School. The red two-story schoolhouse was built in 1922. In the basement was our music room and our school library. Up the wooden stairs were two classrooms and two teachers. Mrs. Licht taught kindergarten through second grade. The other teacher, Mrs. Godsey, taught third through fifth grade.

I will never forget the anticipation of hearing those swings squeaking and kids hollering before I ever attended the school. From the moment I could ride my tricycle down our dirt road when I was around four years old, I would pedal over there about ten minutes before school let out. I would walk straight into the school and climb the wooden staircase to Lori's classroom and knock on the door. Mrs.

Godsey was usually reading a book to her class. She would open the door and invite me in. I walked straight to Lori's desk and sat on her lap, listening to Mrs. Godsey read. I remember her reading *The Lion, the Witch, and the Wardrobe* and being intrigued by a new world deep inside a coat closet.

When the bell rang, one of Lori's classmates would have the responsibility of dismissing the class by calling out each individual's name. One day, Jim called out Lori's name and not mine. We both sat there impatiently, waiting for my name to be called. When he didn't call my name, I yelled out, "Hey, won't you call out my name too?" The whole class burst out laughing. Jim's face turned beet red, and he said, "Dena too!"

On special occasions, Mom and I would walk over to the school when the Schwan's man would show up, and everyone, including parents who brought their toddlers along, would get an Eskimo Pie on a stick, courtesy of Eckley School. The sweet chocolate-covered ice cream melted down our chins in delicious trickles and stained our clothes.

On my first day of kindergarten, I heard my mom calling, "Wake up, sleepyheads!" Opening my eyes, I suddenly remembered I was about to embark on a new adventure. I was officially a kindergartener.

"Come on, Lori, get up!" I hollered across our shared bedroom. "Time for school."

My sister glanced at me with a worried expression on her face, and tears started to stream down her cheeks.

"Mom, Lori is crying!" I shouted. Mom came in and sat on Lori's bed, wrapping her in a tight embrace.

"You'll be okay. By the time the day is over, you'll have new friends!" Mom reassured.

"It's not fair! Why can't Eckley School continue past fifth grade? I don't want to ride the bus to a new town or go to a new school!" sobbed Lori.

"I understand," said Mom. "And believe me, I don't like it either. But this is something we don't have control over. Remember, your best friend Shara will ride the bus with you. She'll be at school too. The two of you will just have to support each other."

Eckley Elementary School only taught through fifth grade. A bus transported the older children twelve miles away to a bigger school in the town of Yuma. This would start a new chapter in their lives and would introduce them to bigger classes and the world of sports.

"Yeah, it'll be fine," my oldest sister, Vonie, piped up. "You can sit with me on the bus if you'd like."

"You're lucky, Dena," Lori wistfully sniffed. "You get to stay here and ride your bike to school."

"I can't wait!" I said excitedly. I ran and jumped onto Lori's bed, giving her a giant squeeze. "I hope you have a good day!" We looked at each other, and in unison, we crossed our fingers, arms, and legs.

"Here, let me help you get dressed and curl your hair," Lori said, quickly changing the subject and moving out of the mushy moment. "You'll be the cutest little girl in kindergarten." She walked over to our closet and pulled out a cotton dress colored with pinks, greens, and yellows. It was her favorite dress of all time. I had admired and wanted it for my very own, ever since it had been handed down from one of our cousins. Now, finally, it was going to be handed down to me!

"It's beautiful! Can I really have it?" I asked, shocked that she would even consider it.

"It doesn't fit me anymore, so you can have it," she said, smiling.

I felt beautiful in my pastel cotton dress. My long blonde hair was curled back against my face. I had brand-new tights and white shoes. My mother placed a small backpack on my back. I was ready for anything and everything.

"Go get your bike out of the shed and take it to the front gate," said my dad, a cigarette dangling from his mouth. "Mom will meet you out front with a camera."

At the back door, I was greeted by Snapper, whose tail was happily wagging. It was a beautiful morning. The doves were cooing and singing in the soft morning breeze. Together, Snapper and I ran down the grass hill to the little white shed. I kicked a heavy rock to the side of the door to open it. Three baby calico kittens came waddling and meowing from underneath the door. They were waiting to be fed and played with.

"I can't play with you today. I've got to go to school," I said proudly. I scooped them up in my little arms and gave each one a kiss on the head. As I put them down, they arched their backs and hissed at Snapper. Snapper remained unfazed and ignored them.

The little shed was dark and cool. I made my way to the purple bike. It had a long yellow banana seat and curved handlebars. The handlebars were perfect for sitting on and riding double. I kicked back the kickstand. I was extra cautious not to step on the kittens that had followed me back into the shed. I began to slowly back my bike out and onto the grass.

"Boo!" shouted a familiar voice from behind me.

As I turned around, I was surprised to see my aunt and uncle standing behind me. My aunt scooped the kittens into her arms and out of harm's way. My uncle backed my bike out of the shed.

"Are you ready to go to sandbox school this morning?" teased Uncle Max.

"It's not a sandbox school; it's kindergarten, Dipstick!" I shot back at him.

"Well, either way, I bet you play with sand. So that makes it a sandbox school," he quipped.

Dipstick pushed my bike to the front of the house. Aunt Joyce and I followed along with kittens tucked under our arms. Snapper happily trotted along, wagging his tail and minding his own business. Then, out of nowhere, Sugar realized that the dog was following her precious kittens. Before Snapper even knew what hit him, Sugar jumped up and scratched his front leg with her claws. The poor dog let out a yelp, and the kittens hissed and scratched their way out of our arms.

Snapper took off running to the house. The cats took off running to the shed. Aunt Joyce and my mother began swearing at my dad and uncle for not being able to stop it. I began bawling my head off. I had red scratches up and down my arms and knew the blood was going to get on my new dress and ruin it.

In the midst of all the commotion, Grandma showed up in her turquoise '57 Chevy Bel Air and parked behind a bus filled with innocent children. The children had their windows down, and they'd witnessed the whole ordeal. We probably looked like a scene straight out of *The Brady Bunch*. Lori was so embarrassed that she turned beet red and refused to get on the bus.

"You won't have a record player in your room when you get home if you don't get on that bus right now!" threatened Dad.

"All right!" she screamed. Vonie grabbed Lori's arm and pulled her toward the bus. Grandma and Mom quickly waved and yelled, "Have a great day! Love you, girls."

After my sisters left, Mom quickly turned her attention back to me. "Stay here while I go get a washcloth from the house. It looks like you could use some Cut-Heal Wound Care, and a Band-Aid too. I'll be right back," she reassured me.

My knees began to shake, and tears poured down my face. I just knew that the Cut-Heal liquid was going to sting my arms. "Please don't," I begged. "It'll hurt!"

"Come on now, Dena!" said Grandma. "You're a big kindergartener now. You can handle a little sting."

"It'll hurt though. It doesn't even hurt now, but putting that spray stuff on it will make it hurt even more."

Grandma shook her head. "Come on, Dena, be a big girl now."

"No!" I screamed. "It'll hurt really, really, really bad!"

Mom came back with the spray. Before I could run away, Uncle Max grabbed my legs and Dad grabbed my arms. "Look at me, Dena. When it hurts, squeeze my finger as hard as you can," demanded Dad.

"But I don't want to hurt you," I cried out.

"You won't hurt me," said Dad.

"Hold still, Dena," said Grandma. "The stinging means it's healing you."

In a matter of seconds, the spray was sprayed, the Band-Aid was on, and as I'd predicted, it stung.

"You had better get going on your bike to school," advised Dad.

"You don't want to miss sandbox school, Kid," commented my uncle, giving me a wink.

"You have a great day at school and pay attention to your teacher," lectured Grandma as she kissed me on the cheek.

Through tear-stained eyes, I jumped on my bike and posed for a picture.

"You be very careful while riding your bike to school. Make sure you watch both ways before you cross the dirt road," warned Mom.

I could already hear the squeaky swings and the kids playing at the school before I even left my house. I promptly forgot about the stinging on my arms and pedaled as fast as I could down the old dirt road. Snapper followed dutifully along behind me.

The merry-go-round. Photo by Shara Berghuis. Used by permission.

When I arrived, I quickly jumped off my bike and kicked the kickstand down. I ran over to the white merry-go-round, which was spinning fast, then a teacher grabbed my arm.

"Hold on there, Dena. You have to wait until it's completely stopped before you can get on. The rule is, only the fourth and fifth graders can push. The rest of you have to sit on the merry-go-round for a fun ride. If I see anyone sitting the wrong way, we will not let anyone back on. Is that understood?" questioned my teacher, Mrs. Licht.

"Yes!" I said.

The merry-go-round finally came to a stop. "Dena, get on," said a boy named Jonathon.

"You can sit between us," offered another boy named Jared.

The merry-go-round was on a slant and was very bumpy, making my teeth shake in my head as it spun around. It was the fastest ride I had ever been on. All the kids were screaming at the top of their lungs.

"Stop, I'm going to throw up!" screamed Jared. No one heard him but me. I could see he wasn't kidding. As I looked at him, his face began to turn green, his eyes tightly screwed shut, and as he tried to lean over the side of the merry-go-round, he lost it. The force of the merry-go-round shot the puke right back at us and splashed me in the face. Chunky vomit ran down my clothes. Luckily, the merry-go-round slowed down enough so that everyone scrambled off. I was so disgusted that all I could do was lean over the side and puke too.

Before I knew it, Jared and I had four adults standing in a circle and gathering around us. Tears were streaming down our faces. My body was shaking, and I tried to talk between breaths. It had been a hard day so far, and it was just getting started!

"What happened?" asked Mrs. Licht, concern and disgust in her expression.

"Jared!" I wailed between sniffles. "Jared got sick on the merry-go-round and (*sniffle, sniffle*) he threw up! He-he threw up all over me. Then I-I got sick and threw up too!"

"Don't worry, Dena," consoled Mrs. Licht. "Mrs. Godsey went in to call your mother. She'll be over here in a few minutes."

Although everyone was standing around us, no one came close or wanted to touch us. Jared still looked green, and tears were falling from his eyes, too. Just as we were settling down, our moms showed up on the scene.

Something funny happens to a child when they are having a bad day. They think they have it all under control until they see their mommies. Then everything falls apart. I'm not sure who got to their mother first, Jared or me. But the playground was flooding with our tears. Our mothers picked us up and hugged us as if we smelled like roses.

"Someday, we will laugh about this," Jared's mom said with a smile.

"Yes, when they are seniors and ready to graduate, we'll talk all about their first day of kindergarten," laughed Mom.

Jared and I gave each other a quick glance. We couldn't understand what was so funny about being so sick, or getting puked on.

"I'll take you back home, give you a bath, and change your clothes," said Mom. I looked down at my colored pastel dress and began to sob.

"I promise I'll try and get it to look like new again," she said soothingly. She picked me up and carried me to the car. Snapper jumped in beside me and began lovingly licking the puke from my dress.

"Snapper, you had better stop that!" yelled Mom. Snapper gazed forlornly at her and whined before laying his head on my lap.

After a quick bath and a change into clean clothes, Mom took my hand, and together we walked back to the schoolhouse. Snapper followed along and sat down to protect my bike. As we entered the building, we climbed the steep wooden staircase to my classroom. In my kindergarten class, there were eight students. Our desks were in a semicircle, with the first and second graders behind us in straight rows.

I felt a little embarrassed walking back into the school after being puked on and also throwing up. I hid behind my mom. Mrs. Licht came over, took my hand, and led me to the semicircle of desks where I was to sit. Then she handed me a sheet of paper with a birthday cake to color. My birthdate was written on the top. We then placed them on the bulletin board so we knew everyone's birthdays.

When school was over, Mom met me outside. She walked behind me while I rode my bike to Grandma's, with Snapper following close behind, as usual. We called out hello to the neighbors as we passed by.

We walked inside Grandma's house, where I sat on the couch while Mom brought me some graham crackers and frosting for a quick snack. Grandma was lying on her bed in the next room.

"How are you feeling, Mom?" asked my mother in a hushed tone as she walked into Grandma's room.

I knew that Grandma hadn't been feeling very well for a while now, maybe even years. She had been at the hospital for such a long time that she'd missed my most recent birthday. I knew it had something to do with cancer, but I still didn't know what that meant. I was just happy I'd gotten the chance to talk with her on the phone when she called from the city hospital. When she came home, she gave Lori and me each a stained-glass bird she had painted during her stay at the hospital. We hung them in our bedroom window. I loved the way the sunlight poured in, and lit up the colors on the glass birds, that reflected off our walls.

Today, Grandma came out of her bedroom in a mid-length pink dress, straightening her short, wavy blonde wig on top of her head. I knew she wore her wig to cover up her gray hair, because that's what she'd told Lori and me when we spent the night with her. She had many wigs of different shapes and lengths. Lori and I once stood in front of a mirror and put them on, pretending we were all grown up. I called her Mrs. Lori, and she called me Mrs. Dena. We both giggled, knowing we looked so funny in these blonde wigs.

"I was feeling better this morning when I was at your house as the kids were leaving for school," Grandma said, sighing. "But this afternoon, I'm just in a lot of pain. Can you come back to the bathroom and put some salve on my back? I have this awful burn from where they did the radiation treatments."

Innocently, I followed Mom and Grandma into the bathroom. The sink was filled with blood and clumps of gray hair. Grandma took off her wig, and to my shock, she was almost bald.

"I've had awful bloody noses since I've been back. And this burn from the radiation is excruciating," said Grandma. "This damn cancer is killing me!"

As she pulled down her dress, I gasped when I caught sight of an angry-looking red burn that ran up and down her back. My mom began to pour some salve onto it. I just sat there in silence. My thoughts went back to a few days ago when I had a bloody nose. Did that mean I had cancer too? I looked down at my arms; my Band-Aids were still intact. My sores were nothing compared to Grandma's.

As I fell asleep that night, I nursed the growing fear that bloody noses turned into that word I didn't understand, *cancer*, which was making Grandma so sick.

I learned three sobering lessons that day. Number one: for sores to heal, you have to make them hurt. Number two: never sit next to a boy on a merry-go-round. Number three: puking is not the best way to make friends on your first day of school.

Later in life, I came to understand that cancer doesn't equate to bloody noses. But back then, I never fully comprehended what it was and how it was impacting everyone in my family. I just knew that cancer made you sick, but I always assumed Grandma would get better over time. After all, my Band-Aids eventually came off and I got better. Wasn't the same true for my brave, beautiful grandmother?

Today I reflect on my own early understanding of cancer, which few people in my household talked about when I was a kid. Back in the 1970s, breast cancer was a private, almost shameful matter. Few people admitted that they had it, and fewer still wanted to discuss the topic.

I feel grateful that so much has changed. I have taken my own children on walkathons for breast cancer awareness, where we have always walked with pride and dignity instead of shame and fear.

Chapter 8

Halloween Fun and Scares

"Be strong and of good courage; do not fear nor be afraid of them, for the LORD your God, He is the One who goes with you. He will not leave you nor forsake you."
—Deuteronomy 31:6

Before long, I stopped worrying about my grandma, and we settled into our school routine. The chilly weather began to set in, and before we knew it, Halloween had arrived. That night, Lori and I bundled up to walk from door to door while we went trick-or-treating. Lori had dressed up as a Raggedy Ann doll, while I dressed up in the cute little clown outfit Grandma had sewn from a colorful polka-dot material. She had even made a cute little cone hat to go with it. It had finally been handed down to me after being worn by many other cousins. I loved the way the colorful material bloomed out at the bottom of my ankles and around my wrists.

That night, as we walked door to door, we heard crying emerging from the old high school. A terrified little girl was being carried outside by her mother. "She's scared to go in there," explained her mother. "The wolf costume looks so real."

Our school janitor, Marvin Tool, and his wife were living in the house that had once been the old high school my mom had attended. I knew why the little girl was scared. For the past couple of years, I, too, was terrified to go trick-or-treating in there.

The old high school Dena's mom attended.
Photo courtesy of the Colorado Genealogical Society.

When I was four years old, Lori had actually dressed up like Little Red Riding Hood.

"Trick or treat!" we'd called out when Marvin's wife opened the door.

"It's good to see you, my dears," she'd said. "But if you want candy, you have to walk over to the chair where the Big Bad Wolf is holding the candy." And then she took our hands and led us to the chair. I gasped as I saw the Big Bad Wolf sitting in the big chair and giving us a gnarly, sharp-toothed grin. With sharp claws and hairy paws, he gripped the big bowl of candy. I just knew he was going to grab both of us and gobble us up right then and there!

I screamed with all my might and ran back to my mom. Lori yelled, "It's okay, Dena. It's only a mask!"

Mom swooped me up in her arms and carried me back to the wolf as I hid my face against her chest and wrapped my legs around her body, holding on for dear life. I didn't want to face this wolf, and I screamed even louder. Mrs. Tool helped pry me off my mom and had me face him. Marvin promptly took off his wolf mask, which scared me even more. When he took off the mask, it looked like that wolf had died, and when he put the mask back on, that wolf came right back to life. I was convinced that at night, our school janitor could turn himself into a wolf.

But this Halloween, I told myself that I was going to be brave, smile, and walk right up to him to get the candy. After all, I was a big kindergartener now, and I knew that a mask was just a mask and nothing more. And that night, I did just that. Smiling nervously, I stuck my hand in the bowl and pulled out some candy. He jumped and shouted, "Roar!" This time, I startled and jumped backward, then I began giggling as he, too, started to laugh at me. It made for a fun and memorable night.

Over time, my fear dissipated during that school year. Sure, like all other small children, I had my moments, but I was quickly learning to be resilient and to face my fears—whether I was scared for myself or a sick loved one.

As I sit on this bench today, I smile at the memory our janitor gave us. Every time I go by this old high school (that has since been made into a house), I remember the old grey wolf.

Chapter 9

Tidings of Christmas

"For there is born to you this day in the city of David a Savior, who is Christ the Lord. And this will be the sign to you: You will find a Babe wrapped in swaddling clothes, lying in a manger." **—Luke 2:11–12**

Before long, the chill of October gave way to the frost and cheer of Christmas—a time I always eagerly awaited. Our entire neighborhood was lit up with beautiful lights and decorated with snow-covered windows from cans of fake snow. Aunt Joyce's house was my favorite of all; this time of year, her house was completely decorated in red, her favorite color. There were even red bows on the door and red ribbons on her Christmas tree.

But best of all, our much-anticipated Christmas program at the school was just around the corner. Music class was one of my favorites, and I was excited to be belting out some of my favorite songs in front of friends and family.

We started practicing our Christmas songs at the start of the school year. And tonight, we were singing "Up on the Housetop," "Winter Wonderland," and "Frosty the Snowman." I had to learn all of those songs, but the one song I didn't have to learn was "Rudolph the Red-Nosed Reindeer," which I already knew.

Ever since I could remember, we had always come to the Christmas program, which was held in the local gymnasium. We would listen to Lori and all her friends sing all the familiar songs, and before the last song was performed, they would invite all the kids who weren't old enough to attend school to come up on stage and sing "Rudolph the Red-Nosed Reindeer" with them. At home, Lori and I would practice until I knew the lyrics by heart.

But finally, tonight *I* was the one who would sing all the songs on stage. Mom made a quick supper of hamburger and homemade french fries while Vonie and Lori helped me into my favorite red-checkered long-sleeved dress, white tights, and sandals. When I twirled in circles, my dress flowed out around me. As Lori curled my long blonde hair, she wistfully said, "I wish I could sing with you. I miss Eckley School."

After eating, we jumped into our station wagon and headed over to the school. I was surprised that the parking lot was full of cars. Even the vacant lot across from the gym was packed. My mom took my hand, and together we walked into the girls' locker room, which sat under the stage. Everyone was talking really loudly, and parents were standing around with their cameras. Mrs. Licht lined us up and instructed us to say *cheese* as a zillion flashes went off at once.

A serious look came across her face, and she put a finger to her mouth. "Children, be quiet and line up," she instructed. "We will walk single file up to the stage, and I will show you where to stand, then Mrs. Flaming will lead you into your singing. Everyone sing loud and strong, okay?"

As we walked up to the stage, I squinted my eyes. A bright light was shining so hard on us that we couldn't even see out into the audience. But I knew people were out there because I could hear coughing and murmurs. We watched our teacher attentively as she led us through all the Christmas songs, which we enthusiastically belted out. Then, before the last song, the little kids from the audience were invited to come and stand by us and sing "Rudolph the Red-Nosed Reindeer." Standing and leading the younger ones made me feel so grown up. But the best part about this being the last song was that Santa had arrived!

When we finished our program, we headed back downstairs to the girls' locker room to meet our parents. I immediately grabbed Mom's hand and led her out to the front hall to see Santa and give him my wish list. For some reason, Lori was not as happy as she normally was to see Santa, and I couldn't figure out why. Then I remembered last year: she didn't get the skateboard she wanted.

As I waited my turn to sit on Santa's lap, Mom began to quiz me. "What are you going to tell Santa you want for Christmas this year?"

"I'm going to tell him I want a Baby Crissy doll!" A Baby Crissy doll was a newer version of the teen dolls that Lori and Vonie already had. This one was large and could wear real baby clothes. Its glossy hair could be pulled out very long. And if you wanted it to be short again, you just pulled a string on the baby's back and—voila!—her hair was back to normal! I found these features magical.

As I approached Santa, I was nervous and excited at the same time. My stomach did little flip-flops as I walked up.

"Have you been a good girl this year?" he asked.

"Yes," I replied as he handed me a candy cane.

"What do you want for Christmas this year?"

"I want a new bike," I proclaimed proudly.

As I climbed off his lap, Mom took my hand and led me into the cafeteria for some milk and cookies. "I thought you wanted a Baby Crissy doll for Christmas. Why did you tell him you wanted a bike?" she asked.

"Because I want both," I said. "And I couldn't decide between them."

Mom sat me down at the kids' table, where milk and cookies were waiting.

My friend Jay looked up at me and asked, "Where are Santa's elves?"

Another boy named John said, "I don't know, but I think they like to eat cookies, so you'd better watch out or you might eat an elf that is in your cookie."

The whole table broke out in laughter. At the same time, I took a large gulp of milk and my laughter turned to choking. Milk streamed out of my nose and mouth, and I began to cry because it stung so badly. Much to my embarrassment, everyone began laughing at me and the mess I had made.

My mom quickly rushed to our table. "Are you okay, Dena?" she asked frantically as I continued sobbing. Mrs. Licht promptly went into the kitchen to get a rag and clean up my mess.

"It hurts, Mommy!" I cried out.

"It's time to go home. Vonie and Lori, get your coats on," she said as she snuggled me into my coat. On our way home, she held me in the front seat of our car. Then, Dad carried me to my room and Mom helped me into my pajamas. I forgot the pain and embarrassment and fell fast asleep.

The next day, the school had a treat for us. "Before our Christmas vacation, we will celebrate with a trip an hour away to the town of Brush, where we will all go skating at the local rink," Mrs. Licht said.

All of the kids from kindergarten through fifth grade piled onto the buses, and our parents followed in their cars. Both Lori and Vonie took a day off from school to come with us. When we arrived at the rink, we stood in the long line.

"Dena, take off your shoes so we can see what size you need," said Mom. After I took off my shoes, my mom handed them to the guy behind the counter, who then handed us the skates. We walked to a bench and sat down, and I nervously assessed the rink.

I had been skating before, but I wasn't very good at it, especially when it came to keeping my balance. Mom helped me push the skates on my feet and tied them tightly. Then she put on her own pair of skates and took my hand.

"I can barely stand on these things," I whined.

It was hard enough to stand on the carpet, but when we stepped out onto the rink, I knew I was going to fall. I had no control over my body, and this frustrated me.

"I'll take you for a few rounds," said Mom with confidence, skating alongside me and holding me up as we went. As I looked around, I realized that most of the kids here couldn't skate very well, which made me feel a little better. My mom let go of me by the wall and skated off. "I'll be back to check on you in a little while," she said.

As the kids who could skate flew past me, I steadied myself against the wall. Before I knew it, a boy about five years older than me came around. I noticed two things: he was not from Eckley, and he was a good skater. I was right in front of him and fell to the floor. He almost fell on top of me. He stopped and reached out his hand.

"I'll help you learn to skate," he said kindly. He took my hand and helped me up. We went really slowly, and he occasionally stopped to steady me.

"It's not like walking. With skating, you glide, so it's more like dancing," he explained. We slowly made it around the rink a couple of times. Then I saw Vonie, Lori, Mom, and Dad watching us.

Vonie and Lori begin to call out in singsong, "Dena has a booooooyfriend!"

My face fell in embarrassment. The boy also seemed embarrassed because he quickly let go of my hand and skated away, leaving me stranded in the middle of the rink.

"He's not my boyfriend! He was helping me learn how to skate!" I yelled across the rink to my sisters so everyone heard.

"You two leave her alone," my mom commanded as she skated over to rescue me.

By the end of the trip, I still wasn't skating very well, and I was tired and discouraged. I did whatever I could to simply not fall down. After a morning of bumps and bruises, we loaded back onto the bus and stopped at a park in the town of Akron to eat our lunch before heading back home.

Chapter 10

Christmas Joys with Family

"Glory to God in the highest, and on earth peace, goodwill toward men!" —**Luke 2:14**

Now that Christmas vacation was finally here, Christmas traditions were ready to play out.

"Tonight is the big firemen's meeting," Dad said one morning over breakfast.

The volunteer firemen were having their annual supper to help fill goodie sacks for Santa. Every year, Santa arrived in Eckley early on Christmas Eve. He rode on the town's fire truck and handed out candy to everyone. The way it was explained to us was that he came to see if the kids were being good, then he returned in the middle of the night to bring us the toys we'd asked for. Dad, Uncle Keith, and Uncle Max were all helping to fill those sacks for Santa's

Christmas Eve's visit. Mom, Aunt Joyce, and Aunt Dolores were also going to help.

"Vonie, Lori, and Dena . . . you girls will have to eat by yourselves tonight! Can you make peanut butter and jelly sandwiches?" Dad asked.

"Sure!" said Lori.

After they left, we pulled out the bread and peanut butter before sitting down at the table to play rummy. The rest of the night, we sat at the table giggling and having a good time. Vonie shuffled the cards for me, since I couldn't do it on my own. Lori was in the process of learning to shuffle—and by the end of the night, she had it all down pat. Vonie played a couple of games with us until her boyfriend, Tom, called in the middle of our game, at which point she left us to play by ourselves. Lori and I quickly became bored with cards and decided to play the staring game instead.

"The object of this staring game is to stare at each other without blinking or smiling. The first person who messes up loses," said Lori. We had played this game before, and neither one of us could hold a straight face for more than two seconds before we were lying in the middle of the living-room floor, rolling around on our backs and giggling so hard that it hurt to even breathe. After a while, we went to the kitchen to get a drink of water, and before long, the big supper at the fire station was over and the filling of sacks for Santa was done. Uncle Max, Aunt Joyce, Uncle Keith, and Aunt Dolores came to our house for a little while.

"Dena, what do you want for Christmas?" asked Uncle Max.

"I want a new record player," I said without hesitating, having added a new gift to my growing wish list.

"I think you need a pacifier!" he quipped.

"Those are for babies!" I protested.

"But you're the baby of the family," he replied. "So I'm getting you a pacifier."

"No, you won't!" I said, taken aback. I turned to my aunt for reassurance. "Will he, Aunt Joyce?"

"I don't know, he might," she said.

"Uh-uh!" I said, crossing my arms over my chest.

"We'll see, Kid," he said with a wink.

When Christmas Eve finally rolled around, a slew of relatives came to our house for a celebration. We were filled with excitement for Santa's arrival at our house that night. We planned to tell him exactly what we wanted him to bring to us when he returned with his reindeer in the middle of the night. All day long, anytime we heard a vehicle driving by, we ran to the living room to see if it was Santa.

"Oh, he won't be here for a while," said Aunt Jean. "You know your dad and uncles have to go help him deliver the sacks of candy, and they haven't even left yet!"

Aunt Joyce chimed in, "Before Santa comes, we'll let the kids open their gifts. All the kids have their own present to open from whoever drew their names during our Thanksgiving celebration."

"Aunt Joyce and Uncle Max have a gift for you, Dena," said Mom with a slight grin on her face. I immediately ran over to open it.

"It's in such a small package," I said, curious about what it could be. With all eyes on me, I sat down on one of our bar stools and immediately began to open up my treasure. My smile quickly turned to a frown and tears began falling from my eyes when I realized that I had, indeed, received a pacifier. Everyone watched and waited for my reaction. They all began to laugh at me. My humiliation turned to pure anger. After all, I was six years old! Not a baby at all, and definitely way too old for a pacifier. I threw my "gift" down on the floor.

"I don't want it!" I cried out.

"Dena, what if you were to use it for your baby dolls?" suggested Julie, always the peacemaker.

"Hmm," I said, my arms still crossed over my chest. I sat there for a moment, thinking about all my dolls in my room. The thought of playing house with them and having a real pacifier to give them was very appealing.

"I could do that, I guess. My one baby doll always has her mouth open, so I bet it'll fit!" I ran back to my bedroom to get my doll. "We can play house now," I announced to my older cousins.

"Well, before you do that, here's another present we brought you," said Aunt Joyce. I tore open the paper to find another package. Inside the box was the chicken game, which was the predecessor to the later Hungry, Hungry Hippo. In this version, chickens attempted to lay the most eggs. My cousins and I had a blast playing the game while the adults had their gift exchange.

"Now it's the adults' turn. Everyone put the present you brought on the middle of the floor, and we'll draw a number out of a hat," instructed Aunt Dolores. "Number one will pick a gift out of the pile and open it. Number two can take the gift away from number one or pick another gift from the pile, and so on. The only rule is that you can't take a gift back from the person who just took it from you. We'll continue like this until all the gifts are opened. Those are the rules!"

The kids turned their attention to the adults to see how it would play out. The men started fighting over some pliers, and the women over some tea towels and a little stuffed animal Aunt Joyce had crocheted. But it was all in good fun; everyone was laughing and having a great time.

After the gifts were opened, my cousin Mike and I became restless as we watched the snow falling slowly to the ground.

"You kids need to get outside," said Uncle Max. "Curt, why don't you saddle up Blaze and hook a sled to him and pull the kids around for a while?"

Everyone agreed and bundled up before going outside, where Curt had Blaze saddled up with a long rope and a sled. Mike and I got to go first. Curt got Blaze into a gentle circle lope out in the pasture. We slid every which way and laughed as we were taken along on the ride. It was one of the best ways in the world to go sledding. I could hear the clip-clop of Blaze's hooves as they hit the snow.

After one ride, we jumped out to let Lori and our other cousins ride. We took turns until we were too cold to move. Our cheeks were bright red and numb from the icy air. Curt eventually decided we'd had enough and took Blaze back to the barn to unsaddle him. Back at the house, hot chocolate and marshmallows awaited us.

Not too long after, we heard a siren and saw flashing lights outside. Everyone ran to the living room, and the adults grabbed their cameras. Santa came striding into our house carrying a big black bag full of goodies. Mom pulled up a chair.

"You have got to be super exhausted from coming all the way from the North Pole!" she exclaimed. "Have a seat, Santa."

Santa still visits every house in Eckley on Christmas Eve and leaves a sack of candy for everyone. Photo by Jan Ekberg.

Mike and I immediately began blurting out our toy requests, but Mom stopped us. "Form a line and don't be pushy," she scolded.

I always felt a little nervous sitting on Santa's lap. Could he *really* see me when I was sleeping, and did he *really* know when I was awake? And why did he come twice in one night? And seriously, how did his reindeer fly?

As I sat on his lap, he seemed familiar to me, but I couldn't put my finger on it. I decided it was because I remembered him from last year.

"Mom says you can't bring me a horse in your sleigh, so I will take a Baby Crissy doll or a bike, please!" I begged.

"We will have to see what is in my sack tonight," he cheerfully announced, handing me a paper bag of peanut brittle, chocolate peanut clusters, candy canes, shelled peanuts, and an orange. Before he left, he handed every adult in the house a bag of candy. As he left, he wished us all a, "Ho-ho-ho and a very Merry Christmas!" He waved goodbye, and I waved back.

As the evening fell, Dad, Uncle Max, and Uncle Keith came back from helping Santa deliver the sacks of candy around our small town on the fire trucks. Everyone began to yawn and look at their watches.

"I guess it's time to go home so Santa can come back," I heard my aunt announce to everyone. They all bundled up to head back home. As a family, we stepped outside to see the twinkling Christmas lights around our tiny neighborhood and said goodbye to our guests. Tomorrow, we would meet each other again at Aunt Nadine's for a big Christmas dinner.

After everyone left, Mom looked at us. "You girls had all better get to bed so Santa will come later when you're asleep," she suggested.

Every Christmas Eve, Lori and I always slept in the same room. We lay there, talking and giggling, trying our hardest to fall asleep in the magic of the night.

The next morning, I nudged Lori awake. "Do you think Santa has been here yet?" I asked.

"Probably, but it's only 4:00 a.m.," she said, squinting at our alarm clock and yawning.

"Let's go see if everyone is ready to get up."

"Okay," she agreed.

The two of us tiptoed to Vonie's room and slowly opened the squeaky door.

"Can't you two wait until it's light outside? Get out of my room!" Vonie yelled.

"You have two hours until it's 6:00 a.m. You get back to bed right now!" my mom hollered from her room as she heard the ruckus.

We walked back to bed and lay there wide awake, talking and laughing until it was finally six o'clock. Then, we promptly jumped out of bed to wake everyone up.

We tiptoed slowly in the dark back to Vonie's room and carefully opened the door. "Go away! I'm still sleeping!" she hollered.

Lori and I made a face at each other and walked into Mom and Dad's bedroom. Mom was lying in bed, and she greeted us with a smile.

"You're too excited to sleep, huh? Fine, we'll all get up. But first, you two go back to your room and let us get ourselves out of bed and get dressed. I'll get Vonie up, and we'll be out to the living room together in fifteen minutes!"

As Lori and I walked back to our room, I could hear my dad groaning and complaining. "This is ridiculous. Why didn't you tell them to go back to bed for another hour or they won't have any gifts to open?" he grumbled.

"Earle, they won't be young forever. Enjoy this time with them," she said, a trace of irritation in her voice.

Fifteen minutes later, we walked out to the tree. Mom went ahead of us and was ready with her camera to get a picture of our eager, lit-up faces.

The stockings were hung on the wall with wrapped presents inside for each of us girls. Below the stockings there were three bean bag chairs: a black one, a red one, and a yellow one. And under the tree was a Baby Crissy doll just for me! Lori received a Play-Doh ice cream set with an ice cream truck, and Vonie received some beautiful jewelry.

There was one more gift to open, just for me. As I tore open the paper, I was surprised to see a pair of red-and-white skates. My excitement grew. After my time at the skating rink earlier that month, I wasn't as scared as I'd been before. In fact, I was excited to get better. I looked outside and saw that the cement was covered with snow, which ruined my plans of skating that morning.

"Why don't you take your skates to Aunt Nadine's house? You could probably learn in her basement, where the carpet is thin. Then you'll be ready to master the cement!" Mom suggested.

Around 9 a.m., we had the living room, which had been filled with colorful wrapping paper, cleaned up and back in order. Mom was peeling and boiling potatoes for our Christmas dinner at Aunt Nadine's.

"Everyone go get dressed and brush your teeth. We need to pick up Grandma before going to Nadine's," said Mom.

When we arrived at Aunt Nadine's, my cousin Janet was on the front steps. "They're here!" she announced excitedly.

"Look what I got from Santa," I said, holding up my new skates. "Mom says I can practice in your basement on the carpet."

"What a great idea, Dena!" said Aunt Nadine, walking out from the house and wiping her hands on her apron. The aroma of turkey wafted from the open door of the house, lingering in the cold air. Some of our cousins were already downstairs playing pool and air hockey. Many of the older cousins were outside taking turns on the go-cart and playing football.

"Dena, let's go downstairs. It'll be awhile before dinner, and you can practice on your skates," said Mom.

"Yeah, I'll help you," said my cousin Janeil.

Downstairs, the jukebox that my aunt had bought a while ago from a café going out of business blared away with '70s music. I practiced gliding around on the soft carpet while jamming out to "Rock Around the Clock." I gained confidence as Janeil stepped in front of me, holding my hands and keeping me upright.

Before long, someone hollered at us from the top of the stairs. "Time to eat, kids!" yelled Aunt Jean. I didn't want to take off my skates, so I got on my hands and knees and crawled up the stairs.

"What are you doing?" yelled Dad. "Get those things off while you eat dinner!"

"All right!" I yelled back. I turned right around and went down the stairs on my butt. I then took the skates off and ran back upstairs in my socks.

Our holiday meals were always served buffet style. I jumped in line behind Mike and Janeil, and my mom stood behind me to help me fill my plate. We could smell the aroma of the turkey in the hot roaster oven and the gravy still simmering on top of the stove. Everyone had big smiles on their faces.

"Oh my gosh," Dad said, sighing. "We're too late getting up here to get our plates. Those kids are going to eat it all!"

"Dad, there is enough food here to feed an army!" said Vonie.

"Hey, you kids, leave us some too!" said Uncle Max, playing along.

As I turned around, I was shocked to see that the plate I'd been filling up had been taken out of my hands.

"Hey, who took my plate?" I asked. At the adult table, my cousin Curt was smiling at me with two plates in front of him.

"I thought you were fixing me a plate too!" he teased.

"Curt, give it back!"

"Give me a glass of tea, and I'll give it back to you," he said.

"Okay," I said with a sigh. "Do you want sugar or plain?"

He smiled. "Just plain."

"Here you go. Now give me back my plate."

"Oh, fine!" he said, smiling at me. I stomped into the living room where the kids' table had been set up. I sat between Mike and Janeil and across from Janet and Lori. We all talked excitedly about what we'd received for Christmas that morning. Unexpectedly, I was the most interested in my new pair of roller skates.

Right after dinner, I took my new skill outside to the small cement patio without falling.

Before the day was through, the chilly weather brought us all back into the house. We snacked on the leftover turkey, mashed potatoes, gravy, and rolls that the adults had heated back up, anticipating a second wave of hunger.

The older teens gathered around in the living room to play their own game of poker while the adults sat down at the main table to play their favorite card game, Oh Shit.

The younger kids stood behind the adults as cigarette smoke circled the table. We were too young to play Poker and too young to play this game with that bad word that we weren't even allowed to say.

I knew that Oh Shit had always been one of my grandma's all-time favorites. All of us kids would run around saying, "The adults are playing that Ole Shoot game again."

"Teach me to play!" begged Janeil. "I want to learn."

"Okay, Janeil, sit by me and I will teach you!" said Grandma.

"Don't let Mom teach her how to play," said Aunt Jean. "She'll just teach her how to cheat."

"Umph, hmm," my mom coughed. "You think that *you* don't cheat? You're not any better!" Mom pointed a finger at all her siblings at the table. "You all cheat," she said, crossing her arms and glaring at each one of them.

"Just sit down beside me and I'll show you how it's done!" Grandma commanded Janeil. "You can be the score keeper while you learn to play the game. And don't listen to them. I do *not* cheat! They're the damn cheaters," she said with a frown.

I stood behind the chair watching everything unfold in front of my eyes. I hoped that someday they would all teach me how to play this complicated game.

That Christmas left an everlasting impression of what Christmas was supposed to be for our big family—as well as the enormous impact Grandma had on us. She was the one who'd passed down her playfulness, sense of humor, and incredible ability to connect with all her family members through the generations.

As a kid, I never thought about how people might be sick at Christmas time. I truly believed that the whole world somehow managed to rejoice on that special day. In my mind, this was the one day of the year no one was ever sick, hungry, or sad. It was the one day of the year that was truly all about love.

Chapter 11

Winds of Change

"For I know the thoughts that I think toward you, says the LORD, thoughts of peace and not of evil, to give you a future and a hope." —**Jeremiah 29:11**

Christmas came and went, and new concerns replaced the warm holiday moments. Several board meetings were organized around the topic of shutting down Eckley School and sending all the kids to Yuma. There just weren't enough kids to keep Eckley going, and they could save money running buses to Yuma twelve miles down the road rather than paying for the school to stay open and hiring more staff.

This devastated my parents, who had both grown up attending a one-room schoolhouse a mile from the farms where they and their families lived. Both of these one-room schoolhouses were in Yuma County. Dad had attended Browning School out by Idalia, and Mom had attended Barns School, north of Eckley. Dad told me that he usually rode his horse to school, while Mom usually walked the mile both ways. When my parents hit their teenage years, they both attended the high schools in the towns nearby. Shortly after Mom graduated in Eckley, they closed the high school and kept only the grade school open.

Both of my parents had such idyllic experiences in each of their one-room schoolhouses, which had offered them the opportunity to grow up in a peaceful and intimate environment. This was why they were so pained by the fact that our town's grade school would be shutting down for good.

After a board meeting one evening, my parents, Uncle Keith, Aunt Dolores, Uncle Max, and Aunt Joyce all gathered around our kitchen table. My mom was in tears.

"This is so heartbreaking," she cried out. "Yuma is so big. Sending Dena to Yuma every day and making her ride that bus means she'll get home late and have to leave early. It's already hard enough to send the older two to Yuma every day. The kids won't get the one-on-one time they need with their teachers. And what will become of that nice schoolhouse just sitting there, rotting away?"

I pretended to play with one of my dolls as I listened to the adults talking, but I also began to wonder what would happen to the schoolhouse. Would it really start to rot? I imagined the floorboards sinking into the earth and the ceilings covered in cobwebs.

"Somehow, we will just have to get used to the idea," said Uncle Keith.

"Yes, but if only they would think of the kids and this community. It's going to hurt this town when the school goes away," grumbled Uncle Max.

"It's going to be such a big adjustment," added Aunt Joyce, sighing.

In retrospect, although the idea of a schoolhouse closing seemed to be something that would only impact families with small children, the truth was that everyone sensed the long-term effects. Besides, this was history in the making: Eckley School had been around for more than fifty years, since 1922, and a tradition was nearing its end. The sense of mourning was real. That night, I was preoccupied thinking about a new school in Yuma, and it took me a while to fall asleep.

I awoke to a beautiful winter morning in February. My sisters and I fell into our regular routine of getting ready for school, then we headed our separate ways—Lori and Vonie on the bus to Yuma and me on my bike to Eckley.

Later that day, when Lori and Vonie stepped off the bus after school, Lori's best friend Shara yelled out of her open window, "Let's meet at the schoolhouse to play!"

The schoolhouse was a local hangout for the kids of Eckley. Many of the children, including teenagers, spent time there. We enjoyed basketball hoops and a nice grassy yard to sit and talk on, as well as a great big playground.

"Mom, can I go over and play at the school?" asked Lori.

"As long as you come home when the lights come on and you take Dena with you," she said.

Lori took our purple bike out of the shed and sat on the banana seat. "Jump on, Dena!"

I stood, straddling the front wheel and facing outward as I grabbed the curved handlebars and pulled myself into a seated position. I rested my feet on the rack that covered the front wheel. Together, we rode over to the schoolhouse with Lori pedaling and steering the bike.

Shara was coming down the road on her bicycle too. Everyone at the school had already left to go home for the day, meaning we had the whole area to ourselves. We parked our bikes on the sidewalk and walked over to the white wooden fence.

Photo of the old school house where we pretended we were tightrope walkers. Photo by Shara Berghuis. Used by permission.

"Let's pretend we're acrobats in a circus, walking the tightrope," said Shara. "I'll walk the white fence, and each of you will take one of my hands to help me across." The white fence was low to the ground and pretty narrow. Shara walked it while holding our hands and eventually lost her balance, jumping down.

"It's my turn," said Lori. She climbed up and balanced herself on top of the fence, then reached out for our hands. She gingerly made her way over to where the fence was supported by two wooden boards. "It's easier to walk on this when it's wider," she informed us. "Let go of my hands. I'll do this myself."

At the end of the two wooden boards, she jumped off.

"I want to try it too," I said.

"Okay, but we have to help you or you'll fall," said Shara.

As I climbed up, I lost my balance and fell before anyone could catch me. I wasn't hurt, but I was flustered and a little scared. This was enough to make me quit my dreams of becoming a tightrope walker.

Feeling a little tired from the long day, we walked over to one of the trees. It was around 4:30 p.m., and the sun was beginning to set. There was snow on the ground, and we shivered slightly from the chilly air. We found the driest area around the tree where the sun had melted away the snow. Huddled together, we sat down and let our imaginations run wild.

"Just think," said Shara, "if we were the only people left on this entire planet. What if when we got home, no one was there? What if they just vanished?"

"What does *vanish* mean?" I questioned.

"It means to disappear," said Lori.

"What does *disappear* mean?" I asked.

"You know, like when we play hide-and-go-seek, but this time you never find anyone."

"You mean if we got home and everyone was gone—forever?" I asked in horror.

"Yes, but it could be fun. Think about it. You would never have to go to school again," Lori said, a dreamy look coming over her face as she pondered the idea.

"And the three of us could eat all the ice cream we ever wanted!" exclaimed Shara.

"I would miss Mom," I insisted, still horrified.

"But think about it, Dena. If we were the only three left on this entire earth, no one would tell us what to do or when to go to bed," said Shara.

"Yes, we could go to Disneyland and never have to stand in line. We could ride any of the rides we want!" said Lori.

"Yes, but who will run the rides or fly the plane to get us to Disneyland?" I asked, not liking the scenario at all.

Both of them frowned, since they'd never considered that. "Maybe it wouldn't be such a great idea after all," said Shara.

"Yeah, I think it could get a little scary if no one else was around," admitted Lori.

"I think I want to go home now," I said.

"Okay," replied Lori, who now looked a little guilty for making her little sister afraid. "I'll see you at school tomorrow, Shara."

Lori jumped on our purple bike, and I jumped back on the handlebars right as the sun was setting. Cold air ran down my spine and the wind stirred my hair as Lori pedaled down our dirt road just as the streetlights began to flicker on.

I remember coming home to a supper of steak and baked potatoes. I was relieved to see both my parents sitting at the table and I felt happy that they hadn't actually disappeared.

Chapter 12

Report Cards and Closing Sale

"And be kind to one another, tenderhearted, forgiving one another, even as God in Christ forgave you."
—**Ephesians 4:32**

The school year proceeded in a fairly uneventful way. Every morning during my kindergarten year, I pedaled my bike to school, unless there was too much snow on the ground or it was just too cold. But on those colder days, my mom would take my hand and walk over with me. Since we lived so close to the school, it was always faster for Mom to walk with me than it was to scrape the ice off the windows of her car.

Our scheduled routine was the same every day. In the mornings, we played outside until the bell rang. Then the fifth graders would raise the US flag on the flagpole by the water faucet outside, and we would stand to say the Pledge of Allegiance before we even set foot inside the school.

We had music class downstairs, and every Tuesday and Thursday we went to the library to check out our own books. I would find books that I knew Lori would read to me when I got home, since we weren't reading in kindergarten.

During our three hours in the morning, we practiced writing our names, coloring the alphabet, and learning our colors. On show-and-tell days, I begged Mom to bring in every dog and cat we owned. Mom would come in each week holding a different animal. I would stand in front of the class and introduce them, then walk around the room so everyone could pet them. When I ran out of pets, I started to beg Aunt Joyce to bring in her dogs and cats, but my mom finally convinced me into taking my Crissy doll and some other toys I owned instead.

Before long, March arrived, and our spring program was just around the corner. I could hardly wait. We'd been practicing every day for our spring program for months, and when opening night finally came, I was so excited! I even had a part to sing all by myself.

All of us had practiced over and over in music class, but during rehearsal, John started singing before he was supposed to. Our teacher had already told him to wait for me to sing before he began his piece. But he kept forgetting. I thought he would remember the night of the actual performance, but no such luck.

I was just getting ready to sing, "I love little kitten, her coat is so warm, and if I don't hurt her—"

But then John started singing and interrupted me. I snapped my fingers across the air and exclaimed, "Darn it!" The whole crowd below me erupted into giggles. The giggling from the audience surprised me, and I couldn't make myself sing any further. Our music teacher smiled and blushed, then began to play our next song to keep everything running smoothly. I glared at John as we moved into the chorus. I was so angry at him for messing me up, even though I knew he was probably even madder at himself.

After the program, Uncle Max and Aunt Joyce came up to me. "Why did you snap your fingers, Kid?" Uncle Max asked, smiling.

"Because John messed me up," I said.

"Well, you all did a great job," said Aunt Joyce as she gave me a hug.

When we arrived home that night, Mom, Vonie, and Lori laughed at me and told me how cute I was when I snapped my fingers. I just stewed in silence because I didn't see anything cute about it. But even though I was initially upset about missing my two minutes of fame, I would later realize that making people smile at my imperfections probably had a more memorable effect than any song could.

The next day was Saturday—and our final parent/teacher conference day of the year. I awoke to the aroma of sizzling bacon, which quickly brought me out of my slumber. Racing to the kitchen, I was greeted by Snapper, who was patiently waiting for food to accidentally on purpose fall to the floor.

Mom greeted me with a smile. "I was just about to come in to wake you. We have a busy day ahead of us. Aside from the parent/teacher conference, there's also a sale going on. The school is trying to get rid of desks and other supplies before it closes at the end of this

REPORT CARDS AND CLOSING SALE

year. You never know what kind of treasures you might find for super cheap!"

Her tone shifted to more serious and thoughtful as she looked carefully at me. "Dena, next year you'll have to ride the same bus to Yuma with your sisters because they're closing Eckley School."

I'd spent the last several months hearing my parents and other family members talk about the old schoolhouse closing. I knew it bothered my mom a lot; she'd even cried about it. I didn't want to go to a different school next year. At the same time, I didn't understand why Lori always said she missed Eckley School. All the kids would be going to the new school with us, and the old school would still be there. But riding on the bus to Yuma every day would mean I couldn't ride my bike or have Snapper or my Tiger cat follow me every day.

"I won't miss Eckley!" Vonie always said. She'd gone to Eckley after my family moved back to town from the mountains, but she loved Yuma and all her friends. She would be out of school next year, as she was seventeen and a junior. Her boyfriend, Tom, was also from Eckley, and he would be graduating this year.

"Hurry and eat your breakfast so we can walk to your school for your conference and see if there is anything at the sale we might want to buy," Mom ordered us.

Together, my sisters and I walked over to the school with Snapper and my Tiger cat.

"I can't wait to see what they have at the sale today," said Vonie. "I brought my money I raised from babysitting."

"Me too," said Lori. "I hope I can find some good books."

Before we even left the house, we heard the echo and rhythm of the squeaky swings and kids playing on the playground. When we arrived, we climbed the wooden staircase to my classroom, which was littered with treasures. I opened my eyes wide. They were selling so many things: books, desks, chalkboards, crayons, and pencils. They were even selling Christmas trees and ornaments.

"You girls look around and see if there is anything you want to buy," said Mom.

It felt as if Christmas had come early. We eagerly began grabbing everything in sight. I found an old wooden bat, a baseball, and some paints. Lori found a desk that opened at the top. We ran back to Mom with our requests.

"I found this dry-erase board. I'll pay for it myself," said Vonie, smiling. "Now I can write my schedule and hang it up in my room."

"This will help you stay organized," Mom said, impressed.

"Mom, we want to buy all of this. Is that okay?" Lori and I asked.

She nodded. "The prices seem cheap enough. I brought twenty-five dollars to spend. If we buy a desk, we'll have to walk home and bring over the pickup. I'll pay for the items now. Then we'll leave them here and walk across the hall for your conference and come back and pick them up later," she said.

Mrs. Licht greeted us as we walked across the hall. I thought she was absolutely beautiful, with her dark hair and dark eyes. Plus, she always had a smile on her face.

"Good morning, Dena!" said my teacher. "How are you this morning?"

"I'm fine," I said, all the while eyeing the freshly baked chocolate-chip cookies that lay on a big platter.

"Help yourself, Dena!" said Mrs. Licht.

I eagerly grabbed a cookie and bit into the gooey, warm, delicious . . . horrible, no-good cookie! I stopped in my tracks. What I had thought was a chocolate-chip cookie was actually a raisin cookie, and I *hated* raisin cookies.

"Dena, go and spit it out in the trash can," Mom said, grabbing my hand to lead me to the can, obviously embarrassed by my behavior.

My teacher frowned and regained her posture. "It's okay. I should warn people that they're not chocolate chip," she said, placing the cookies on a higher shelf. "Dena, why don't you and your sisters go outside and play while your mom and I have a talk?"

My sisters and I took off down the stairs to the playground where all our friends were. But before we left, I could hear Mrs. Licht talk to Mom. I stopped and lingered just outside the door to listen.

"I hate to be the one to break the news to you, but we need to discuss a few things about Snapper. The other day, our janitor went to move Dena's bike to the other side of the school and Snapper bit him. So we're not allowing Dena to bring Snapper to school anymore."

I frowned but didn't say anything as I heard Mom's response. "That dog wouldn't hurt a flea! If he bit someone, then he was only protecting Dena's bike. He follows her everywhere. I can't bear the thought of tying him up every day. Besides, all the kids love him!" she pleaded.

"Well, that's the problem, Mrs. Ekberg. If this dog bites any kids, we'll have a lawsuit on our hands. And we don't want that," said Mrs. Licht.

Mom sighed. "Okay, I agree with you that we can't take any chances of him biting anyone. I will somehow find a way to tie him up." She quickly changed the subject. "So how's Dena doing in school?"

I perked up my ears to listen to what my teacher said. I liked to go to school and spend time with my friends, and I also enjoyed learning new things, but I would much rather be outside than stuck in the schoolhouse trying to learn to read and write.

Mrs. Licht replied, "She seems to enjoy her time here and has made good friends. She loves to play outside and ride the merry-go-round. She takes turns well, and she's obedient. As far as schoolwork, she's doing well, but she's having trouble remembering the sounds of the letters and writing the alphabet. I'm wondering . . . if I were to send some worksheets home, would you have time to help her?"

"That shouldn't be a problem. Lori and Dena play school a lot. Today we're buying one of those desks the school is selling. We'll set that up in their room so they can play school. If I show Lori what she needs to work on, then maybe they can play and learn at the same time!"

"That would be great. Make sure you have her look at the picture, then really emphasize what the letter sounds like and practice sounding it out. Other than that, she's doing superbly and should get caught up in no time!"

I felt that this was good news for me, so I happily skipped back downstairs and ran out to the playground to play with my friends.

Mom and Mrs. Licht came to meet us outside on the playground when they were finished talking. The sun was shining brightly, and spring was in full swing. Some of the leaves were beginning to reappear on the trees. There were lots of kids outside, either playing on the merry-go-round or waiting their turn to get on. Their parents were inside at the sale, discussing what the future would hold for us at a different school next year.

As Lori and I approached the playground, my friend Pati stopped me. She was a tall, blonde girl a year older than me. She looked at us and said, "You can't get on the merry-go-round until you have a rock for a ticket."

"Yeah!" said Jay, who was also older than me and a little bossy.

"This is an airplane, and you need to have a ticket to get on. The bigger the rock, the longer the ride," said a girl named Julie Z who was in my class.

Looking all over the playground, I finally found some rocks out past the basketball court. I excitedly ran over to Julie Z. "I found one!"

She shook her head. "That's not big enough. It won't even get you off the school grounds!"

That seemed silly. Why wouldn't this rock be big enough? But I didn't say anything. Frowning, I ran back to the basketball court to look for much bigger rocks. Lori and I both found two more rocks that dwarfed the ones I'd found earlier. We ran back to the merry-go-round. "Will this take us both to Disneyland?" I asked.

"Sure, hold on while we stop the plane. As soon as the plane stops, you can jump on for a wild ride!" said Julie Z, who stood tall and yelled at the older kids in the middle. "Stop the plane! We have more tickets!"

"Hold on a minute!" said Vonie as she and Tom came running over. "Everyone get on and we'll push."

Everyone jumped on, given the authority of two high schoolers telling them what to do. Tom and Vonie began pushing the merry-go-round really fast before jumping on the bars in the middle. This merry-go-round was a fun and bumpy ride that never disappointed. It sat on a slope, so when you rode it, you felt yourself inching up the slope and then sliding down again. It felt like flying. We were going so fast that our hair whirled around our heads and our heads spun. Everyone started yelling and laughing, until something louder than us began whistling through the air. Sirens were going off down Main Street. The merry-go-round came to a screeching halt, and everyone quickly jumped off, eager to see what was going on.

"I hope it's not serious," said Mom, bringing her hands to her face in concern. I rushed over to her with my hands over my ears.

"What's going on?" asked Vonie.

"I don't know," replied Mom.

Looking toward the west, we saw a glimpse of siren lights. The blaring sound had everyone's full attention. Living in a small town, we didn't usually hear sirens. When we did, the first thought that raced through everyone's minds was, *Who are they for?*

A minute later, our janitor came out, hurriedly walking toward Mom. "You have a phone call you need to take in my office," he informed her.

Mom took a deep breath and smiled a fake smile. "Stay here with your teacher, and I'll be right back," she ordered us.

The siren was still loud and very close now. I could feel my heart racing. Honestly, I wasn't really worried about anyone but myself. And right now, I was more than a little scared, but mostly of the loud noise. We all stood by our teacher with our hands tightly clasped over our ears. After a little while, the sound died down. A few minutes later, Mom come back outside.

"Come with me, kids! We need to go home right now! Some things have come up, and we need to hurry!" she said, obviously trying to hide her own fear under cover of motherly orders.

Mrs. Licht looked at my mom with a quizzical and concerned expression. "Is everything okay?"

"I'll fill you in," the janitor told her.

My sisters and I grabbed each other's hands and jogged back home with Snapper and Tiger cat following close behind.

As a child, I had no idea what was going on or why we had to leave the school so soon. I had no idea that the ambulance had anything to do with what would take place in our lives over the next few months. The schoolhouse shutting down was symbolic, but that was just the beginning.

In retrospect, remembering the hypothetical scenarios with Shara and Lori about living alone, without adults to boss us around, I realize that our imaginations couldn't stamp out the love that was in our hearts. All that was yet to come prepared us for the huge transitions in our later lives . . . and made us appreciate our parents and families on a much deeper level.

Chapter 13

The Hard Fall

"And those who know Your name will put their trust in You;
For You, LORD, have not forsaken those who seek You."
—**Psalm 9:10**

I remember Dad and Aunt Joyce were already waiting for us when we arrived at the house after hearing the sirens. Vonie, Lori, and I climbed in the backseat of our maroon station wagon with Aunt Joyce, who lifted me up and sat me on her lap. With her right hand, she took her long, red-painted fingernails and gently rubbed them up and down my arm. It was a comforting, tickling feeling. Her left arm was around my waist, holding me close to her. Her eyes were teary, and I could feel her shaking as she began to tell the story of what had happened to Uncle Max that morning.

Dad was driving faster than usual as we headed to Wray Hospital, fourteen miles east. Lori scooted closer to us, and Aunt Joyce embraced her in a hug too. Mom sat sideways in the front seat, facing my aunt, whose voice began to shake as she told the story.

"Max was shingling a two-story house this morning when he lost his balance and suddenly slid off and landed on the ground. The little boy who lives there, Jamie, found him and ran to tell his dad."

I was in awe as I listened to the story.

Aunt Joyce continued, "They called the fire hall and the ambulance to go out. They're pretty sure he broke at least his legs and maybe his ribs. I knew you were at the school, so I called you and then ran over to your house. They say he is still talking, but he's in a lot of pain. They might be transporting him three hours away to another hospital."

I sat in silence as I took in the news: Uncle Max had been hurt and now was in the hospital. I didn't understand what this meant, but I felt scared. I pictured him all bloody without a leg, and a feeling of dread came over me. I didn't want to go to the hospital to see him. And I didn't know what to do to make Aunt Joyce feel better. The worst thoughts were running through my head. I felt helpless.

When we arrived at the hospital, we climbed out of the station wagon and walked into the waiting room. The receptionist already knew who we were and had been waiting for us to arrive. "Follow me," she said.

Dad looked back at my sisters and me. "You stay here and be quiet and good. We'll come back to get you later."

Looking over at the bookrack, I saw a purple children's book with Casper the Friendly Ghost on it. I took it over to Lori. "Will you read this to me?" I asked. She nodded, seemingly relieved to have something else to focus on other than the fact that our uncle was in the hospital. We sat down on the floor and began reading the story. We heard some people come into the waiting room, and as we looked up from the book, we were surprised to see my aunts Nadine and Jean come in with our cousins Lisa, Greg, Janet, Janeil, and Mike.

"Are they in the room with Max?" asked Aunt Nadine, who hurried over when she saw us.

"Yes," said Vonie. "I think it's pretty serious. Julie and Curt are back there as well."

"I can take you back to the other waiting room!" said the receptionist when she saw the adults. "But the kids are going to have to stay here."

"Vonie and Lisa, you are in charge of the kids for a while. Why don't you take them outside to play?" Aunt Jean suggested.

All of us walked outside, where a cement wheelchair ramp curled around to a bench.

"Let's have a race," suggested Janet.

"Okay," agreed Vonie. "You and Lori stand at the top, and when I say go, run to the bottom and touch Lisa's hand. Whoever gets there first has to challenge me. Now, ready—one, two, three, stop!" she yelled.

Both Lori and Janet took off on a sprint and then stopped, laughing as they headed back to the top. Everyone else burst out laughing too.

The next time, Vonie counted to three and said, "Go!" Janeil, Mike, Lori, and Janet took off racing to Lisa, and both Janet and Lori got there at the same time.

"Tie!" Lisa called out.

At that moment, the door at the top of the wheelchair ramp opened. Dad, Mom, Aunt Nadine, and Aunt Jean walked outside and called us over to them. "We need to talk to all of you. They're taking Uncle Max to Denver in an ambulance. He broke his legs, pelvis, and hip, and they have to go to the city hospital to fix him."

I couldn't even imagine what it was like to have all those bones broken. I wondered if Uncle Max could move any part of himself at all.

"Is it the same hospital that Grandma had to go to?" I asked, concerned.

"It's in the same city but a different hospital," replied Mom, rubbing my forehead with her hand in a comforting way.

"He'll be gone for a while, and he wants to say goodbye to all you kids before he leaves in an ambulance," said Dad.

I began to cry uncontrollably. "I don't want to see him!" I cried out, feeling my heart race in panic.

Mom frowned. "And why not, Dena?"

"Because, because!" I spluttered. But I just couldn't answer. All I could think of was blood running out of him all over the place. And I tragically pictured him missing a leg. I didn't want to see such a horrible sight. But I also didn't know how to tell the adults about my fear. "I just don't wanna go in there," I said, biting my nails. I shook my head stubbornly and continued to cry.

"It's okay, Dena," said Dad. "I'll carry you in."

As he picked me up, I hid my face in his shirt. Lori stood right beside Dad and grabbed hold of my hand.

"I don't really want to go in there either," she said.

Mom put her arm around Lori and motioned us all to go ahead of her, patting all the kids on the back. "It will be fine," she reassured us.

Everyone followed close behind. My face was still buried in Dad's shirt as we walked into the hospital room.

Aunt Joyce came up to me and gently stroked my hair. "Dena, it's okay. Look up," she whispered.

I did so hesitantly. Julie and Curt were sitting next to the window. Uncle Max was lying on a hospital bed with a sheet covering his legs. I breathed a sigh of relief; I didn't see any blood at all. He looked peaceful, like he was resting. Dad set me down on the ground.

"Hi, Kid, and all of you kids," Uncle Max said, a little smile playing over his lips. "Now, I'm going to be gone for a while. All of you had better be good. Don't get into any trouble or get hurt. The last thing I want to see is one of you kids in a hospital bed beside me while I'm recovering. Kid, you keep going to sandbox school and be good. I'll see you when I get back."

"Okay," I responded shyly, not knowing what else to say.

"All of you need to stand out in the hallway," said a doctor sternly, who had just come into the room. "We need to prep him for his trip to Denver and give him some pain meds to help him sleep on the way there. You should say goodbye now."

We waited for a long time as we stood in the hallway, trying to remain still and quiet. But it was hard for me, a six-year-old, and Mike and Janet, two ten-year-olds, to be quiet. Aunt Jean dug into her purse and handed us each a sheet of paper and a pen. We scribbled on some paper until Uncle Max was wheeled out to the ambulance. I saw Aunt Joyce give him a kiss on the forehead. "I love you," she whispered.

Standing around the adults, I listened closely to the plans they were making. "We will head back home and get packed, then head to Denver to take Joyce, Curt, and Julie to the hospital. It's about a three-hour drive from home. We'll leave the kids at Grandma's house and come back tomorrow," said Mom.

Finally, after what felt like an eternity, everyone was ready to leave the hospital. We waved to our cousins and walked back to our station wagon. Aunt Joyce rode back to her house with Curt and Julie in Curt's pickup. I sat in the middle between Vonie and Lori.

"Will Uncle Max ever walk again?" Vonie asked.

"I don't know. We'll just have to wait and see," Mom replied, tears forming in her eyes again. The rest of the way home was very quiet. I was still picturing Uncle Max with his legs cut off and bloody. But I tried to take that out of my mind, since that wasn't how he'd looked when I encountered him in the hospital. I hoped with all my heart that he'd be able to walk again.

"Before you kids go to Grandma's, we'll stop by our house so Vonie can feed and water the horses. Lori, you can feed the cats while I feed Gidget and Snapper," said Mom.

I recall how terrified I was, and the crazy thoughts that went through my mind, thinking his legs was ripped off. I can still feel the comfort and security of Uncle Max's words to us before he left. "All of you had better be good. Don't get into any trouble or get hurt. The last thing I want to see is one of you kids in a hospital bed beside me while I'm recovering. Kid, you keep going to sandbox school and be good. I'll see you when I get back."

Chapter 14

Safe Under Grandma's Umbrella

"Come to Me, all you who labor and are heavy laden, and I will give you rest. Take My yoke upon you and learn from Me, for I am gentle and lowly in heart, and you will find rest for your souls. For My yoke is easy and My burden is light."
—**Matthew 11:28–30**

Thinking back to my uncle's accident, I realize moments that knock us down come and go in our lives, but during the rain, there is an umbrella to keep us safe from the storms.

Grandma was our umbrella. And she would be the one to give us kids a sense of solace after what had just happened.

Arriving home, Mom hurriedly packed some overnight clothes in paper bags and ran around the house getting chores done while preparing for our night away.

"Mom, can I take my doll over to Grandma's?" I asked.

"That's a great idea. Grandma says she has a surprise for you. She's been wanting you to bring over your Crissy doll for a while," said Mom. "Lori, why don't you take the original Crissy dolls with you, as well? Maybe you can do their hair."

Snapper and Gidget began barking, and I realized that Grandma had pulled up outside in her car. "I decided to come get the girls to save you some time!" she said as she embraced my mom. "Now, when you go over to pick up Joyce, Curt, and Julie, give them a hug for me. And you be careful going into Denver," she instructed. "Girls, are you ready to go to my house?" she asked, turning over to us with a smile.

Mom gave my sisters and me a hug and kiss. "I love you girls. You be good for Grandma, and we'll see you tomorrow!" she said.

Grandma's dog, Chico, greeted us at the door as we walked into her house, but I didn't ever pet him because he was a grouchy Chihuahua.

"Since you're here early, let's have some fun!" Grandma said, clapping her hands together excitedly. "We'll make a waffle batter mix for breakfast in the morning."

We followed Grandma into the kitchen, where she dug out her tattered and torn cookbook from a drawer. It was thick and heavy. She instructed us to go into the bathroom to wash our hands. Then she got down on her knees and pulled out three glass bowls, her yellow mixer, and some measuring spoons and cups from her bottom cabinets. Afterward, she pulled out all the ingredients the recipe called for.

Lori read the first ingredient: "Three eggs separated. What does *separated* mean?"

"It means you separate the yolk from the whites. Let me show you," said Grandma. She took three fresh eggs out of the carton. "These eggs came from Uncle Keith's chickens. They are a different color than what you normally buy in the store. See? They're brown. And because they're fresh eggs, the yolk inside will be a dark orange."

She held one egg and gently cracked it against the counter to break it apart. She then took her thumbs and pulled apart the shell, splitting it in two.

"Put your hands over the bowl that you want your egg whites to fall into and pour the yolk to the other side of the eggshell. Just let the egg whites fall into the bowl, and keep dumping the yolk back and forth into each side of the eggshell until the egg whites are completely separated from the yolk. Then dump the yolk into another bowl and put the shells in this bucket to use as nutrients for our plants around the house."

I tried to keep all of her instructions in my head as Vonie and Lori followed her closely. Lori accidentally dropped a yolk in the bowl but it didn't break, and Grandma was able to scoop it out with a spoon.

"Here, Dena and Lori, take these two eggs and try to break them yourself, just for practice," she said, handing us two bowls to separate them into as we sat at the kitchen table. "It takes a lot of practice to get this down pat," she continued, smiling at us.

Lori and I sat at the table as we practiced breaking the eggs and separating them.

"Next, we beat the egg whites with a blender until they become frothy," said Grandma. "You can do that, Vonie."

Vonie stood at the counter with the electric blender for about five minutes, beating the egg whites until they started to resemble whipped cream. Lori and I quit what we were doing to watch the blender spin. It was fun to watch the egg whites change before our eyes.

"Now, Lori, you can take the blender from Vonie and beat the yolks in this bowl. Dena, here is a three-quarter cup. I'll pour milk into it, and then you pour the cup of milk into the yolks."

Standing on a chair so I could reach, I gently poured the milk into the egg yolks and watched the creamy white liquid swirl into the bright yellow.

Grandma took a pan out of her cupboard and placed it on her gas stove, turning on the fire. She took a stick of butter out of the refrigerator and stuck it in the hot pan to melt it. Then, she poured the butter into the milk. Next, she handed Lori a carton of sour cream, a spoon, and another three-quarter cup. "Lori, spoon out sour cream to fill the cup, then put it in with the other ingredients.

"Really? You put sour cream in the waffle mix?" I asked, wrinkling my nose.

Lori looked at me, and we stuck out our tongues. "Yuck!" we said in unison.

"Oh, girls, sour cream is what makes this recipe so good. You've had my waffles before. I've always put sour cream in them. You'll absolutely love them, I promise. Just wait till the morning, then you'll see."

While we worked on the waffles, Vonie sifted together one-and-a-half cups of flour, two teaspoons of baking powder, half a teaspoon of baking soda, and a tablespoon of sugar.

Grandma continued to instruct us. "Now we bring it all together in this bowl. Lori, dump the wet ingredients with the dry ingredients and use the blender to mix it together."

After it was all mixed, Grandma smiled at us. "There is a secret ingredient missing, and it will never be written down. You have to remember it. Two teaspoons of vanilla."

"Vanilla?" Lori and I both asked.

"Yes, vanilla!" Grandma poured the dark liquid into a teaspoon and let us smell it.

"Mmm, it smells so good!" I closed my eyes and breathed it in. It smelled warm and sweet. As some spilled onto the counter, I took my index finger to scoop up a little taste.

"Don't taste it, Dena! It may smell good, but it tastes awful," cried Lori.

"Too late," said Vonie. I spat it out, grimacing as I tried to get it off my tongue.

"Get to the sink to spit it out," Grandma said, lifting me up to the sink and giving me a glass of water. "Now, Vonie and Lori, don't forget to fold the egg whites gently in. Tonight, they'll sit in the fridge; then, in the morning, we'll chop up pecans and cook everything in our waffle maker. After that, we'll pour syrup on top. Ta-da! Grandma's famous waffles!"

I was still a little confused. "Grandma, why do we put vanilla and sour cream in the waffles if they taste so bad?" I asked.

"Because when you blend the right ingredients together, they complement each other and make everything taste good," she explained. "If you think about it, that's how all of us are. We each have good and bad inside us, but when we work together in life, we complement each other through our good."

"And that makes us all better, right, Grandma?" asked Lori.

"Right," said Grandma, folding us all into a hug. I buried myself against her skin, which smelled faintly of perfume. After the long day we'd all had, it felt really good to be in her presence. Grandma's kitchen was a million times better than that hospital!

"Now that we're done making waffles, I'm going to lie down for a while. I'm awfully tired," said Grandma. "You girls can play with the baby clothes I brought up from downstairs. Dena, they'll fit your Crissy doll. The thing that's special about these clothes, girls, is that they were your mom's when she was a baby. I put them all in this green suitcase for you. In the suitcase, you'll find some combs, brushes, and ponytail holders. You girls dress your dolls up and do their hair while I go rest."

"I just want to lie down with my book," said Vonie as she grabbed an afghan my grandma had crocheted, along with a soft pillow, and lay down on the yellow couch.

"Let's play with the dolls," said Lori. "How do you want her hair to be today?" she asked, pretending to be a hairdresser.

Pretending to be the doll, I answered back in a squeaky voice, "I want long hair and a ponytail."

"Long hair and a ponytail," Lori repeated. "I'll do it!"

After Lori styled my doll's hair into a ponytail, she took out both her doll and Vonie's doll and brushed each into a ponytail: one long, one short. Then we went through the suitcase of clothes. We took them out and lined them all around the living-room floor, matching tops to bottoms and trying them on my doll.

"I wish these clothes would also fit the original dolls," said Lori sadly.

"That's okay, Lori. We can both try all these clothes on my doll and redo the hair," I said.

That evening, Grandma came out of her bedroom not looking so well. Her skin was pale, and she had dark circles under her eyes. "I'm not feeling my best," she admitted. "I feel sick enough to throw up! Vonie, I'm going to have you make PB&J sandwiches for the girls, and I'm going back to bed. Make sure you put the food away and be in bed by 9:00 p.m."

Grandma then put Chico outside and stood by the door until he wanted back in. "You girls make sure you shut these lights off before you go to bed. Lori and Dena, you can sleep in the guest room. Vonie, you can sleep downstairs or on the couch," she suggested.

That night, while I was tucked in bed in the guest room, I thought about Uncle Max without a leg and Grandma throwing up. Life felt scary and out of control. I couldn't help but miss my mom and dad.

The next morning, Grandma was up before anyone else. By the time we got to the kitchen, she had already started a pot of coffee and fried up some bacon to go with our waffle mix.

Lori and I walked out to the kitchen in our pajamas. Vonie was already in the shower.

"It smells so good, Grandma!" I exclaimed.

"Yes, it does! We'll have company here in a little while. My sisters and brother will be here visiting, and some of your cousins will come by later. So hurry and eat your waffles and bacon, then go get dressed!"

Even though there was sour cream in the waffles, not to mention the yucky vanilla, they tasted delicious—especially with the pecans and syrup, alongside the salty bacon from Uncle Keith's pigs.

The sun was shining, and we went outside to play. Gradually, people started to show up at Grandma's. I knew all these old people. They were always happy to see us. They said they liked to watch us run around, and they wished they had our energy—whatever that meant.

In a little while, Aunt Jean, Aunt Dolores, and Aunt Nadine showed up with some of our cousins. All of us younger kids stayed outside to play. Behind the garage was a vacant lot. Janeil took a rake and began raking away the weeds. She made a couple of bare spots and proudly said, "Let's play house! These bare spots will be our beds, and over here will be our kitchen." We all began to play house, making do with whatever was in our presence. And if we didn't have something, our imagination did the trick.

Later, Greg and Mike found a way to climb to the top of the garage roof by standing on top of the railing of the fence in the front yard. Everyone followed suit, except me. I was too little to jump up there. I ran into the house, begging for someone to please come out and lift me up. My great-uncle Myron came out and assessed the situation.

"Whatever possessed you all to get up there?" he asked, laughing at us. "Dena, I'll help you up!" He lifted me high above his head and sat me down on the edge of the roof. I used my strength to crawl up the steep incline to the top of the garage.

"You kids be careful up there!" hollered Aunt Jean, coming out of the house to see what the heck I had been talking about. "Uncle Max told you all that he doesn't want anyone getting hurt like he did. And what's the first thing you kids do? Go climb up on top of the garage," she scolded.

"Oh, they're not that high. If this was a higher building, I'd be concerned, but they'll be okay," said Great-Uncle Myron.

"Okay, you kids! You can play up there, but you help Dena get down when she wants," said Aunt Jean, shaking her head disapprovingly.

We continued to stay up there for a while, waving at all the traffic that drove down Main Street. Some of the people who drove by knew who we were and slowed down to do a double take. A little later, Grandma came out with her camera and took a picture of us all sitting on top of her garage. "I want more pictures with you kids. Why don't you all come down?" she suggested.

I scooted to the edge of the garage, and Great-Uncle Myron lifted me down to the ground. All my older cousins jumped straight off, challenging each other to see who could jump the farthest.

"All the grandchildren need to follow us out back to take some fun family pictures," Grandma ordered.

In the backyard was a three-ring pyramid of huge tractor tires with dirt in them. This was Grandma's flower bed, but the flowers hadn't bloomed yet. As we walked by the lilac bushes, I noticed they were in full bloom. I stopped and picked a couple of dark-purple lilacs for the picture, as I had done many times before this.

"Dena, you stand by Great-Aunt Illa," said Grandma. I hung my head low. I was scared of Illa because she always yelled at me. But I did as I was told and went over to stand by her.

"Dena, put that flower down for the picture," Illa sternly told me. I immediately dropped it to the ground.

"Dena, don't drop that flower that you just picked," scolded Grandma.

At this point, I didn't know what to do, and my tears began to fall. Great-Aunt Olive came to my rescue as my older cousin Diane put her arm around me. Great-Aunt Olive picked up the flower and held it. "It's okay, Dena," she said. "We'll take it into the house and put it in a vase of water. But first, let's take some more family pictures. Dry your eyes, smile, and say cheese."

After the adults finished snapping pictures, they headed back inside.

"We'll make some Kool-Aid and snacks for you kids, then we'll holler for you when it's all ready," said Aunt Nadine.

We were all hungry and thirsty by the time we got back inside. As we walked into the house, all the older adults were sitting around the living room drinking coffee. We devoured the Kool-Aid and graham crackers, which were smothered in frosting. As we walked into the living room, the Beach Boys were on TV singing, "Ba, Ba, Ba, Barb, Barbara Ann."

"Hey!" said Lori. "This is what we were listening to the other day when we were at our other cousin's house on our dad's side. Our cousin Donna started calling, "Dena Bob-Bob-Bob!"

"Hey, Dena Bob!" said Greg.

"Dena Bob," said Aunt Jean. "I like it!"

"Yeah," said all my other cousins. "From now on, you're Dena Bob. That's your new nickname."

Ever since, I became Dena Bob. Many people began calling me either Dena Bob or Bob. And it stuck, even when Uncle Max and Aunt Joyce came home, although I would always remain Kid to my uncle.

As I glanced around the room, something amazing began to happen that I took for granted at such a tender young age. It was as if the essence of time stood still. I realized that each person had a glowing bright light above their heads, like a halo, and a radiant ring around their bodies. The older generation was glowing brighter than everyone else. Their lights all ranged in color from bright purple, to green, to blue, to red. Even the kids had them.

I had seen these lights before, when I'd come here with my mom a couple of months ago. On that day, all of Grandma's siblings were sitting in the living room drinking coffee. I really didn't know what the lights were, just that they were beautiful. But never had I seen them in the rainbow colors that were here, in this moment. I stood in amazement, watching as the halos shone and the ring of lights danced around them as if they were alive and playing.

"Lori, don't you think that all these lights are beautiful?" I asked.

"What lights?" she asked, confused.

"Don't you see them?" I asked, surprised.

"No, I don't know what you're talking about!" she replied, tossing her hair and turning back to everyone else.

I didn't mention it to Grandma, or anyone else, because I realized I was the only one who could see them. In retrospect, I believe that I was seeing auras, or the spiritual imprints of the human soul, shining brightly. I know from experience that children are generally more attuned to the spiritual realm than adults are because they aren't seeing through the filters of the experiences and expectations they've built up over the years.

As an adult, I feel it was a gift that I could see those colors. I believe I was attuned to the people around me.

In Daniel 12:3, it states, "Those who are wise shall shine like the brightness of the firmament, and those who turn many to righteousness like the stars forever and ever."

No wonder the older generation was shining so brightly; they were leading our generation to righteousness. It was a magical moment, but little did I know that from that point on, the lights of people's auras would stop randomly appearing to me. As time wore on and I began to learn about the fragile, temporary nature of life firsthand, my innocent outlook gradually gave way to adulthood—and to a more practical way of thinking about my family and the world.

Chapter 15

Kindergarten Work Ethic

"Train up a child in the way he should go, even when he is old he will not depart from it." **—Proverbs 22:6**

Overall, kindergarten was a year of adventure. Many people believe that you will never remember this time in your life. But as I sit in this exact spot of my childhood, the memories are right there—just as if the moments happened yesterday. I can almost hear the school bell ringing, as well as the sounds of screaming, laughing children on the playground.

I was still in kindergarten when Uncle Max came home from the hospital. He still had a long road ahead of him. He had a broken pelvis and two broken legs. He was in a wheelchair and came home to a house that was not wheelchair accessible. Coincidentally, his home therapy nurse was the same woman whose house he'd been shingling when he fell.

I knew things were a little tense by the time Uncle Max was ready to come home. He was the breadwinner of the family, but because he was now in a position where he couldn't work for a while, this put him and my aunt in a financial bind. Bills kept coming in and piling up.

Aunt Joyce had been working for the past year. She and my mom had been running a small café in Eckley. They rented a tiny building from the couple who owned the town's bar, which sat right next to the café. They called their place the J&J Café, which stood for Joyce and Jan. The bar that sat next to the café was the J&B Bar, which stood for John and Betty, the couple who owned and operated the bar.

By the time Uncle Max was released from the hospital, the café had been closed for a while. Aunt Joyce had been at the hospital with Uncle Max and wasn't able to help run the business. But now, both Aunt Joyce and my mom were eager for their work to begin again, right where they had left off.

The day Uncle Max was released from the hospital, my parents drove to Denver to bring him home. In the station wagon, the seat folded down so Uncle Max could comfortably lie down in the back.

When the station wagon approached Uncle Max's house, it was late in the afternoon. I had spent my morning in kindergarten and the rest of the afternoon with Grandma, but Lori and Vonie were barely stepping off the bus from school.

Arriving home with a wheelchair in tow was a huge challenge. The doorways were too small for a wheelchair to fit through, so our family had to carry Uncle Max into the house. This made Uncle Max feel bad, but everyone was more than willing to go the extra mile to help him in his time of need. Luckily, his wheelchair could be folded when not in use, which made it easier to get it through the front door.

When I came running into the house to greet him, Uncle Max was already situated in his wheelchair with pillows. How he did it, I'll never know, but as I walked into the living room, he had a huge smile on his face.

Toby, his trusty dog, was lying right beside him on a pillow. "Good to see ya, Kid," Uncle Max greeted me. "Are you still passing sandbox school?"

"I'm almost a first grader," I replied proudly.

"I heard you have a picture of yourself that you're going to give to me to hang up in the shop to scare all those mice away," he said, winking.

"No, I gave Aunt Joyce a picture, not you!" I said. "You can't have a picture if you are going to use it in your shop to scare those mice away."

"Aww, come on, Kid, you can help your uncle out!" he protested.

"No, Guy, you can't have a picture of me," I said as I playfully stuck my tongue out at him.

"Dena!" hollered my aunt from the kitchen. "Come have a pop with your mom and me."

"When you go in there, Dena, tell Aunt Joyce that I need her for a minute, would you?" my uncle requested.

I walked into the kitchen, where my mom and Aunt Joyce were working on some bills from the hospital. They smiled up from their paperwork, but I saw my aunt wipe away a few tears. I didn't know at the time they were concerned about the bills, but I knew Aunt Joyce was upset.

"Guy needs you, Aunt Joyce," I said, sitting down at the table and flipping the tab open on my can of pop.

"Oh, dear!" exclaimed Aunt Joyce. "I can't always hear him when he needs me, so I wish he would speak up."

"I know what we can do!" I said, a light bulb of inspiration flashing through my mind. "Let's give him a bell. Then, when he needs you, he can ring it!"

"Good idea, Dena!" she replied enthusiastically. "Let me look through these drawers and see if I can find one. I know I have quite a few. Yes, here's a bell! Let's go tell Guy!"

I grabbed the bell, which was shiny and made a tinkle sound, and ran back to my uncle's wheelchair. "When you need something, ring the bell and we'll come help you," I said, happy that I'd come up with a solution that would make both Uncle Max's and Aunt Joyce's lives easier.

"Good idea, Kid. You make a good nurse," he complimented me.

"You had better watch it or he'll put you to work as his nurse," warned Aunt Joyce jokingly.

"I can be your nurse!" I said, jumping up and down with excitement. I loved the idea of being given the responsibility of taking care of one of my favorite people in the world.

"Well, I need to go to the bathroom," he said matter-of-factly. "What we are going to have to do is take the office chair that has wheels on it and push it in here. Can you do that, Kid?"

"I think so," I said, realizing that he wouldn't be able to get his wheelchair through the kitchen and into the bathroom.

Mom and Aunt Joyce both went into action and pushed him to the office chair that I had pushed to the doorway. He used his hands to maneuver himself out of the wheelchair and onto the office chair, keeping his legs stretched out. Mom and Aunt Joyce carefully pushed the office chair over to the bathroom. I eagerly followed along with the bell and handed it to him.

"When I'm done, I'll use this bell to alert you," he told me with a wink.

Mom put her hand on my back and guided me back to the kitchen table while Aunt Joyce stayed in the bathroom a little longer. When she came back, she saw the look of anticipation on my face. "He said he'll ring the bell when he's done," she reassured me. I patiently waited to hear the tinkly sound of the bell. When I did, Mom and Aunt Joyce instructed me to wait by the refrigerator. Once again, they both had fake smiles plastered on their faces. I knew they were fake because they didn't seem to smile until I started talking.

To everyone's surprise, Uncle Max was able to move himself back to the office chair and even place the blankets over himself before anyone else could get to him. He was smiling and obviously proud of himself. As they wheeled him out to the hallway, I ran over to him so I could push the office chair back to the wheelchair in the living room. As I pushed him back to the wheelchair, he helped by using his arms to prop himself against the cabinets. He was able to situate himself back into the wheelchair.

After all of this, he looked at me carefully and said, "I have a proposition for you and your mom to consider. Since Dena is home by 11:30

from sandbox school every day, maybe she could come and be my nurse until Joyce comes home from work around two in the afternoon"

Of course, I loved the idea. A smile stretched across my face. "That sounds like a great plan! I want to be your nurse! I can do it! Will you let me, Mom?"

"Well, if Dena wants to do it, that sounds good to me, too," said Mom.

"Okay, let's give it a trial run. Go into the kitchen and tell me if you hear my bell."

I walked into the kitchen; immediately, I heard the bell ringing from the other room. I went running back to the living room. "At your service! What do you need?"

"A glass of water," he replied.

"Coming right up!" I declared, running into the kitchen. Aunt Joyce already had a glass of water for me to take to him. I tiptoed back to the chair, trying not to spill any of the contents.

"Here you go," I said.

"Thank you!" he replied.

I walked back into the kitchen to sit down again. No sooner did I sit down than the bell began frantically ringing again.

I rolled my eyes this time and yelled, "What do you want now?"

"The newspaper!"

"It's right here, Dena," said Aunt Joyce. Both my mom and aunt were smiling in amusement as I jumped down from the bar stool and took the newspaper over to Uncle Max.

"Do you need anything else?" I asked sarcastically while handing him the newspaper.

"No, I'll let you know when I do."

Once again, I walked into the kitchen to sit down—and he rang the bell again.

I ran back and asked him in exasperation, "What do you need *now*?"

"A pencil!"

"Oh, all right, Guy. I'll get you a pencil."

When I walked back to the kitchen, Aunt Joyce was ready for me. She handed me a pen, pencil, and small notebook. She and my mother laughed out loud. "Now, take this back to his wheelchair and tell him you're going on a break!" suggested my aunt.

I walked back to the living room and handed him the pencil, the pen, and the small notebook. Then I put my hands on my hips, tired of my uncle's antics. "Here you go! And now I'm going on a break!"

Before I was even to the kitchen, the bell went off again.

I turned right back around with a huff and stared at Uncle Max, who was smiling innocently. "I told you I'm going on a break, so what do you want now?" I demanded.

"I wanted to let you know that you passed my test. You can be my nurse starting tomorrow."

"I thought I was your nurse today?" I asked, confused.

"Nope, you're in training today, but tomorrow you start," he said.

I laughed. I felt really proud of myself for passing his test.

"I passed the test! I passed the nurse's test," I said, skipping back to the kitchen.

The next day after school, I raced home, pedaling my bike as fast as it would go. When I got home, I ran to the clothesline to unleash

Snapper. I had to climb up on the doghouse to reach the leash. He was so happy to see me. I jumped down to the ground and let Snapper lick my face. I knew how much he hated being tied up now that he couldn't accompany me to school, so I was relieved to be able to cut him loose.

Mom came out of the house and took my hand. Together, we walked over to Uncle Max's, with Snapper following close behind. My mom had a basket of food she'd made for our dinner.

"Hi, Guy," I cheerfully said, walking in and kicking off my shoes. "We brought you some dinner. Mom says you need to eat to get well, you know."

"Did you fix it, Kid, or did your mom?" he inquired.

"My mom did. I was at school. I don't have time to fix you a dinner, silly!"

"You mean you were at sandbox school. In that case, I'll eat it."

I just rolled my eyes at him, although I was happy that we'd be eating together.

"Before you eat, why don't you draw a picture? I'll let you do this every day you're here," he said. He took a marker and handed it to me to let me draw sunny pictures with flowers all over his cast—which everyone who came to see him also started doing.

"I don't know if you noticed, Kid, but your socks are on the wrong feet," he said, pointing down to the floor.

I looked down at my feet, alarmed. But then I realized he was just pulling my leg. "No, they're not!" I protested. "It doesn't matter which sock goes on which foot!"

He just winked at me in response.

"Here, let's get the two of you something to drink," Mom said. "Then I'll help Dena get you to the restroom before I leave. I'm heading down to J&J Café to run the afternoon shift so Joyce can come home by two o'clock. Do you think you're ready to be a nurse, Dena?" Mom asked.

I didn't hesitate. "Of course! I'll be a great nurse!"

After he was back in the wheelchair, Uncle Max asked me to set up a TV tray next to him so we could begin eating. I sat next to him while he was propped up with his legs stretched out on the bars of the wheelchair. We immediately wolfed down the delicious fried-hamburger sandwiches, chips, and apples my mom had fixed. We also drank the bottles of Pepsi she'd packed with our dinners. Both Toby and Snapper waited for something to fall to the floor accidentally on purpose. I watched as my uncle took pieces of his sandwich and gave each of the dogs a treat.

"Can you turn the TV to Channel 6? You like *Sesame Street*, right, Kid?"

"Yes, I like it a lot."

"It seems like a good show, but I noticed you didn't bring me any cookies. You don't suppose Cookie Monster ate them, do you?" Sitting there for a minute, he asked, "Maybe you're the Cookie Monster and you ate them before you got here?"

I laughed out loud. "I didn't eat them, Guy. And I'm not a Cookie Monster. I'm a people. Maybe *you* ate them!"

"Well, there are some cookies in the cookie jar if you would like to bring some to your patient," he said. "Don't forget to grab some for the Cookie Monster . . . I mean, for yourself!"

I happily skipped into the kitchen and dug into the cookie jar, bringing each of us two Oreos.

Watching *Sesame Street* and feasting on our Oreo cookies, I quickly fell asleep on the couch in Uncle Max's living room. But I immediately woke up, startled, when I heard the bell ring.

"What is it?" I asked, rubbing my eyes.

"What are you doing? You can't fall asleep on the job! I'm bored. Let's play tic-tac-toe."

I frowned. "I've never played that game before," I said, yawning. "I've never even heard of it."

"Well, it's easy. Just go get some paper and a pencil and I'll show you how to play."

I came back with a paper and pencil, and Uncle Max drew two lines going down and two lines going across.

"You want to be an *X* or an *O*?" he asked me.

"What do you mean, an *X* or an *O*?" I had no idea what he was talking about.

"Well, you pick a letter to be, and we take turns drawing in these squares. If you can make them go all the way down, across, or diagonal without me blocking you, you win. But if I can block you, I win."

I quickly started to get the hang of it, although I'm pretty sure Uncle Max let me win a couple of times.

After I became really good at tic-tac-toe, we decided to play Go Fish. Halfway through the game, Aunt Joyce came in and wanted to play too. We played until Lori walked in through the back door. She'd just come home from school and wanted to see what we were doing. Vonie had been dropped off at the café to work. Since it was such a nice day out, Aunt Joyce suggested that we go outside and play on the tire swing that hung from the giant tree in their front yard.

"Here, Dena, climb on top and I'll twist you up!" suggested Lori.

I held on as tight as I could while Lori twisted up the tire swing. The rope got tighter and tighter as the swing wound higher and higher. Then Lori let go and jumped back. I took a spinning ride that left me dizzy and mesmerized. I watched the world turn faster and faster. When I was done, Lori and I traded places; I twisted her up higher and higher, then ran out of the way as she circled her way down.

For the next couple of afternoons, I watched *Sesame Street* with Uncle Max and played the role of his nurse. One day, I climbed on top of the counter and stood up to reach a plate before jumping back down like Superman. I was fine, but I must have made a big crash because Uncle Max hollered from his chair, "Are you okay? You need to stay off the counters! I don't want you to end up in a wheelchair like me!"

Unlike his usual cheerful self, he sounded angry, which made me go quiet. Later that afternoon, he told my mom he didn't want me to come over by myself anymore because if I couldn't reach something, he didn't want me climbing the counters and getting hurt.

Now I realize this was his way of telling me he needed some time to himself, but I was okay with that. Besides, I missed my friends, and they missed me.

Chapter 16

The J&J Café

"Her children rise up and call her blessed. Her husband also, and he praises her." —**Proverbs 31:28**

It wasn't long before I was put to work again. After I lost my job as a nurse, I became a waitress. I started going to the café with my mom in the afternoons after school.

"Mom, I'll take orders!" I said in my bossiest six-year-old voice.

"Oh no, you won't! You don't even know how to spell or write anything down," she said, frowning at me.

"But I can remember and then tell you, and you can write it down," I protested, giving her puppy-dog eyes.

"Oh, all right," she gave in. "But only when family comes in."

"Fine!" I agreed, a little disappointed.

This small café was in a tiny white building with two separate rooms for dining. Neither of the rooms was very big. The front room had a long bar with four bar stools and two tables, while the back room had four tables. Each table had four chairs around them. Still, tiny as it was, the café was packed with people for breakfast and dinner. My favorite meal on the menu was bacon, toast, and french fries.

That day, I sat on the tall bar stool in the front of the café just watching and waiting for family to come in; finally, Uncle Keith, Aunt Dolores, Aunt Jean, and Aunt Nadine came in with Janeil, Mike, Janet, and Greg.

"Hi, guys, boy am I glad to see you!" I said excitedly, hopping down from the bar stool and following them to their table with a pen and a pad.

"What are you kids doing here?" asked Mom in surprise. "Didn't Wray School have class today?"

"No," said Aunt Jean. "It was teacher's work day, so we decided to come here for lunch and visit all of you."

"What do you want to eat?" I asked as they sat down.

"Why don't we take a look at the menu?" suggested Uncle Keith.

"Oh, a menu," I said, rushing to the counter to grab a few. Even though I didn't know how to spell anything but my name, I could kind of sound words out. I knew that *bacon* started with a B, *hamburger* started with an H, and *french fries* started with an F.

Mom came and stood behind me as I wrote my letters down to indicate what they wanted. "First off, let them order their drinks," she instructed me. "Then you can help me bring them out, Dena."

I asked them what they wanted and repeated it in order, writing down the first letter it sounded like. Walking back to the kitchen, I told Julie and Diane—who both worked there—exactly what everyone wanted to drink. My mom stood behind me and listened to make sure I got it right. "Surprisingly, she's spot on," Mom proudly said.

Mom filled the drinks and let me carry out Janeil's and Mike's first. She put the rest of the drinks on a tray and walked out behind me. I handed the pops to my cousins very carefully. Then I ran back to the counter to get my pencil and pad. Mom stood behind me, writing everything down as I took down the first letter of each item they ordered. Then, both of us walked back to the counter, tore off the green piece of paper, and placed it on the nail that was sticking up on a board. When all their food was ready to be taken out, Mom handed me a basket of bacon, french fries, and toast, then told me to sit down by my cousins and eat with them. (If it isn't already obvious, nutrition was not a big concern when we were younger!) Then Mom delivered everyone's food and brought me a Pepsi.

Mike and I began laughing as we took straws and tore off the end of the paper before blowing it at each other, sending straw paper flying across the table. Janeil and Janet quickly joined in the game. We giggled at one another until two cops walked in and sat next to us. They were in full uniform, and both had handguns in holsters on the side of their belts, in addition to handcuffs and handheld radios.

Mike and I looked alarmingly at them and then at each other. Mom came over to our table and wagged her finger at us. "You two had better be good or they'll throw you in jail," she said. All the adults looked at each other and exchanged sly grins, while we kids immediately settled down. Mike and I stopped laughing, sat straight in our chairs, and did as we were told.

"Hello," the cops said, smiling at us. Mike muttered a hello, while I bowed my head and tried to hide from them. After they left, Mike and I breathed huge sighs of relief.

"You need to leave a tip," Mom said, walking over to our table and taking out some quarters from her apron. "Take these quarters and put them in your glass. We'll trick the dishwasher people!" Both Mike and I eagerly put coins into our cups.

It was getting late in the afternoon. The bus stopped outside, and both Vonie and Lori came in and put their backpacks down.

"How was your day at school?" Mom asked as she gave them both a hug.

"It was good!" said Lori, who looked over to see the whole gang sitting down and eating. "Hey, Janeil, Mike, Janet, and Greg are all here! What are you doing here?"

"We didn't have school today, so we came by," said Janeil.

"Let's go outside to play," said Lori, wanting to take advantage of everyone's presence.

"First, you and Vonie take your bags outside and put them in the car. Afterward, Vonie, you can clear off this table," Mom suggested.

As Vonie and Lori came in after putting their bags in the car, Janeil met them at the door. "You have to try this new flavor of pop the café got today. It's called Vanilla Coke, and it tastes really good."

"You mean vanilla also tastes good in pop?" I asked, remembering that it tasted really good in waffles but terrible alone.

"Yes, you need to try it!" Janeil said.

"Here, let me squirt the vanilla flavoring into it," said Vonie. As we tasted it, we all agreed that it was delicious.

"Now let's go outside to play," suggested Janet.

Outside, at the back of the café, was a long, green horse wagon with steel wheels. Lori insisted that the wagon had probably been sitting outside for a hundred years, and we all agreed that it was fun to play on.

"Here, Dena, I'll boost you up!" said Janet.

There was a bench on the front of the wagon where I imagined the driver of the team of horses would sit in the old days. We played out there the rest of the afternoon, pretending we were cowboys and Indians. We took turns sitting in the front seat so we could pretend we were the ones driving the team of horses. Half the fun was climbing up and down from the wagon. However, Janeil, Lori, and Janet quickly got tired of boosting me up every time I got down.

"Stay up or down, but pick one!" Lori shouted at me.

It wasn't long before we tired of playing on the wagon and walked over to the J&B Bar. A green merry-go-round sat on the northeastern side of the bar. The older kids pushed as we went for a ride. Although we were allowed to play on the merry-go-round, we weren't usually allowed to go into the bar. There were always a lot of cars there, and Mom and Dad told us to stay away from the parking lots so we wouldn't get run over by "tired" people (which I later came to realize was code for drunk or tipsy people!).

That night, as we settled into the evening, Vonie came up to me. "Dena, you had better not put change in the glasses at the café anymore because we about dumped the coins down the drain. What if we didn't see them?" she said, clearly upset.

Mom looked up at Vonie with a sly grin. "Actually, it was my idea to do that," she said, laughing.

"Why, Mom?" she asked, her frown turning into a smile at my mom's sneakiness.

Lori and Dad also started laughing.

"Okay, Dena! Once was fun, but don't do it again," Mom instructed me. "We don't want to make Vonie mad!"

As a kindergartener, and the youngest child in my entire family, I wanted to feel valued and important. I believe that's why Uncle Max asking me to be his nurse was so important to me. At the café, I wanted to show that I could be helpful too. However, the J&J Café didn't stay open very long. Aunt Joyce eventually took a new job as the town clerk down at Eckley's town hall, while my mother stayed at home to take care of us kids. The café simply wasn't a financially stable business. It didn't bring in enough income to pay for the extra help that was needed when Vonie and my cousins were at school. However, what it did bring was a lot of fond memories to the community.

Chapter 17

Memorial of Summer Memories

"To everything there is a season, a time for every purpose under heaven: a time to be born, and a time to die; a time to plant, and a time to pluck what is planted; a time to kill, and a time to heal; a time to break down, and a time to build up; a time to weep, and a time to laugh; a time to mourn, and a time to dance; a time to cast away stones, and a time to gather stones; a time to embrace, a time to refrain from embracing; a time to gain, and a time to lose; a time to keep, and a time to throw away; a time to tear, and a time to sew; a time to keep silent, and a time to speak; a time to love, and a time to hate; a time of war, and a time of peace."
—**Ecclesiastes 3:1–8**

Summer routines and traditions always seem to repeat themselves year after year—even to this day. Our kids continue to start the summer off where they have joined the local 4-H and become a part of their Memorial Day service. This tradition of honoring our veterans has given our children a deep sense of respect for our land, our freedoms, and for those who served, fought, and died for us. The week that follows is always a week-long Bible school session where they learn that our salvation in Jesus was paid at the cross of Calvary.

When I was a child, every one of my mom's siblings hosted family gatherings during the holidays. In the summer, my mom hosted Memorial Day and Aunt Jean hosted the Fourth of July. Altogether, it was those carefree days with family that we all looked forward to.

The water tower we ran under.

On the last day of school, before our summer vacation and before Eckley School was closed for good, I walked into my kindergarten class for the final time. Mrs. Licht stood in the front of the classroom. "All right, kids, today we have a special treat for you! The town is turning on the water tower for all of you to play under. We'll walk over there together. I need each of you to pair off in threes and hold each other's hands."

Julie Z, Dusty, and I excitedly teamed up to walk down the dirt road and across Main Street to the town hall. Our parents had known about this surprise and sent us to school with sack lunches, flip-flops, shorts, and towels.

When we arrived, our parents were standing with their cameras, ready to capture the moment. All of us kids stood under the water tower as the maintenance man walked into the watershed. "Are you ready?" he hollered at us.

"Yeah!" we all screamed. But we were all shivering because it was a chilly morning—not really suitable weather for getting wet. Standing there in our summer attire, we heard the water begin to move in the tall tank above us. Then it made a loud noise like thunder. The water began spraying out from above us, pouring down like rain and drenching us from head to toe. We took off running through the weeds and down the hill. Our screams of laughter soon turned to horror when a few of us ran into a bunch of small cactus plants. I cried out in pain as one of the plant's needles went deep into my toes. My mom heard my cries and came sprinting down the hill. She scooped me in her arms, getting herself drenched in the process, and carried me back up the hill to the white picnic table. She dug deep into her purse and found some tweezers. Then she began to gently pull the needles out of my feet and toes as another adult grabbed hold of my hands and reassured me that everything would be all right.

Before long, more mothers were carrying their children to the picnic tables. We screamed in pain and shook with fear as the adults worked together to dig the needles out of our toes. As soon as the needles were pulled out, we rushed back under the tower and back down the hill, our bodies shivering from the cold and our lips turning purple. This time, we were more careful about where we stepped.

Now that school was officially out, Memorial Day weekend was here and summer vacation began. Uncle Max was still in a wheelchair, but he was making great progress. Through his physical therapy sessions, he was beginning to put weight on his legs. Over the next couple of weeks, the physical therapist told him he could go straight to crutches. This put us all in a good mood.

This was a special weekend with many family gatherings. Grandma's sister, Great-Aunt Olive, and her husband, Great-Uncle Wallace, were here from Denver to put flowers on family graves as they did every year. They stayed with Grandma over the weekend. Every Sunday before the Memorial Day service, we took fake and real flowers out to place on the graves. My granddad's grave was always so beautiful when all of our aunts and uncles decorated it with their colorful bouquets of flowers. That afternoon, I bent over to smell the fresh lilacs that had been placed in a vase beside the gravestone. Then Lori and I stood beside Grandma for a picture. After the picture, I took off running across the burial ground. Grandma grabbed my arm and stopped me from going any further.

"Dena," she scolded with a pained look on her face. "You need to listen to me. We are standing by the gravesite where my husband, your granddad, is buried. See, he died, and when he died, his whole body stopped working. He stopped breathing and talking, and then his spirit left his body and he went to heaven. His body is underneath the ground, right here. When you walk over it, you are standing on him."

Grandma and Dena at the cemetery.

Because I never knew my granddad, or anyone who had ever died, my understanding of Memorial Day was very shallow. But I heeded my grandma's warning and began tiptoeing around, scared of stepping on anyone underground.

As we were ready to leave the cemetery, I jumped into the back seat of our station wagon with Lori. Our mom was up front beside my dad.

"I know that next year we'll be putting flowers out for Mom," she said, sobbing and wiping away her tears.

"Grandma is dying, isn't she, Mom?" Lori asked, her voice serious.

No one answered Lori.

Deep breathing and soft weeping were the only sounds we heard on the way home. I hadn't thought about it in a long time, but the idea of Grandma dying had me worried. My stomach was in knots, but it felt safer to keep my thoughts to myself than to upset my mom even more.

On Monday morning, we were up early to attend the Memorial Day services at the cemetery. For a quick breakfast, Mom took a can of biscuits from the refrigerator and poked a hole in the center. Then she fried them in our deep fryer and rolled them in a bowl of sugar—just the way we would have them at the J&J Café. We eagerly ate the sugar donuts and washed them down with a glass of milk.

As we walked out to the car, Lori ran up to Mom. "Mom, can Dena and I ride our bike out to the cemetery?" she asked.

"I suppose you can," Mom said reluctantly. "But I feel you'll be safer if I ride my bike with you, since there's going to be a lot of traffic this morning. Earle, you drive the car and take the extra flowers I picked this morning to put on Dad's grave."

Lori pedaled our purple bike as I rode up on the handlebars.

When we arrived, we parked our bikes against the cemetery fence and walked around with family and friends while marveling at how beautiful the graves were. The purple lilacs stood out to me. I closed my eyes and deeply breathed in the sweet aroma of flowers all around the graves. I felt happy that our deceased loved ones were being celebrated with such beauty. I made sure to stay away from the graves that I might accidentally step on anyone lying under the ground.

As the services began, the American Legion veterans came marching up to the flag in their uniforms, carrying their guns. I noticed that one of them was my great-uncle Pat. Silence fell over the crowd. Everyone stood to face the flag, placing their hands on their hearts. Out in the distance, two girls played "Taps" on the trumpet. The sound was both beautiful and eerie.

"This is for the veterans who have fought and died for us. We are honoring them today," whispered Great-Aunt Olive to Lori and me. "I'm always so frightened when they do their 21-gun salute and the guns go off. Would you and Lori stand beside me and hold my hand?" She smiled down at us.

Lori and I stood on each side of her and eagerly grabbed her hands. As the American Legion veterans began their forward march, our anticipation grew.

"Ready!" they shouted.

I could feel Great-Aunt Olive's hand gripping tighter around mine.

"Aim!"

I could feel her take a deep, deep breath.

"Fire!"

All three of us held our breaths while our hearts skipped a beat at each shot that was fired.

Later that day, everyone gathered at our house for a family potluck picnic with fried chicken and all the trimmings. Some of our extended family, including Mom's first cousins, Nedra, Wayne, and Dani, along with Paul, Karen, Lynne, and Dawn came for the day. My aunts and Mom were busy in the kitchen making all the food.

"You kids can make a dessert," Mom suggested. "I bought all the ingredients to make scotcheroos. Janet and Lori, you can do that."

I looked around at all the activity and breathed in the sweet-smelling air. My mouth watered in anticipation of all the treats.

Despite the somberness of the Memorial Day service, the rest of the afternoon was a fun family occasion that included playing Marco Polo and jumping on our trampoline while the adults gathered around outside, talking about life and telling stories about how my granddad was hurt fifteen years ago when he was on a horse that threw his head back. The horse then knocked into my granddad's head, giving him a concussion. "He never was the same after that," Aunt Joyce sadly said.

Before everyone left for home that evening, they helped put away the chairs and tables and also assisted my parents in cleaning up the dishes and yard. We were tired and went to bed early that night.

The next week we started Bible school at our local church. That Monday morning, we arrived with the many other loud and excited children. The adults separated us into age groups to learn about God. I was excited to be here because I usually didn't go to church. Sometimes, Lori and Janet went with Grandma, but Grandma said it was too hard to keep me quiet for that long. But this time, it was only for kids, which seemed way better than regular church.

The adults divided us into teams. We would get points for bringing money, knowing our daily memory verse, bringing a friend, bringing a Bible, and learning the pledge of allegiance to the Christian flag, the American flag, and the Bible. The team that received the most points at the end of the week would win a prize—for example, a Precious Moments poster to hang in their bedroom.

I was pretty good at all of this. I was lucky because on Tuesday, Julie's stepson, James, came for the summer to stay with his dad, and he promised he would come to Bible school with me. That meant he'd be coming as my friend; therefore I would get extra points for bringing him. Plus, our cousin Janet was staying with Lori, so Lori got points for bringing a friend too.

Bible school was so much fun. We drank Kool-Aid and ate cookies. We also played games like Drop the Hanky, which was basically like Duck, Duck, Goose. But today, while standing in a circle, my screams of laughter became screams of terror. A burning hot sensation started to run up and down my leg. When I looked down, I realized I was standing in a pile of red ants and getting bitten—a lot.

My cousin Diane took me by my hand and quickly pulled me away from the ant pile. Then she carried me downstairs to the bathroom. Another teacher came into the bathroom with some baking soda in a bowl.

"Here, put some water in this bowl to make a paste to put on her bites," said the teacher.

I continued crying as Diane put baking soda on my bites. Then another grown-up came in to help. I was surprised to see that it was my grandma. By chance, she was there bringing cookies she had baked and donated to the church for the Bible school kids. She picked me up and held me for a while.

"You're going to be okay, Dena," she said, murmuring and nuzzling me against her face. I felt comforted and began to calm down. The pain gradually lessened, and Grandma sent me back to my classroom to listen to a Bible story.

As we sat around the table, Kathy, a high-school helper, began to tell us about a man named Jacob. "We are going to learn about Jacob's ladder," she said, holding a colorful biblical image of a man with a ladder reaching to the skies. Kathy told us that Jacob was on a journey and was getting tired, so he stopped for the night because the sun had set. Taking one of the stones, he put it under his head and lay down to sleep.

"Now, who would want to use a rock for a pillow?" she asked all of us.

We all touched the backs of our heads and winced. "Nooo, that would hurt!"

"Well, Jacob didn't have a pillow like you and I do, so he used a rock," said Kathy. "But as he slept, he had a dream in which he saw a stairway resting on the earth, with its top reaching way past the clouds to a place called heaven, and the angels of God were ascending and descending on it. Now, who can tell me what heaven is?"

"I can!" I shouted out. "My grandma says that my granddad went to live in heaven, and my mom says my grandma will be going there soon too. That's where people go when they die." Some of the other kids looked at me with surprise. I hadn't missed a beat, and I didn't know enough about death to be sad about it.

"That's right," said Kathy. "If you ask Jesus into your heart, you can go and live in heaven when you die. Now, way above the ladder stood the Lord, and he said: 'I am the Lord, the God of your father Abraham and the God of Isaac.' We all know that God is the father and Jesus is the son, and then there is the Holy Spirit. He is three in one, right?"

All of us six- and seven-year-olds looked at each other, confused. I'd heard Jesus' name before. I knew he lived in heaven and could see us down here, and that He was God. But I didn't really understand what this all meant.

"Well," Kathy continued, "In John 14:6, Jesus says, 'I am the way, the truth, and the life. No one comes to the Father except through Me.'" Kathy walked behind each of us and touched us on the shoulder, asking us all the same question. "Dena, do you know that Jesus loves you?" she quizzed. "He made you, and He loves you very much. And He died on a cross for you."

I looked up at her with a serious expression on my face. "I don't think He knows me," I said, kind of shocked that she would think Jesus could love me if we hadn't even met before.

"Yes, He does," she insisted. "He made everything in the universe, as well as the stars, the moon, the trees, the water, the animals, and even you. In Psalm 139:13, it reads: 'For You formed my inward parts; You covered me in my mother's womb.' And in verse 15, it says, 'My frame was not hidden from You, when I was made in secret, and skillfully wrought in the lowest parts of the earth.' What this means, Dena, is that even while you were in your mommy's tummy, you were being created in His image, being made by God Himself. So of course He loves you."

A little bolt of excitement shot through me as I sat in awe and thought about who Jesus was and what this all meant. I felt happy to think that someone I couldn't even remember meeting actually loved me.

"And if you ask Him into your heart, then when you get older and die, He will take you to heaven," said Kathy. "Everyone who wants to ask Jesus into their heart, bow your heads, close your eyes, and fold your hands. Then repeat this prayer with me: Dear Jesus, I know You love me, and You want me to belong to You. I ask You into my heart. Amen."

We solemnly repeated after her, then we heard the big bell begin to ring. We rushed upstairs, where we sang songs of praise. My favorite song was when one side of the church would stand up and sing "Hallelujah" and then sit down while the other side sang "Praise Ye the Lord." We took turns and sang as fast and loud as we could, trying not to get mixed up when the song would change from "Praise Ye the Lord" to "Hallelujah." The fun continued, because at the end of each Bible school session, the high-school kids would perform a puppet show about our lesson of the day.

After thinking about what I learned that day, a clear picture of Jesus popped up in my mind. I pictured Him taller than the clouds, made out of shiny brass, gold, and steel. His head had a glowing crown, and on His spine was a beautiful, shining brass stairway with golden rails that you climbed when you died. It would take you straight to the gates of heaven.

The week at Bible school went as quickly as it came. On the last day, we put on a program for our parents and grandparents. Then, we dragged our parents all over the church, showing them all the arts and crafts we'd created. Everything we'd worked on sat in a box so we could take our handiwork home. The treasures we'd created would soon turn to trash. Except for the plaster of Paris handprint sculpture we had created. For many years it hung on our Christmas tree as a reminder of that special week.

Chapter 18

Fourth of July Blasts

"Stand fast therefore in the liberty by which Christ has made us free, and do not be entangled again with a yoke of bondage." **—Galatians 5:1**

As the summer continued, it wasn't long before my favorite holiday, the Fourth of July, was here. Aunt Jean and Uncle Neil always had a big picnic so we could watch the fireworks that were set off just west of their home in Wray.

When we arrived, the narrow street was jam-packed with vehicles on both sides. Uncle Max and Aunt Joyce were already there. Grandma was there, too, lighting up the place with her beautiful smile.

Uncle Max was beginning to use his crutches, as he was becoming stronger. All the kids began hopping around on them. I was too small to use them properly, so I found a way to improvise by putting my arms around the bar where he gripped with his hands, then placing my hands down below.

My cousin Mike stood in the empty lot next to his house, lighting firecrackers. After playing with Uncle Max's crutches, Lori and I ran over to watch him.

"Hey, Dena, here's your favorite one that you liked last year," he said as he lit a small black dot that began to grow. It resembled a black snake coming out to get you. Then, before long, it turned to ash.

"Hey, that's cool. Let's do another one like that!" I suggested.

"I have a whole sack of firecrackers to do. Let me do this one. Everyone stand back—this is a twizzler," he announced.

"Is that the one that spins on the ground and makes a loud buzzing noise that chases you?" Lori asked, alarmed.

"Yes, that's the one," replied Janeil.

In anticipation, we stood way back and watched Mike light it. After that, he ran back to where we were standing. It made a whizzing sound as it twirled in colorful circles. All of us were ready to run when it bounced off the ground and came right toward us. It made a couple of jumps and then, just like that, the fire died out.

"That one always chases me!" Lori shouted.

"Let's do more firecrackers later when it gets dark out," said Mike. "We can go ride motorcycles now."

Mike backed his motorcycle out of the shed. "Hop on!" he said.

I jumped on, and we took off as fast as he could go. He had a small area that he used to jump over logs in the empty lot beside his house. I'd been on these jumps before, and I'd since learned to balance myself when my butt went flying off the back seat. It was scary and exciting at the same time. We continued to ride up a hill that led to a bridge over the railroad tracks. Making sure there were no trains coming, we rode down the center of the tracks, over the bridge, and back down the other side of the hill. Then we rode over another bridge where a small river ran beneath us. This led to the baseball field, where many people were gathering for the fireworks that night. Mike and I waved at everyone as we rode around the baseball field and then back to his house the same way we'd come.

Back at the house, the grill was smoking and the smell of hamburgers lingered in the air. We noticed that more family members had shown up. Lori and Janeil were riding the air-pump scooters on the street. Mike ran into his house and brought out his bow and arrow, and many of my older cousins started to target shoot on the east side of the house.

As the evening set in, many fireworks were being set off by teenagers around the town, and when I saw them go off in the air, I ran to Mom, shouting, "They're starting!"

"No, Dena, they're not starting yet. Those are just kids having fun. When it's completely dark, the real show will begin," she patiently explained.

Finally, when it was dark out, the adults took lawn chairs to the west side of the house as giant booms began to echo through the canyons. I followed my older cousins to the end of the lot, where it felt as if the whole sky was lit up right above me. I looked up in awe, engulfed in a shower of colors that gradually faded and disappeared, only to reappear again in the next heartbeat. It was as if they were putting the whole show on just for me.

Tuckered out from all the excitement, I fell asleep on the way home. Our cousin Janet came to spend the night with us. By the time we arrived in Eckley, some of my older cousins were setting off their own fireworks down at the softball field. Mom and Dad parked and woke me to watch their display. I sleepily looked on, smiling at the radiant colors.

As we drove home, Lori asked, "Mom, can we sleep out on the trampoline?"

"You can get the sleeping bags out, but Dena, you had better sleep in the house," she said.

I frowned. "Why can't I sleep outside too?"

"Because you need more sleep, Dena," Lori and Janet said in agreement.

After Mom tucked me into bed, I waited until I knew for sure that my parents were asleep. Then I snuck outside to where the girls were talking on the trampoline.

"Dena, you're not supposed to be out here!" they both scolded me in small whispers.

"I know, but I'll only be out here for a little while!"

Sitting on the trampoline, we looked up at the sky in our small, dark town. We could see the stars clearly, and we could hear the irrigated sprinkler on the cornfield north of the house. We could also hear the busy nearby highway, with all its cars and trucks whizzing by. Next door, a dog was barking, and two cats by our shed were hissing and yowling.

Over by the barn, we heard the horses neighing back and forth with their hooves stomping as they tried to shake off the pestering bugs, and we heard the zapping of the bug catcher going off.

"Dena, you had better get in the house before Mom and Dad figure out you're here," said Lori.

"They just said I couldn't sleep out here. They didn't say I couldn't come out for a visit," I pointed out.

Soon enough, though, the three of us got to giggling so loudly that my parents heard my voice from their open window.

"What the heck is Dena doing out there? You get in here right this minute!" yelled my dad.

Mom came out in her long blue robe. "You kids probably need to come in. I can see it's getting cloudy. The stars aren't as clear as they were a little while ago, and the wind is picking up." She helped us grab the sleeping bags and took us into the house. "You girls can sleep in the living room. I'll get Dena another sleeping bag."

This time I had no trouble falling fast asleep. But I woke up when I heard a loud noise and felt my dad picking me up. I didn't quite understand why Dad was picking me up, but I wasn't concerned. I lay my head on his shoulder and proceeded to fall right back to sleep. Then I felt as if I were dreaming and hearing fireworks go off again.

After a while, I heard my mom yelling. It dawned on me that we were all standing in the back bathroom. As I became more aware of my surroundings, I realized there was fear in her voice, but I wasn't sure what was going on or why everyone was screaming. Mom, Dad, Vonie, Lori, Janet, and I were all huddled together. I wasn't scared, but I came to realize that my parents were. I finally woke up enough to hear the loud noise, which sounded like a freight train coming through our house, driving right on top of our roof.

At that moment, I became scared. It was so loud, I couldn't even hear myself crying. For about fifteen minutes, hail and wind swept through our house. "With this loud noise, I believe we may be experiencing a tornado!" Dad screamed out so that we could hear him.

I really didn't understand what a tornado was, but if this was one, the sound was terrifying. I began to cry and clutch my dad, who was also shaking. Lori and Janet were hugging each other tightly, and Mom had her arm around Vonie and both the girls.

This scared me even more, and I began to panic. When the wind and hail finally quit, an eerie silence settled in.

"We have to find some flashlights in the utility room," Mom said. "Everyone hold hands and follow me."

She bravely tiptoed in her slippers, leading us through the dark hallway and into the wet utility room where the rain had come through underneath the door. In the complete darkness, she found two flashlights in the cabinets above the washer and dryer. Handing a flashlight to Dad and holding one herself, she led us to the living room while shining a light on our sleeping bags. We were all in disbelief. Where we had previously been sleeping on the floor, glass from the bay windows was strewn about. I shivered as I realized that we would have surely been cut up had we remained there during the horrible storm.

The next morning, we saw that tree branches had fallen all over the trampoline and all over our yard. We had a lot of cleaning up to do. Mom and Dad had to call the insurance company to come out and assess the damage. And before long, we had a new bay window.

As an adult, I remember that night as if it happened yesterday. I was a child who usually obeyed my parents. However, I didn't obey that night. Instead, I allowed my curiosity to get the best of me by going out to the trampoline. Had I not done so, my mom might never have come outside and realized that a bad storm was brewing. She might never have shepherded us to safety inside the house. No one ever confirmed it was a tornado, but my dad swears that the way the tree branches came down, it had to be. Whatever the case, it was a climactic moment in what had mostly been a serene and carefree summer—and a sign of some of the storms that we'd be weathering together as a family in the near future.

Chapter 19

A Moment of Change

"Likewise you younger people, submit yourselves to your elders. Yes, all of you be submissive to one another, and be clothed with humility, for 'God resists the proud, but gives grace to the humble.'" —**1 Peter 5:5**

Mom and Aunt Joyce were talking one day shortly after the storm. "It seems like when it rains, it pours. Not only did we lose our windows, but the hail ruined my garden, and now, with going back to school and sending the kids to Yuma, everything just feels a bit stressful," said Mom.

"But thank the Lord we're healthy. I'm still worried about Mom though. She's doing well with her treatments, but she's been fighting this cancer for a very long time. I hope she can continue to fight it," said Aunt Joyce, sighing. "Then there's Max. He's still on crutches but continuing to heal. And the bills . . . Oh, good Lord, those hospital bills!"

Mom comforted Aunt Joyce by patting her on the shoulder. I didn't know anything about the bills, but I was glad that Uncle Max seemed to be recovering swiftly—so much that he was back to work at the grain elevator on his crutches.

One Saturday, Aunt Jean, Janeil, and Mike came to visit us. "Kids, we're heading down to the elevator to see how Aunt Joyce and Uncle Max are getting along. While we're there, you can get a pop," announced Aunt Jean.

Uncle Max was unloading a truckload of corn when we arrived. If he weren't on his crutches, no one would have ever known that he was hurt. He was his usual happy, playful self when he came out to greet us.

"Can we play over at the storage units?" Janeil asked.

"Sure, but you keep an eye on the trucks! Remember that even if you see them, it doesn't mean that they see you," lectured my mom.

After walking over to the storage units, we climbed a long cement walkway with cement stairs in the middle that separated the units.

"Let's pretend that these are our houses, and between each step is a different house," suggested Janeil. I, on the other hand, was content to climb the stairs and run across the cement walkway.

After a while, the adults came out to check on us.

"Come here, kids!" said Uncle Max. Climbing the stairs on his crutches, he unlocked one of the doors to the storage unit where he kept sacks of feed that he sold for livestock. In one corner of the dark building was a stack of white salt blocks and a stack of brown mineral blocks for cattle and horses.

He took a white salt block that glistened in the sun. With a hammer, he broke it into several pieces. "Here!" he said as he handed each of us a piece of salt block to suck on. "Now you need to come over to the elevator for a pop, because this salt will make you thirsty!" All of us kids loved to lick the salt blocks, except Janeil, who shook her head in disgust.

Back at the elevator, my uncle took a key out of the cash register and unlocked the pop machine. "Everyone, tell me what your favorite drink is," he said as he handed each of us a can of our choice. I snapped open my Pepsi and enjoyed the cold, prickly feel of the soda as it trickled down my throat.

"Okay," Mom said after a while. "All of you hand me your salt blocks and I'll save them for later. You can't have too much salt in one day, you know!"

Uncle Max handed us a pencil to pass around. "Each of you put your name on the block and then put them inside this paper sack to save for later," he advised. "You'll get sick if you eat too much!"

Mom looked at all of us. "Kids, today we're taking off to go school shopping in Sterling. All of you need to jump in the back of the station wagon!"

Sterling was an hour-and-a-half drive from home, but it was the only place that had a variety of stores to buy clothes, cleaning supplies, and school supplies. We always shopped at K-Mart, Gibson's, JCPenney, and Woolworth. Woolworth was my favorite store. As we entered the front door, we ran to the back of the store to see all of the animals. They sold all kinds of birds as well as gerbils and fish. We watched the fish swimming in their tanks and marveled at all the pretty parakeets. A lady who worked here was cleaning the tanks. When she noticed us, she told us all about the animals in the store.

"I'm getting thirsty," I told Janeil after listening to the lady talk for a while. The store had a restaurant, and the scent of food was wafting over to us.

"I don't have any money, but we can order water for free. Let's go sit at a booth, and we'll all get water," Lori suggested.

"You can order water for free?" I asked, surprised.

"Sure, you can do that anywhere!"

All four of us headed to the booth and sat down without any adults. When the waitress came to our table, she asked, "What would you like?"

"Water," said Janeil

"Water," said Lori.

"Water," said Mike.

"Me too. I want water," I reiterated, feeling like an adult for ordering myself.

"Okay, that won't cost you anything," the waitress said, smiling.

We were all having a great time pretending to be adults. Mom, Aunt Joyce, and Aunt Jean came and sat behind us in a different booth.

"When the waitress comes back, you can order some food," suggested Aunt Joyce.

Janeil stopped the waitress as she walked by our table. "This time we'll order food, but the people behind us will pay for it," she said, pointing behind her.

Mom, Aunt Joyce, and Aunt Jean began giggling. "That's what they think," said Aunt Jean with a conspiratorial smile.

"Yeah," piped in Aunt Joyce. "Don't let them fool you. They know how to wash dishes."

After a delicious meal, we watched my aunts and my mom all grab for the ticket when the waitress set it on the table.

"I'll get it," said Mom.

"No, I'll get it this time. You got it last time," insisted Aunt Jean.

"Oh, you brought me up here on your gas and you got it last time. I'll pay this time," said Aunt Joyce.

"You're not paying for our kids!" said Aunt Jean and Mom.

"Oh, poop," said Aunt Joyce, realizing she was outnumbered.

"I've got the ticket right here, and I'll pay for it," Mom said calmly.

I watched my aunts closely, and I saw them both secretly place money inside Mom's purse without her noticing. Then everyone threw loose change out for a tip for the waitress.

We continued to shop for bargains that afternoon. But it didn't take long for our smiles to turn into frowns when a lady came back over the loudspeaker. "Is there a Jean, Joyce, or a Jan anywhere in the store? You have an urgent call in our office from home. Repeat: Jean, Joyce, or Jan, you have an urgent call in our office."

"Oh no!" Mom groaned. "What could it be?"

They all began to run to the front of the store, and all of the kids followed. Mom hurried over to the lady who was talking over the intercom.

"I'm Jan."

"Yes, come into the office. A girl named Vonie needs to talk to you on the phone."

"Oh, that's my daughter! Did she say what's up?"

"No, she just said it's urgent."

Mom walked into the office as we stayed outside, eagerly waiting to find out what was going on. When Mom came out, she had a worried expression on her face. "They had to take Mom by ambulance to Wray," she said, the frown on her face getting more pronounced. "She can't stop throwing up, and they're giving her an IV for dehydration. I guess we need to finish up here and head back home!"

We all rushed back to the aisle with the backpacks and lunch boxes. We grabbed some crayons, pencils, and folders, then headed to the counter to pay and drive back home.

On the way home, it was quiet until Aunt Jean spoke up. "This is a slow-moving cancer. She was diagnosed in 1977; here it is, 1979, and she's still fighting hard. I didn't think she'd last a full year last year, but I just don't know how much longer she can hold on."

When we got to the hospital, the kids stayed outside to play. When Mom and my aunts came outside, they were happy to announce that Grandma would be back home tomorrow morning.

At home, Mom made some chicken noodle soup that she took over to Grandma's, and Vonie spent a couple of nights with her to keep her company while she was recovering. Grandma felt that even though she was sick, she could still live her life at her house and be completely independent.

"I don't want to be a burden to anyone!" I heard her say to Mom one day.

Mom broke down in tears. "You're my mother, and I love you. You will never be a burden to me!" It was a comforting moment that helped put me at ease, because it made me realize how lucky we were to have one another—especially in life's most difficult moments.

Soon, it was the last day of summer and the day before my first day at my new school. My friend Pati, who lived next door to my grandmother, invited me over to play at her house. Pati was a year older than me, but we always had so much fun playing together. She had all these small cooking pans and a pretend kitchen that sat outside by her swing set. We usually turned on the water hydrant to make the dirt wet, and then we'd proceed to make chocolate mud pies.

"I'm going to make a chocolate mud pie for Grandma," I announced.

"And I'll make her a mud chicken casserole," said Pati.

After we had scooped our mud into our pans, we sat them inside her toy oven, counted to thirty, then took them out and promptly walked over to my grandma's and knocked on her door. When she opened the door, there we stood, dirty from head to toe, each of us holding our mud pies and casseroles. Grandma's smile widened as we explained why we were there. "Our treat will help you feel better, Grandma," I quickly added.

Grandma stepped outside and took the spoon from us and pretended to eat the casserole and pie until they were all gone. "Yum! These are the best mud chicken and mud pies I have ever tasted in my whole life, and they make me feel so much better," she said, smiling and patting us both on the top of the head. "Why don't the two of you walk over and rinse your hands in the hydrant?"

Pati and I walked over to the hydrant and turned it on at full speed, placing both of our hands in the water and getting each other drenched in the process. Grandma came over and turned down the hydrant before handing us a clean, dry towel right from the clothesline.

"You two stay outside for a second while I run inside and get you a treat," she said. Pati and I walked back to the front porch, leaving a small mud trail behind us. When Grandma came back, she handed each of us two chocolate-chip cookies. Then she sat down between us as we eagerly ate our cookies and rocked back and forth on the porch swing, "I sure do love the two of you," she said brightly.

"Thanks for the cookies, Grandma," I said. "Now Pati and I are going back to her house to bake more mud pies."

"Thanks for making my day, girls!" said Grandma.

After a moment of hugs, Pati and I took off running back to her house as fast as we could as Grandma stood on her front porch waving at us. We had the best of times pretending we owned a café and that we were the cooks. (I had been inspired by my mom and aunt.)

That night, after I came home from Pati's, my family and I sat down for supper.

"You all need to take a shower tonight to get ready for school in the morning," said Mom. "And you will have to wake up early to get on the bus to go to Yuma. All of you will ride the same bus, but you'll switch buses when you get to the high school. There are three different schools in Yuma. Dena, you will go to Morris Primary North Elementary School as a first grader. Lori, you will be at Middle West School as a seventh grader. And Vonie, I just can't believe you're a senior this year! Where has the time gone?" She smiled, but her eyes were teary.

Chapter 20

New Chapter in School

"Let no one despise your youth, but be an example to the believers in word, in conduct, in love, in spirit, in faith, in purity." —**1 Timothy 4:12**

My sisters were already used to the long trek out to Yuma each day, but my stomach was in knots as I thought about the gigantic change ahead of me. I couldn't just ride my bike a few blocks away and be where I wanted to be. This was a big adjustment, and I didn't quite know how I felt about it.

The next morning, there were two separate buses in Eckley to pick up the kids. On the west side of Main Street was one bus, and on the east side was the bus that my sisters and I would ride. That morning, I stepped up to the steep incline, pulling myself up with the handle bar. I followed Lori, with Vonie behind me. I felt really small walking down the aisle on the bus, wondering where I was supposed to sit. I finally found a seat in front of my friend Julie

Z. As I faced the front, Julie Z reached across my seat from behind me.

"Hi, Julie Z," I said, turning completely around in my seat to talk to her.

The bus driver, who was also Julie Z's uncle, eyed me from the big mirror. "Dena, sit the right way in your seat, please!" he scolded. I turned around to face the front and then scooted over by the window, where I could talk to Julie Z between the crack of the window and the seat, out of the bus driver's sight. The brown seats were so high, I could barely see over them.

Julie Z's cousin, Kirk, who was in high school, continued to watch the bus driver (who was his dad) through the mirror. Then, when he wasn't looking, Kirk grabbed Julie Z's arm and picked her up, sitting her right beside me in my seat so the two of us could continue talking. Pati, who was a second grader, got on the bus at the last stop and crammed in next to us so we were all sitting together.

Being with my friends made the drive not so scary or long. Before we knew it, we were at the high school. The high school was a long building with a pretty green hill in the front. On the south side of the school, there was a long curved driveway in the shape of a horseshoe where the buses parked. In the center of the driveway was the parking lot. That morning, many teenagers were hanging out by their cars with their music blaring away as they waited for the bell to ring for the first period.

Before the bus driver opened the door to let Vonie and some other high schoolers off, he gave us an announcement: "The middle-school kids, fourth through eighth grade, need to stay on this bus, but the students in third grade and under need to step off the bus and get on the one parked right behind us."

As he opened the door, we let the high schoolers go on ahead of us. "Goodbye, Vonie!" I said as she walked off the bus. The younger kids then got out. I looked up at the tall bus we'd just gotten off of and felt so small. Shara and Lori had rolled down their windows and were waving at us. I waved back. Julie Z, Pati, and I stuck together like glue as we climbed the steep stairs of the new bus. We all felt a little scared of the unknown day ahead of us.

This was such a new experience. I didn't know what to expect or what I would do to make friends. When we arrived at the new school, it seemed massive, and all of a sudden I wanted to be back at the little red schoolhouse in Eckley.

As we walked off the bus, a teacher came up to us. "I'm Mrs. Kork. Are you first graders?" she asked.

"I'm a second grader," said Pati.

"I'm a first grader," said Julie Z.

"Yeah, me too," I chimed in.

"I will show all three of you where to go," she replied, leading us down a very long hallway. Before we got to the end of the hallway, there was a ramp we had to walk down. At the end of the ramp, the teacher stopped to show Pati where the second-grade classes were. Pati gazed at us with longing in her eyes, almost like she wished she, too, were a first grader so she could stay with us.

We could hear a lot of commotion coming down the hall as we followed the teacher. I widened my eyes. There were so many kids in first grade! Walking down a long hall, we came to a great big room;

on each corner of this giant room were four classrooms and four teachers.

It was pure culture shock. In our Eckley kindergarten class, there were eight kids total. Today, Mom had informed me there were eighty first graders.

"To start off, we want all of you to sit in the big room on the floor in lines," announced a teacher.

"Criss-cross applesauce your legs, and be quiet so you can hear us when we call your names!" ordered another teacher.

Then another teacher walked in front of us. When she began talking, I realized it was my favorite teacher of all! Mrs. Licht had gotten a job as a first-grade teacher in Yuma. I was so happy to see her that I jumped up and ran to give her a hug. She gave me a squeeze back, smiling. "Good to see you this morning, Dena, but you need to go sit down with the other students," she instructed me. Obediently, I took my seat next to Julie Z. Mrs. Licht then asked us to stand back up, place out right hand over out heart, and say the Pledge of Allegiance.

We all stood with our hands over our hearts as we recited the Pledge of Allegiance. "Good job," said Mrs. Licht. "We all seem to remember this from last year!"

As the teachers began calling our names to come up and get a name tag, Julie Z and I were separated. She got to go with Mrs. Licht, who apparently was not going to be my teacher. But I was happy to see that another friend from kindergarten, Dusty, had ended up in the same class as me.

Our teacher led us to her classroom. "I'll have each of you sit at a desk," she said. "My name is Mrs. Standsfield." Mrs. Standsfield had a smile that made me feel welcome. Her long, dark hair curled against her face, and her cheeks and lips were red. She had a blue scarf around her neck and wore a pretty red sweater, complemented by black leggings and a navy-blue skirt. I thought she was beautiful.

"Here is the book we will be working on. When you turn to the first page, you will see a boy on his bike. Is everyone on the first page?"

I turned to the first page, but I didn't see a boy on a bike.

"Does everyone see a boy on a bike?" she asked again.

I was too shy to say I didn't see a boy on a bike; instead, I saw kids on a swing set. I sat in silence, not wanting to mention that my page was different.

Finally, the little boy behind me raised his hand. "Teacher, my book is different. It has a boy riding a horse."

I was relieved that the kid behind me was also seeing something different from our teacher, even if it wasn't the same picture that I saw. I gathered the courage to raise my hand too.

"Mine has kids playing on swings!" I said.

Finally, Ms. Wynter, the teacher's aide, came over and looked at our books. "Uh, Mrs. Stansfield, these books look the same on the outside but are different on the inside. One is a second-grade book, and this one here is a third-grade book!" she explained.

"Okay, tomorrow I will get you both a new book. I will have to talk to the second-grade and third-grade teachers and see if they have any first-grade books." She sighed, clearly upset that her day wasn't going as she had planned.

Before long, the bell rang. "It's time to eat lunch," said Ms. Wynter. "Everyone line up in two lines; boys stand behind Mrs. Stansfield, and girls stand behind me. We will stop by the bathroom, where I want everyone to go in and wash their hands."

I was taken aback at how small the toilets and sinks were. I'd never been in such a tiny bathroom before; it looked like it was made for tiny people. Mrs. Stansfield stood at the door, watching to make sure we all washed our hands. Then we all lined back up behind our teachers.

It gradually became louder as we walked toward the cafeteria. I could feel my heart racing, as there were easily over a hundred kids, with the first and second graders eating together. I had never seen so many kids in one spot. Sitting down to eat, I glanced around at all the kids. I felt scared, as if I could feel everyone watching me. I worried that they would break out in taunts and laughter at any moment.

A teacher came to our table. "You need to hurry and eat," she warned us. "The third graders will be in here in about five minutes, and we need to get out to recess."

I looked down at the bean burrito on my cafeteria tray. It didn't look very appealing. But Dusty had been eating it, and she seemed to like it.

As the teacher walked away, I went to take a bite of my burrito. As soon as I did, the same teacher came back. "Everyone take your plate up to the kitchen to be washed and then head outside for recess," she instructed. Although I hadn't taken so much as a bite, I decided I wasn't hungry, so I hurried and dumped my tray.

Outside, the Eckley girls quickly bonded in a tight circle and held hands. My friends Jamie and John were relieved to find us.

"Can we join, too?" asked Jamie. I was about to let go of the hands to let the two boys in when Julie Z piped up, "No, this is a girls' circle, so boys can't join."

I felt a little sad but went along with her rules anyway. "Yep, this is a girls' circle, so boys can't join!" I repeated. But honestly, they were my friends, and I really didn't see any harm in letting them join.

At that moment, Mrs. Licht came over. "You will let Jamie and John join your circle or you will not be in a circle any longer!" she scolded. The other girls sighed in disappointment but obeyed. I promptly let go of Julie Z's hand, and Jamie and John joined in, making our circle much bigger.

By the end of the week, we fell into our new first-grade routine and began making friends with some of the Yuma kids. I also learned to eat fast during lunch because I knew I wouldn't get any food at all otherwise. It got to the point that I was doing it everywhere. Even at home, Mom began to scold me for shoveling in the food. "Slow down, Dena! You're going to make yourself sick eating that fast!" But the habit had been formed, and old habits are hard to break.

Chapter 21

Tough Transitions

"Jesus Christ is the same yesterday, today, and forever."
—**Hebrews 13:8**

My first-grade year in a new school seemed to be flying by. Before we knew it, Thanksgiving break was here and we were heading out to Uncle Keith's and Aunt Dolores's for our Thanksgiving meal.

That morning, my dad woke me up. "You need to come out to the TV and watch the Thanksgiving Day parade with us. It's very pretty."

As we were watching the parade, I heard my mom gasp with laughter in the kitchen. "Really? Oh my gosh, Vonie, that is a beautiful ring! When did he propose to you? Earle, you better come in here. Vonie has some news."

Lori and I eagerly followed Dad into the kitchen, where Vonie was sitting on a bar stool, her left hand extended. On her left ring finger was a shiny new diamond ring. A great big smile stretched across her face. "He proposed to me last night!" she said.

My dad was speechless, and shock came across his face. For a long while he just sat there, contemplating what to say to her. He finally blurted out the only thing he could think of. "You know you have to finish high school before you get married, young lady!"

"I know I do!" Vonie shot back to my dad, her smile melting into a frown.

"Married?" I asked in shock. "Vonie is getting married!"

"That means you will have a new brother, Lori and Dena. Tom will be your brother-in-law," said Mom.

I was excited for a wedding, and I really liked Tom, who always played games with us.

"Wow, I'm going to have a new brother," I said. I also knew that I would get the job as Vonie's flower girl at her wedding. I had been the flower girl for many of my older cousins' weddings, and sometimes they called me "Flower Girl" when I talked on the CBs at Uncle Keith's house. I couldn't wait for Vonie's wedding!

"Let me see your ring, Vonie," Lori said excitedly. "Oh, that's beautiful! When did he propose?"

"How and where did he propose?" asked Mom.

"Last night, before he dropped me off after the movie," Vonie said.

"When are you planning this wedding?" asked Dad, a very concerned look on his face.

"We're waiting until after I graduate in June," Vonie replied, a dreamy look in her eyes.

"You're not pregnant, are you?"

"No, I'm not pregnant, Dad!" Vonie screamed.

"Earle, she's not pregnant. What is the matter with you?" screamed Mom. "Can't you just be happy for her for once? You're ruining the moment with all of your questions. Can't you see she's in love? We knew this moment would happen before we were ready, but oh, I'm so happy for you, Vonie!" She enfolded my sister in a big hug. "Just think, we will have so much fun planning the wedding. I bet Aunt Joyce and Aunt Jean will even make your bridesmaid dresses."

"I suppose that if you marry Tom, it will be a big, expensive Catholic wedding!" my dad huffed. "Can't the two of you just go to the justice of the peace and get married there, like your mother and I did?" I knew my dad hated to go anywhere fancy that required dressing up, and he wasn't all that fond of weddings.

"Earle, she is going to have a beautiful wedding, and we are going to help her pay for it," Mom said, pointing a warning finger at my dad.

"What does a ring have to do with a wedding?" I asked, totally confused.

"When people get engaged, the boy asks for the girl's hand in marriage with a diamond engagement ring. Then when you get married, another ring, the wedding ring, will go beside it or around it. Then you wear it forever," said Mom.

"Did Dad give you a ring, Mom?" I asked.

"Yes! See, my engagement ring and my wedding ring are fused together. I hardly ever take it off. Your dad has a ring too.

"Yes, I do!" said Dad with a smile. "I only have the wedding ring, though, because only girls get the engagement ring. Your mom bought this one for me when we got married. I wear it all the time, but it's been years since I've actually looked at it. It's a pretty silver wedding band." He held it out, a look of fond remembrance on his face.

"Vonie, I get to be your flower girl! I've had lots of practice with all our older cousins. I promise I'll do a good job!" I said.

"Yes, I guess so, Dena," she said, wrinkling her nose as if she didn't really have any other option. "You'll be our flower girl. And Lori, I want you to stand up as a junior bridesmaid with me."

"I would love to!" she said, giving Vonie a hug.

"This is great news, but now we need to get ready to go to Uncle Keith and Aunt Dolores's house for Thanksgiving dinner. No one say a word about this during dinner, do you understand?" said Mom.

"Yes," Lori and I both responded, running our fingers across our lips as if we were zipping our mouths shut.

Our whole family was at Uncle Keith's, and my older cousins were in the shop playing basketball. I sat down to watch them. Later, more of our cousins came out to the shop, where some tables for dinner were set up just for the kids. All of us younger kids got to eat in there and be as loud and messy as we wanted.

As we sat around the table with my older cousins, Janeil had a question. "Is Vonie going to college after she graduates?"

Lori and I looked at each other, not knowing what to say.

At seven years old, I didn't think before I spoke. "No, she and Tom are getting married," I blurted out.

"She and Tom are getting married?" asked my older cousins, Tim and Kenny, who were sitting at the table behind us. "Really?"

"Dena, you weren't supposed to say anything!" Lori glared at me.

I immediately covered my mouth with my hands. Before we even went back to the house, the news had spread like a wildfire out of control.

"Dena, I'm going to kill you!" Vonie said. "That announcement was for me and Tom to make, not you. Just for that, you're not going to be my flower girl in my wedding." She flounced off in tears.

Grandma walked over to Vonie and gave her a hug. "That's the best news I've heard all day. I'm so happy for both of you. And you will forgive your little sister before the wedding, I'm sure of it," she said, taking Vonie's cheeks in her hand and kissing her. Then she gave Tom a hug too. "Welcome to the family, Tom!"

Then, after smoothing the ruffled feathers, Grandma turned to me. "Dena, this is a lesson for you to learn when to keep your mouth shut. Now, go give your sister a hug and tell her you're sorry!"

I walked over to Vonie with my head down and tears in my eyes. "I'm so sorry. If you don't want me as your flower girl, I understand."

"It's okay," she said with a sigh. "But in the future, when I tell you to keep your mouth shut, can you do it?"

I sniffed as the tears fell down our cheeks. "I'll try," I promised.

Everyone got up and started congratulating them. The family slapped my dad on the back and shared their joy with my parents. Aunt Joyce came behind me and gave me a big hug, and I sat on her lap as she rubbed my back.

"We were wondering if you and Aunt Jean could make the bridesmaid dresses," Mom asked her sisters.

"Of course!" they piped up.

"We can try to get the material before Christmas and work on it through the spring if they're getting married in June," said Aunt Jean. "It will be here before we know it."

That night, I felt bad about spilling the beans to our family about the wedding, and I had a hard time falling asleep. But Vonie eventually forgave me, and the celebration of the holiday seasons continued.

Chapter 22

Graduation Ceremony and Wedding Bells

"Therefore what God has joined together, let not man separate." —**Mark 10:9**

As a child, I recall that the transition from winter to spring felt like it took forever. In truth, though, May came around pretty quickly. For Vonie's graduation, Mom made dinner reservations at a new restaurant in Yuma. Afterward, we drove over to our great-aunt Velma and great-uncle Pat's house so Vonie could change into her graduation gown and Lori and I could change into our new dresses—which had been purchased especially for the occasion.

Every year, Great-Aunt Velma invited all the graduates to stop by her house and take a picture. Great-Aunt Velma had been a teacher in Yuma for many years, and she usually knew all the kids who were graduating. She was the scrapbook queen of the '70s and '80s. She and Great-Uncle Pat lived close to Yuma High School and right behind the 7-Eleven store. We always stayed with her when we had any school activities.

When we arrived, I asked Mom, "Can Lori and I go get a Slurpee?" Whenever we came here, we'd always walk to 7-Eleven to buy a Slurpee by ourselves.

"I suppose, since it's just a Slurpee and it's very hot outside. Here's a dollar. Hurry back, because you need to change and get ready for the graduation," she told us.

When we got back, I could tell that Dad was impatient. "You didn't need a Slurpee! We have to leave in twenty minutes, and you haven't even changed yet. Now get upstairs! These Slurpees are going in the freezer until after the graduation."

Mom helped us change into our new dresses, and when we came down the stairs, we all stood beside Vonie for family pictures. Then we went outside and stood by the big tree before heading to the sidewalk for another photo.

"Okay, this is good for now," said Great-Aunt Velma. But somehow, I knew it wouldn't be the last picture of the day.

"Now, about tonight," said Great-Aunt Velma, looking straight at Vonie and a couple other seniors who had shown up to take a traditional senior picture for my aunt's scrapbook. "I know you seniors always have a big party after graduation that continues until early in the morning, but just be aware, when you pull up to 7-Eleven and go behind the building to pee, you are right below our bedroom window. We not only see you, but we also know who you are!"

Lori and I looked at each other and began to giggle. Vonie was visibly disgusted as she glared over at her three male classmates. "You know it's always the boys who do that, not us girls!" she said in her defense.

"We need to get over there, *now!*" said Dad. We all piled into our car and drove to the church parking lot across from the high school. Vonie jumped out and ran ahead of us to get to her destination before graduation. The gym at the high school was packed with people as we walked in. Many of them greeted my parents and gave them a hug, congratulating them on Vonie's graduation. My mom was wearing her beautiful cotton pink-and-teal dress and red lipstick. She looked gorgeous. But I was bored and hot as I waited for fifty-five seniors to graduate—not my idea of a good time.

I sat between Mom and Dad on the bleachers.

"Dena, why don't you come and sit between Lori and me?" suggested Mom. I didn't know why it mattered, but I noticed Mom grab Dad's hand and hold it tight. Listening to the speeches was tiring and I mostly zoned out, but when they called Vonie up to receive her diploma, my mom started crying. To my surprise, I saw Dad take a handkerchief out of his pocket and dab his eyes. Lori and I began to tear up too. I think Vonie's graduation was harder on Lori than me. I only teared up because everyone else was crying.

When the ceremony was finally over, we stepped out into the common area where it felt much cooler. But as people began to go outside for a breath of fresh air, they gasped at the sight before their eyes. While we were inside at the graduation, a big cloud of dust from the eruption of Mount St. Helens had made its way to Colorado and other surrounding states. Dust had settled over the entire town and covered every car for miles around. I didn't quite know how far the ash had traveled. Kids excitedly used their fingers to draw pictures and write their names on the cars and the sidewalks. Lori and I began drawing on the front steps of the high school, and my dad snapped a picture of us. Now, everyone was taking pictures. Some people were excited, and others were almost terrified and in a state of shock. It was a strange but symbolic moment as the ashes settled over the town.

In the weeks following Vonie's graduation, our attention quickly turned to her wedding. Aunt Joyce and Aunt Jean were sewing the bridesmaid dresses and my flower girl dress. Lori began fixing our hair every night to practice how to wear it for the wedding and to see what would look best. Great-Aunt Cleota was working on the flower arrangements out of her own flower garden.

On June 13, the night before the wedding, we were at the rehearsal practicing how and where to stand the next day.

"I really don't need the practice," I assured Vonie and Tom. "I've been a flower girl so many times for our older cousins, so I already know what to do. But the ring bearer doesn't know what to do, so he needs some practice."

The ring bearer was Tom's nephew, Jason, who was only four years old.

"Jason," I said to him, "you have to hold my hand when we are walking up the aisle, but not on the walk down, because I have to throw the flowers."

But Jason didn't really listen to me and flat-out refused to hold my hand. In fact, he refused to walk down the aisle at all, which bothered me. "Come on," I insisted. "You have to do this. It's your job!"

My mom swiftly grabbed me by the arm, pulling me out in the hall to talk to me. "Every wedding is different, Dena. And you still have to practice. Also, be nice to Jason. You are not his boss!" Mom scolded me.

By the end of the night, I was walking down the aisle all by myself. Even Jason's mom and dad couldn't seem to make him do his job. *I sure hope he decides to do it tomorrow*, I thought.

After we finished practicing, a summer storm came rolling in and the electricity went out. Everyone stood in shock, mumbling to themselves, while someone dug in their purse and found a flashlight. "Surely it will come back on in a little while," someone announced. An hour later, the lights were still off.

"What will we do now? We can't decorate this place tonight without the electricity!" Mom shrieked.

"We will have to wake up early and decorate tomorrow morning," said Dad, a hopeful note in his voice. But more than a few of us were worried. On the way home, my mom was in tears.

"We'll never be ready for this wedding tomorrow!" she cried in despair.

The next morning, everything felt rushed. Aunt Joyce and Aunt Jean came over to help us into the beautiful dresses they had made. My long dress with pink flowers fell off my shoulders and went down to my white sandals. My dress matched the bridesmaid dresses, except their dresses were baby blue.

Tom's family was Catholic, so the wedding was held at the Catholic church in Yuma. The church was regal and beautiful with its dark maroon carpet and stained-glass windows. In the front was a statue of Jesus dying on the cross. It was awe-inspiring and a little disturbing.

Thankfully, on that day, everything came together smoothly, as many people were there to help my mom decorate for the wedding. In hindsight, it may have been God's plan for Mom to go home and get some rest, because today she was completely refreshed.

Our parents came to give each of us a hug before the ceremony started and before my mom would be ushered to her seat.

"All three of our girls look so beautiful," Mom said with a smile through her tears.

"They sure do," Dad replied, dabbing at his eyes with a handkerchief.

At exactly 2:00 p.m., the music started to play and my heart began racing. I realized I was more nervous than I thought I would be. Lori was too. She got to walk down the aisle with one of her classmates, Jim, who was Tom's brother. Lori's long blue dress flowed off her shoulders and down to the floor. Her dark hair was curled back against her face. She looked so beautiful, and so did Vonie in her long white gown with a long white train reaching to the floor. Her blonde hair matched the white of her veil.

Since all eyes would be on me, I didn't want to mess up. Being the flower girl, I got to watch each bridesmaid walk down the aisle before me. I heard Lori take a deep breath and mumble the words,

"Here I go," with a huge smile plastered on her face. Vonie then motioned for Jason and me to go ahead of her when "Wedding March" started to play on the organ and the whole congregation stood up and faced us. Jason was standing in a brown suit. And this time he eagerly followed me down the aisle. Dad and Vonie followed close behind, and I made a trail for her with the purple petals I threw out of my white basket.

As excited as I was at the beginning, it was a long ceremony, and I quickly grew tired of standing up there and listening to the priest talk. Jason began moving around and lying on the floor. As he came closer to me, I whispered, "Stand up, Jason." The next thing I knew, an adult grabbed him and made him sit with him. *Great*, I thought to myself, *now I have to walk back up the aisle alone.*

As I watched my new brother-in-law lift the veil over my sister's face and kiss her, I reflexively put my hands on my hips and stuck out my tongue. "Ooh!" I said. The congregation erupted into laughter. Looking at Lori, I could see tears starting to form in her eyes at the realization that our sister wouldn't be under the same roof as us from now on. I could tell that it was hitting her harder than it hit me. After all, I was still at the age where I didn't worry about what would be; I only focused on the moment at hand.

The priest introduced them to the congregation as Mr. and Mrs. Tom Weaver. Then someone stood Jason back up next to me. I grabbed his hand and the two of us walked out of the church together, following Vonie and Tom to where we stood in the wedding line so everyone could tell us how cute we were and what a great job we had done.

The photographer began taking a bunch of family pictures. I watched Vonie as she called my grandma up to stand beside her. Grandma was in a beautiful pink dress. They both hugged, and Grandma whispered, "You look beautiful," and gave her a kiss on the cheek.

After the cake was cut and they smeared it into one another's faces, Vonie announced that she was going to throw the bouquet. Whether it was a setup or not, she turned around and tossed it behind her, and it landed right in Lori's hands.

"I caught it, Vonie! Did you see that, Mom? I actually caught it," she said, laughing in disbelief.

"That doesn't mean that you are the next one to get married out of these beautiful ladies," giggled my mom, "but it might mean that you are the next sister to get married."

While everyone was enjoying their cake and mints, Jason and I went outside and played with the new toys we'd received for being in the wedding. This would actually be the beginning of a great friendship.

Before Vonie and Tom walked out of the church, two of his sisters began to hand out little sacks of rice for us to throw at the bride and groom. They came out of the church, hand in hand, both with big smiles on their faces as they ducked their heads down, trying to keep the rice from getting in their eyes. They left in Vonie's gray Chevy Chevelle, which was decorated with dangling pop and beer cans and shaving cream on the windows that announced, "Just Married, Tom and Vonie." After they left, Mom and Dad went back into the church to clean up alongside Tom's parents.

When we arrived home that evening, Mom talked Dad into driving to Wray that night to eat at a fancy new restaurant called The Sand-Hiller to relax and unwind. Lori and I felt so grown-up. We ordered a fancy kids' drink called a Shirley Temple; it arrived in a tall glass with a cherry inside. We ate halibut by candlelight as we sat in fancy wooden chairs. The waitress was decked out in a beautiful red dress. With the four of us sitting around the table, exhaustion and the realization of Vonie being married began to sink in. I caught Mom wiping away her tears as we ate in the calmness of the quiet room.

Vonie's wedding was full of deep emotions and fun. Aunt Dolores was the family cake decorator who not only made Vonie's cake but, many years later, made Lori's and mine too. Aunt Dolores always told me that my cake would be the last cake she would ever make, because she was retiring after her youngest niece was married. Of course, such a day felt vague and far, far away in my eyes.

Chapter 23

When Life Unfolds

"Cease listening to instruction, my son, and you will stray from the words of knowledge." **—Proverbs 19:27**

That summer, we mostly stayed busy (and I did my best to stay out of trouble), but we also dealt with the huge adjustment of Vonie getting married and moving out of the house. We saw them often, but it felt strange not having her in the next bedroom at night. Still, they made it a priority to come to our house every Sunday for our famous fried-chicken dinner rituals.

One Sunday, after our big family dinner, Mom said that she was really tired and she went to take a nap as the rest of us began to play a game of rummy. Unfortunately for me, I was losing.

"We need to finish this game so we can spend some time over at my parents' house," said Tom.

My feelings were hurt; I didn't want them to leave so soon, but I didn't know how to tell them. I wanted them to stay and keep playing with Lori and me, but I was too proud to actually admit it.

"Dena, you lost anyway!" Vonie said impatiently.

That's when I lost control and began screaming at the top of my lungs. "Fine, just leave! This game is stupid and not fun. You were never fun when you lived here. I'm so glad you're married and don't live here anymore!" Much to my surprise, tears began to fall out of both Vonie's and my eyes.

"Let's get out of here, Tom," Vonie said, angrily wiping her face with her hand.

As they left, I ran into my room, crying. I felt even worse than before because now I'd upset my sister and didn't know if she would ever come back.

"What happened out here?" asked Mom, who'd woken up to the ruckus. "Why did they leave so soon?"

"Because Dena told Vonie that she's glad she doesn't live here anymore!" said Dad, shaking his head.

"Dena, why would you say such awful things to your sister?" Mom asked, confused.

Deep inside, my heart was broken, but I didn't want my parents to know that I missed Vonie terribly.

"I don't know," I lied as the tears fell down my cheeks.

"You can sit in your room and think about this!" she said, shaking her head.

I decided that the next time I saw Vonie I would pretend nothing happened and would be extra nice to her. Then, maybe she wouldn't be so mad at me anymore.

Before the next Sunday dinner, the fight was water under the bridge and was never mentioned again.

The next Friday afternoon we were at Aunt Jean's house. We had spent all day running around with my mom, Aunt Joyce, and Aunt Jean while they were shopping.

"Before we get our groceries, we'll drop you kids off at the park. But you all stay away from the river—and no crossing the bridge. Janeil and Lori, you watch Dena. Is that understood?" scolded Aunt Jean.

The shopping center park. Photo by Wray Library.

"Come on, Dena, we won't let anything happen to you!" said Janeil. Jumping out of the vehicle, we all raced to the wooden castle in the middle of the playground and climbed the wooden stairs. I grabbed hold of the pole and slid down like I was a firefighter; then I climbed back up the wooden stairs again and flew down the high slide.

"Hey, I'll push you on the tire swing," suggested Janeil. "Get on and lay across the swing on your back with your feet sticking out." she said.

As she began to push, I felt as if I was going to fall off. I started to scream as she kept pushing me higher and higher. Then it felt as if I was going to hit the castle. As Janeil let go of the tire swing, a rush of adrenaline flooded my body Then, just like that . . . I felt like I was flying over the river. My stomach had that tickling butterfly feeling, and it felt amazing. I giggled and asked her to keep pushing me. I refused to let anyone else take a turn.

"Dena, you will get off and let other people take a ride right now!" screamed Lori.

"Oh, all right," I said reluctantly. I jumped down and followed Mike through the yellow cement tunnels when we heard a horn honking. Mom, Aunt Joyce, and Aunt Jean were back to pick us up.

"Mom, can I spend the night with Janeil tonight?" Lori asked as we jumped into the car.

"Yeah, Mom! Do you care if Lori spends the night?" Janeil turned to Aunt Jean. "Sure. You can ride back home with your dad tomorrow evening," said Aunt Jean.

Mike and I looked at each other with the same thought. "Then can Mike spend the night with us?" I suggested.

"Sure, I don't see why not," Mom replied.

"Well, in that case, I guess I will come up tomorrow to bring Lori home and pick up Mike," said Aunt Jean.

That evening, our favorite show was on Channel 3: *The Dukes of Hazzard*. Mike and I were glued to the TV as we watched General Lee racing down a dirt road. After an hour, it was over, and my mom wanted to watch her favorite show, *Dallas*. Mike and I had called Aunt Joyce earlier and asked if we could come over to her house after our show was over on Channel 3 so we could watch it again on Channel 10. Just as soon as the show ended, we both raced out the back door and ran straight through the path leading to Aunt Joyce's back door, just in the nick of time to hear the theme song.

"You made it just in time," our aunt said. "I made some popcorn and poured some Pepsi for the two of you."

Mike and I sat in the living room on the couch with a big bowl of buttery, salty popcorn between us, drinking our Pepsis while watching the exact same thing we had just seen an hour ago unfold in front of us. Aunt Joyce was generous enough to watch *Dallas* on the late station just so she could have us over for company.

After the show was over, it was pitch-black outside. "You'd better run fast or the bogeyman will get you," warned Uncle Max. We thanked Aunt Joyce for her hospitality and ran as fast as we could through her backyard in total darkness. Uncle Max had me convinced that there really *was* a bogeyman out to get us.

That night, Mom put out two sleeping bags in front of our TV. When Mike spent the night, he always liked to wake up early and watch Saturday morning cartoons, which started at 4:30 in the morning.

"Aunt Jan," he asked, "will you come and turn on the TV at exactly 4:30 in the morning so we can lay here and watch?"

She gave him a funny look but was used to this request. "Okay, will do!"

Early the next morning, Mom came out and turned on the TV. We both watched *The Flintstones* as we lay there only half awake.

Later that day, Aunt Jean brought Lori back with Janeil. It was a beautiful, sunny day, so Mike and I got out our bikes to ride around the block. Later, we came back into the house to ask if we could ride farther then just around the block.

"Mom, can Mike and I ride over to the pig barn to see Cinnamon and Fritz?" I asked. Last year, we had taken Vonie's horse Cinnamon out to Aunt Nadine's for a month so she could get a baby in her tummy. And in March, she had a baby colt that Vonie named Fritz. To give them more room to run and more grass to eat, we put her right by Uncle Keith's pig barn.

"That would be fine. But you know the rules. That colt is a little wild and likes to kick. You both stay out of that pen," she warned.

We agreed and rode over to Uncle Keith's pig barn.

"Hey, they're clear over on the other side of the pasture, so let's just leave our bikes here and cross to get over the gate," suggested Mike.

"But we're not supposed to get in with them," I protested, remembering my mom's warning.

"They're pretty far away from us, so it's okay. We can see them better if we just cross through here."

It seemed like a reasonable idea. "Okay," I said.

Cinnamon saw us coming and walked over to greet us. Fritz, however, was somewhat ornery as we climbed on the fence to pet him. We had to watch him because he opened his mouth wide, like he was going to bite us. But when I screamed, "Don't bite us," it scared him and he backed away from us. Then the two of them stood between us and the other gate, gently grazing away.

"Now we will just have to wait for them to move before we can cross back over and go home," said Mike.

As soon as Mike said that, we heard a giant clap of thunder and saw lightning fork across the sky.

The horses looked up from grazing.

"We'd better go," I said in alarm.

"Yeah, let's make a run for it!" said Mike.

The next thing we knew, hail was coming down in pea-sized pebbles. Cinnamon and Fritz became more and more riled up. The more they began to move and run, the more scared we were to cross between them to get to the other gate. The hail began coming down a little harder. Finally, Mike said, "Now! One, two, three . . . run!"

We both jumped off the fence and raced across the pasture between Cinnamon and Fritz. I was running as fast as I could, but I could barely keep up with Mike. We jumped and climbed the next gate. Then we jumped down the other side and grabbed our bikes, pedaling as fast as we could as the hail turned to hard rain that whipped against our faces. When we arrived back to the house, we were soaking wet, muddy, cold, and clearly rattled.

"My God, where have the two of you been? We've been looking all over for you and hollering your names!" Mom said huffily. "Aunt

Jean is driving around looking for you as we speak! What were the two of you thinking?"

I sighed, knowing I couldn't lie to my mom. "We got in with Cinnamon and her colt, and they were running around when the hail hit, and we were too scared to pass them. We finally made a run for it."

She sighed. "Dena, you know you're not supposed to get in that pen with her. You're grounded from your bike for a week! Both of you need your butts kicked, I swear. Now go change clothes, Dena. Mike, your clothes will just have to dry on you as you think about what the two of you did."

I felt bad for getting in trouble, but as the days went by, my punishment was lifted and the fun of summer continued with my love of animals that was encouraged by my family.

With Vonie married, the house felt a little quieter and lonelier than before, especially when we would sit down at the kitchen bar for meals. The empty chair was a heavy reminder that someone very important (even if I never told her so myself) was missing. As if not having her live at the house anymore was hard enough, Dad decided to sell Cinnamon and Fritz. I really wanted to keep Cinnamon so I could ride her. But the decision had been made. And while the pain took a while to heal, as time had proved over and over, I was strong enough to get through it all.

Chapter 24

Life Stumbles

*"Have I not commanded you? Be strong and of good courage; do not be afraid, nor be dismayed, for the L*ORD *your God is with you wherever you go."* —**Joshua 1:9**

One Saturday morning, the phone rang. I heard my mom talking. "Yes, I'm sure she would love that. We will see you in a little bit." As she hung up the phone, she smiled at me. "Go get your cowboy boots and jeans on. Your cousin Julie is bringing over Chiefer for you to ride this morning!"

I hurried and finished my cereal and ran back to my closet to grab my boots and Western shirt. As I raced outside, I spotted Julie coming down our road on Chiefer.

"Hi, Dena," she said, waving at me. "I figured you'd like some time to ride this morning. Hop on," she said as she climbed off Chiefer.

I walked over to Chiefer and lifted my left leg high into the stirrup. Then I grabbed hold of the saddle strings and used my strength to pull myself into a standing position. I swung my right leg over, pulling myself up by the saddle horn. I was still too small to reach the stirrups when I sat in the saddle, but I was pretty proud for pulling myself to the top.

"Now you can ride around by yourself for a while," said Julie.

"Wait, I want a picture," said Mom, running back into the house to grab the camera. When she came back out, Aunt Joyce was there with Julie.

"I'll take your picture," said Aunt Joyce. "Jan, you and Julie both stand beside her."

The photo Julie painted specifically for this book. Used by permission.

I sat tall and smiled for the picture, with both Mom and Julie standing on either side of Snapper and me. Then I turned Chiefer around and walked out of our driveway with Snapper following loyally behind. It was a beautiful fall morning, and I could hear kids playing on the playground. Without a care in the world, I headed toward the sound of laughter.

As I passed by the school, I saw two older boys, Clayton and Troy, swinging on the swings and then jumping out of them. I continued riding past them on the road, sitting tall and royally, and then I turned Chiefer around at the next block. I quickly noticed a tangled-up barbed-wire in a ditch. I dutifully avoided it and stayed on the road.

I continued riding two more blocks west, where Linda, our next-door neighbor, was visiting a friend down the road. They were out in the yard watering flowers. I didn't really know the other lady, but she had always been friendly to me. Then I saw her walk toward the mailbox. I put Chiefer into a trot toward her so I could show her my horse and talk to her.

"Hi," I said excitedly, showing off my cowgirl skills.

"Hi," she replied with a weird tone in her voice. "I'm going to ask you not to ride around here because there are dogs around this neighborhood that may scare your horse."

"Oh, he's not scared," I insisted.

"I still don't want you to ride around here. You need to go back home," she warned me again.

Not understanding why she was being so strict, I hung my head low and turned Chiefer back toward the school where the boys were swinging on the swings. I got to the end of the block and turned around again, heading right back toward the house. I doubted any dogs would chase me. Besides, my mom hadn't told me I couldn't ride over here. But as I got closer to the yard, I saw some dogs across the street coming straight toward us.

The next thing I knew, Chiefer did a full one-eighty and turned, running full speed toward the schoolhouse again. I had no idea this horse could run so fast! My heart was racing as fast as Chiefer's hooves were hitting the ground, and my hair flew away from my face as I rode along, holding on for dear life. I felt as if I might die. I could feel

Chiefer's muscles beneath my saddle moving with power and might. As his hooves hit the ground, my heart beat against him in a fast drumming motion. I began screaming at the top of my lungs. But the louder I screamed, the faster he ran. Ahead of me, I saw the tangled barbed wire lying in the ditch. I ordered myself to hold on until we'd passed the barbed wire.

As soon as I felt that we'd passed it, either I let go and slid down Chiefer's side or flew off his back. My worst thought was that no one would find me. It happened faster than the speed of light, but it felt as if time had stopped and everything was occurring in slow motion. It was as if I were having an out-of-body experience.

Then, just as if someone had shut off the lights, everything went dark. I lay there in the ditch, crying, unable to move. The air was knocked out of me, and I was having a hard time breathing. The next thing I knew, I was being carried up the front steps of our house.

"She fell off her horse," cried Linda and the other lady she'd been visiting with. Both of them were carrying me; one had a hold of my legs while the other one supported my shoulders and head.

"Oh my gosh, is she all right? Here, let's lay her down on the couch," said my mom, grabbing the purple pillow from the back of the couch and propping my head up.

Confused and disoriented, I opened my eyes. I was still crying while everyone was standing around me.

"My back hurts," I cried out. My mom sat me up on the couch and lifted up my shirt while Aunt Joyce, Julie, and the Linda inspected me.

"Wow, you really scratched it up, didn't you?" said Mom as they all shook their heads in disbelief. "But you'll be okay," she quickly added, kissing my forehead.

Thank goodness I missed the barbed wire, I thought to myself.

"We need to talk to you alone before we go," said Linda. They all walked to the back bedroom, and I heard Mom gasp. I could tell that she, too, was crying.

"Joyce and Julie, you need to come back to the bedroom for a moment!" she hollered back at them. I could tell something was up, and I figured I was in trouble because I hadn't done what they had told me to do. I had been told not to ride back to where they were—and I'd done it anyway.

I bet I'm in big trouble now, I thought to myself.

When the four of them came back to the couch, I waited for them to start yelling at me. But instead, they all came over and gave me a hug.

"You'll be okay," they said with big, fake smiles on their faces. I could tell they were fake because they were *big* smiles through teary eyes.

Mom took a washrag and washed my face. A knock on the door interrupted my crying. It was Clayton.

"We brought your horse back to you," he said, a look of concern on his face.

"Thanks for bringing him home," replied Julie.

Outside, Troy was riding Chiefer back and forth in front of our house. He looked so gentle, it was hard to believe I fell off of him. Julie came over to check on me. "Are you going to be all right?"

she asked me, tears in her eyes. I didn't understand why she was crying.

"Yes, she'll be fine. When you ride, you eventually fall!" said Mom.

"Well, I'm sorry you fell off, but I'm glad you'll be fine," said Julie.

"Thanks for bringing Chiefer over for Dena to ride. When she feels better, we're going to eat dinner in Wray with Earle and Max," said Mom. "Joyce is coming with us if you want to come along after you unsaddle Chiefer."

"I think I'll take Chiefer down to the arena and ride him for a while and make sure he realizes he's not allowed to take off like that. I'll give him a good workout," Julie said. "You all have a nice dinner with my dad and Uncle Earle!"

After I felt better, we headed to the Riverside Café in Wray, where we met up with Dad and Uncle Max. "Tell your dad what happened today," said Mom.

"I fell off Chiefer this morning," I replied, still moving slowly from my scraped-up back.

"Well," said Uncle Max sympathetically, "real cowgirls get back in the saddle when they fall off. You'll be good to ride again before you know it!"

"Sure," I said, unconvinced. I honestly wasn't certain I would ever be able to ride again, although I guessed that Uncle Max knew a thing or two about getting up after a fall.

When we were leaving the café, I climbed in the back seat and waited for Mom and Aunt Joyce as they said their goodbyes to

Uncle Max and Dad before they both went back to work. From the window, I could tell that something was bothering them. I could tell from the expressions on their faces that, whatever it was, it upset Dad and Uncle Max too. I saw Uncle Max take a handkerchief out of his pocket and wipe his eyes as he looked at me sadly through the window.

Boy, they really must be mad at me for not obeying our neighbor lady, I thought to myself. *I'm going to be in big trouble later.*

On the way home, Aunt Joyce and Mom were extremely quiet as they kept peering back at me to see if I was okay. From the way they were acting, it was as if they were expecting something worse to happen.

When we got home, I walked into the house and hollered for both Snapper and Gidget. But only Gidget came to greet me. "Where's Snapper?" I asked.

"I don't know," said Mom in a choked-up voice. "Why don't you go outside to play?" Walking outside, I began hollering again for Snapper. He never came. I began looking all over and under everywhere, including the dog house. Snapper was nowhere in sight.

"I want to go look for him on my bike," I insisted.

"I'll go with you," replied Aunt Joyce. The two of us set out to ride around town looking for him.

I cried out continually, "Here, Snapper. Where did you go?" The whole time, I was in quite a bit of pain from my back being scratched up. I have no idea how I rode as far as I did.

It wasn't much longer before Aunt Joyce said to me, "Dena, I can tell you are in a lot of pain. I think we need to go home now."

As we walked in the door, my mom greeted me with a hug. "You didn't find him, did you?" she said, sniffing. "I guess he must have run away."

I burst into tears as I fell into her loving embrace. The pain of not finding Snapper was only matched by the pain of my scraped-up back. The next few nights I cried myself to sleep, not really believing my dog was dead, but worried he was lost and wondering how to get back home. I wasn't quite buying the fact that he ran away.

I learned the cold, hard truth one day during my senior year in high school, when I innocently asked, out of the blue, "I wonder whatever happened to Snapper?"

My mom looked me in the eyes. "Do you really want to know the truth?" she asked tearfully. This time, we cried together as she apologized for lying to me so many years ago. "I just couldn't bear to see my little girl with a broken heart, and I figured that if you didn't know the truth, your heart wouldn't be as broken. I'm so sorry!" she said with a hug, releasing years of guilt through her tears.

I discovered that Snapper had been buried in a box out in our pasture that day by Julie, right after we left for Wray. The dogs hadn't been after Chiefer; they had been after Snapper.

That summer was full of changes and deep loss. Losing Snapper was a tough experience, and perhaps my first major heartbreak, as he'd followed me everywhere since I was four years old. Not knowing whether he was dead or alive made it hard for me to sleep, at least for a little while.

Chapter 25

Hospital Visitation

"Jesus said to her, 'I am the resurrection and the life. He who believes in Me, though he may die, he shall live. And whoever lives and believes in Me shall never die. Do you believe this?'"
—John 11:25–26

One day, my grandma got sick and was sent to a hospital in Denver. Reflecting back on that time, it was full of question marks and confusion. I was eight years old, and although I'd heard her talk about each celebration or event we experienced as being her last, it was beginning to feel like she wasn't really going to die. After all, we had said it over and over again through the years, and it never ended up happening.

I didn't know at the time that this moment would be the last I would see her before she passed away. Now, as an adult, I know where Grandma's fear came from when she was on her deathbed: she felt terrible guilt about all the children who had slowly watched her die.

Moreover, she didn't want them to remember her in a state of slow decline.

"Wake up!" my mom said, walking into my room early one Saturday morning. "We're heading to Denver to see Grandma in the hospital. She's feeling really sick."

In my childlike innocence, I felt like this was more of a field trip than a somber occasion. "I can't wait to see her. She'll be so happy to see me too!" I hurriedly jumped out of bed and got dressed. It was 5:00 a.m. and the sky was still dark, but it would take us three hours to get to Denver, which meant we had to leave soon.

In the stillness of the morning, headlights shone through my window, and Gidget began barking. Vonie and Tom pulled up outside so they could accompany us. I walked out to the kitchen, where Mom had placed three kinds of cereal on the bar and was popping pieces of bread into the toaster. "What do you want for breakfast, girls?"

"We want Lucky Charms," Lori and I both agreed.

By 5:30, we'd eaten breakfast and were off to Denver in our new yellow Dodge. I sat in front between Mom and Dad, while Lori, Vonie, and Tom squeezed into the back.

"Before we go to the hospital, let's stop at a K-Mart and go inside for some items," suggested Mom. "You need some quiet toys to keep yourself occupied while we're visiting Grandma."

I found some Weebles, while Lori picked out coloring posters with markers for both of us.

Back in the car, Mom said, "When we arrive at the hospital, there may be a possibility they won't let you or Lori go in, so we might have to take turns going in to see Grandma and being outside with you."

I wasn't a fan of hospitals; to me, they were just big, boring buildings where I was expected to be quiet all day long. When my cousins were around, we always had fun playing outside on the grass, but it was less exciting when it was just Lori and me.

At the front desk, Mom asked the receptionist if we could go to Grandma's room with her.

"As long as they're her grandchildren, you can take them up!" she replied. I was happy to hear the news. It had been a couple of months since my last visit with Grandma, which felt like a lifetime.

The big hospital had several floors, and we got to ride in the elevator. This was the first time I had ever been on one, and it made my stomach tickle as the elevator went straight up. I giggled.

"Shush, Dena!" hissed Vonie. "We're in a hospital where people are sick and trying to rest!"

"Yes, Dena, when you go into the room, you have to be quiet and good. Do you understand?" Mom asked, her voice serious and slow.

I didn't see what the big deal was. "Fine," I grumbled.

"If you're not quiet, the nurse will give you a shot!" my dad warned, which immediately shut me up.

We walked into Grandma's room and found her lying in bed.

"Hi, Grandma!" I greeted her, but I didn't get a response in return. She seemed a little dazed. I noticed she was hooked up to many machines and was blankly gazing out the window.

"Lori and Dena, why don't the two of you take the toys you bought from K-Mart and go to the other side of the room to play with them?" Mom said.

Lori and I sat on the floor. I played with the Weebles while Lori colored the posters. It was fun at first, but as the day dragged on and we just lingered in the stuffy room, I became restless. There was a lot going on that I didn't understand—things I was oblivious to.

"Vonie and Tom, would you mind taking Lori and Dena outside for a while?" asked Mom, exchanging a strange look with my oldest sister. Vonie quickly nodded and took us outside, where Lori and I stepped out onto the luscious green grass, which was dotted by towering trees.

"Let's play tag," said Tom. "I'll be *it*." Both Lori and I took off running around trees, trying to ditch him. We played outside for a while, but then Mom came out, crying, with Dad right behind her.

I had seen Mom cry many times before, but this felt different.

"What's the matter?" I asked. But she wouldn't even look at me, which confused me even more.

Tom softly took my hand. "Let's go back to the grass and you can show me the somersault you've been working on," he suggested. I looked over my shoulder at my dad, who was standing behind my mom with a helpless look on his face.

"Mom doesn't want us here," I heard her tell Vonie. "She told us to leave because she doesn't want us to see her dying. We drove all the way up here and now she's telling us to go? I can't bring myself to walk out of here, knowing this is the last time I'll ever see her. What am I supposed to do?" She turned and sobbed into my dad's shoulder.

I felt a pit in my stomach. I was just as helpless as my dad looked. I wanted to wave a magic wand over the entire setting and make my mother happy. And although I loved Grandma, the thought of her dying was too much to bear. All I knew was that my mother was crying as if nothing would ever be okay again. And there was nothing I could do about it. I couldn't understand why Grandma wanted us to leave. It made my heart hurt.

"Let's get out of here and get something to eat," suggested my dad.

"How about a Mexican restaurant in town called Casa Bonita? It's super entertaining. It even has caves and a cliff diver," said Tom.

"That sounds good," Dad said, relieved. "We need to do something fun to get our minds off this for a while."

"But I don't like Mexican food!" I protested. "It's too spicy. Let's not go there!"

"Dena, they have American food too," Tom reassured me. "You'll love this place."

When we arrived at Casa Bonita, I could see a large pink building that looked like a castle, with a shallow pool and a waterfall in the front. We parked our car in the parking lot and walked to the water.

"People can throw coins in to make a wish," said Dad, digging in his pocket for some loose change to hand us. As I tossed in some coins, my thoughts lingered on my mom.

"What did you wish for, Dena?" asked Dad.

"I can't say, or it won't come true!"

There was a long line outside, and it took a good twenty to thirty minutes to even get inside the building. But once we were in, the long line was still endless. I was hungry and thirsty, so I began to whine. "This is taking forever! I just want to go eat someplace else!"

"I'm so hungry I could eat a horse," Lori whined.

"We are here now and we're not leaving," said Mom, clearly annoyed.

"You two stop complaining or you'll sit in the car while we eat," warned Dad.

About an hour and a half later, we finally came to the place where we ordered our food. Mom ordered two tacos and a Coke for me. Then we followed our waitress into a whole new world. As she led us to our table, we walked through a dark room with pretty white lights along a carpeted pathway. I could hear splashing water and the sound of people laughing and screaming. The cool surroundings made me feel like I was actually in an underground cave. Rocks with holes to hide in surrounded us. There were people playing the banjo and singing "Happy Birthday" in Spanish, while girls in big skirts kicked up their heels and danced to the music.

Despite my hunger and annoyance, I smiled. Everyone seemed to be happy here. I looked over at my mom, who was also smiling as she watched our faces light up. This made me very happy, because I could see that the wish I'd made outside was working. And for a moment, all was well in the world.

"Before they bring us our food, let's go for a walk by the pool. There's a bridge out there, and we can walk right up to the water," said Tom.

We followed Tom to the fake illuminated palm trees that surrounded the pool. A man in a gorilla costume was chasing a forest ranger. They ended up way above the thirty-foot waterfall, which rushed into a deep pool below. Before we knew it, a diver stood above the waterfall and dove straight into the water below, right next to where we stood. I gasped in astonishment as he quickly climbed out of the water and waved to us. The crowd let out a giant breath of relief and began to clap delightedly. I, too, clapped with joy.

We continued walking up some stairs to another bridge straight behind the towering waterfall. We stood there until the diver went down again, this time doing full back flips into the water. In perfect form, his body shot downward, right past us, into the water. Again, the crowd burst out in cheers.

We continued walking through the caves. We eventually came to a place called Black Bart's Cave where a sign warned us: "Enter at Your Own Risk!" The cave resembled a big dragon with its mouth open wide, its red eyes staring down on us, and its gnarly sharp teeth ready to devour us. We reluctantly walked inside, where skeletons and glittering treasure awaited us.

"You go first, Lori!" I said.

She grabbed my hand. "We'll go in together!" I could feel her hand shaking as we held each other tightly, scared that the dragon would come alive and crunch down on us.

Tom was ahead of us, and Vonie was behind us. Soon, I lost sight of Tom. "Where did he go?" I asked, worried. Then, all of a sudden, someone jumped out and grabbed Lori's and my arms. Both of us immediately screamed in terror, but when I heard Vonie and Tom laughing, I realized it had been Tom who'd scared us. I pretended to be angry; inside, though, I was laughing.

Finally, we reached the end of the cave where a puppet show was taking place. I joined a group of kids on the bleachers and began to lose myself in the spectacle.

A little later, Dad came in and announced, "It's time to eat, kids!" In the next room, we sat down to eat and could hear the sound of a fake gunfight in the background as we devoured a plate of sopapillas—sweet doughy bread filled with honey—which we were all trying and loving for the first time.

I looked over at my mother, whose face was still glowing with happiness. I smiled too. It felt like the storm I'd encountered earlier had passed for good.

By the time we left Casa Bonita, darkness had settled in. We had a long journey back home. I sat between Vonie and Tom in the back, and Lori took her turn up front between Mom and Dad. I was just starting to doze off when I heard Mom begin to cry. My eyes shot open. I was so confused! I thought Casa Bonita had made everyone happy again and that my coins in the wishing well had worked.

Maybe it only works while you're there, I thought sadly. I didn't realize at the time that just because someone is smiling doesn't mean they're happy.

Chapter 26

Death's Sting

"Blessed are those who mourn, for they shall be comforted."
—**Matthew 5:4**

Over the next couple of weeks, it felt that life was falling back into place. But one night, as I lay fast asleep in Lori's bed, the phone rang. I heard my dad answer and give out an audible gasp. "Yes, I understand! We've been expecting this call for a while. Thanks for letting us know," he said quietly, not wanting to wake anyone.

I heard him hang up the phone, then I heard Mom begin to cry. The sound of her footsteps came into the hall, and the light that she turned on poured into our darkened room. I was awake enough to understand what was going on. As I lay there in bed, I felt empty. I wasn't sad that Grandma had died, but I did feel a twinge of guilt for not feeling sad. Beyond that, I didn't want to face my mother's hurt again. When she walked into our room, I pretended to be asleep.

"Wake up, Lori and Dena!" she said, shaking us. I moaned a little and turned over, closing my eyes and hoping she'd just leave me alone.

"Lori, Dena, come on, you need to wake up," she insisted. "I have something to tell you."

I continued to lie perfectly still, hoping that I was convincing in my slumbering state. Mom tried to sit me up, but I was dead weight in her arms. She sighed and gently lay me back down. I didn't want to hear what I already knew, because I didn't know what I would say in response.

Lori, however, immediately sat up.

"Grandma died tonight," my mother softly informed her.

I heard my sister take a deep breath and begin to cry. My mom reached across my body and pulled Lori to her in a hug. Dad picked her up and sat her down on the ground. I didn't want to be held. I didn't feel sad, and I didn't want to see Mom crying. Stillness engulfed me, and I concentrated on my steady breathing: in and out, in and out.

"Dena's not waking up, so we'll let her sleep," said Dad. The three of them walked out to the hall, and the lights went out. I took a deep breath. I was finally alone, sheltered in the darkness with my thoughts, and wide-awake. I began to imagine my grandma as an angel with wings. I pictured her flying to me and then lying down beside me, telling me that she loved me as she held my hand. I imagined her kissing me on the forehead and telling me that she was going to heaven now, so I needed to be good. In my mind, I said, "Goodbye, Grandma." I wondered why everyone else was feeling so sad. I believed she was happy to be going to heaven to join my granddad.

Listening closely, I could hear Gidget barking. Outside my window, I saw car lights pulling up to our front driveway. I heard the voices of Uncle Keith, Aunt Dolores, Uncle Max, and Aunt Joyce. People kept coming, including Vonie, Tom, and Julie. As I heard the murmur of their voices and tears, I was glad that I was tucked away snug and warm, alone in this dark bedroom.

"Where's Dena?" Aunt Joyce asked.

"We tried to wake her up, but she wouldn't budge. So we decided to let her sleep," said Mom tearfully.

"That's okay. She's where she needs to be," said Aunt Joyce. "She'll learn about this tragedy soon enough."

In a little while, Lori came back into bed and snuggled next to me, putting her arms around me. I felt safe nestled next to my sister, and I was glad she'd come back to me. Together, we fell into a deep sleep.

Early the next morning, Mom came again to wake us. "Wake up, Dena, there is some news I need to tell you."

"It's not good news, either," said Dad, bracing me.

"Last night, while you were sleeping, Grandma died and went to heaven," said Mom softly.

I acted like I didn't already know. I genuinely didn't know what to say. I simply fell into my mom's embrace and hugged her while she played with my hair and cried on my shoulder.

"You two can stay home from school today if you want to," she said.

"But Mom, my eighth-grade class is going on a field trip to Denver today, and we're going back to Casa Bonita again. I don't want to miss it. Can I stay home tomorrow?" Lori asked.

Mom smiled between her tears. "Yes, you may do that! You go and have fun. Dena, how about you?"

I had a feeling that Mom wanted me to stay. I looked up at her and said, "Yes, I want to stay home from school today with you."

"That's fine, but just know there will be a lot of crying. We're all headed to the farm, and you're probably going to be the only cousin out there. Why don't you go take a shower and get ready to leave? Uncle Keith and Aunt Dolores are fixing breakfast, so we'll eat there after Lori gets on the bus."

After Lori was on the bus, Mom and I drove out to the farm. Dad said that he needed to keep working, as he knew he'd have to take time off for the funeral.

We walked into Aunt Dolores and Uncle Keith's house a little later, and Aunt Joyce came up to me and pulled me into a tight hug. "Dena, get a plate of food. There's bacon, eggs, toast, and hash browns. Do you want orange juice or milk?" She looked at me, concerned, although there was no need. My hunger hadn't gone anywhere, and my stomach growled as she mentioned all the food that was on the table.

"I'll take orange juice," I said.

I sat on my aunt's lap as if I were four years old again and ate my breakfast. I think it was more comforting for her than for me, but I was happy to be with my family—even though I didn't fully understand their sadness. In the next room, Aunt Jean and Aunt Nadine thumbed through photo albums together.

"Dena!" said Aunt Jean and Aunt Nadine, obviously surprised to see me there as they came in from the living room, wiping their tears away. "We were going to bring our kids with us, but they all wanted to go to school. I guess we should have brought them to play with you."

They looked a little guilty, but I quickly reassured them that I didn't mind being the only kid there.

"Joann and her family should be here by the evening," said Aunt Jean, changing the subject.

Joann was my one aunt who lived far away, and all of her four children were grown up. I didn't know them as well as all my other cousins. But Aunt Joann and Aunt Jean were the twins in my mom's family. There was a funny story they told us whenever they got together. When Grandma had the twins here in this house, they didn't know she was carrying two. My granddad walked into the room where she was giving birth and went to sit in a chair. The first twin was lying there, and Granddad just about sat on her, not realizing there were two. Everyone always laughed at the story, although the idea of my granddad sitting on a baby was a little scary to me.

After finishing my breakfast, I went outside to explore.

"The wagon is down by the barn if you want to get it!" yelled Uncle Keith as he watched me from the front porch. I headed down the hill between the rows of trees, toward the barn to where the little red wagon was sitting. I stopped and looked up at the white V connected P quarter circle painted on the red barn. It made me wonder what the V connected P stood for and who had painted it there.

Then I pulled the wagon back to the top of the hill, pushed it a little way down the trail, and jumped in, bracing myself for the fun and bumpy ride to the bottom. I steered the wagon with the handle bar. The last time I'd done this, Janeil, Lori, Janet, and Mike had been with me, and we'd taken turns riding down the hill and pulling the wagon back up. Today it was still fun, but I felt a little lonely.

Down at the bottom of the hill, I took the wagon and began pulling it back up again. It was around 10:00 a.m., and the sun shone brightly between the treetops. I wondered what it was like for my mom, aunts, and Uncle Keith to grow up here, riding horses and raising cattle. I never knew my granddad, but my mom always said he was the reason I loved horses so much. A peaceful feeling came over me as I imagined my grandparents reunited and sitting at the top of the trees, watching over me as I played.

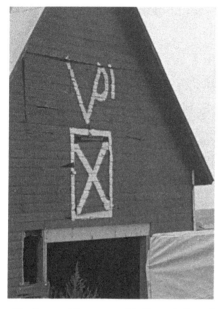

The barn with my granddad's cattle brand VP quarter circle.

I decided to walk back to the house. The adults were sitting around the table, talking in quiet tones as I walked in. I decided to climb the stairs to the tiny bedroom and get my cousin Diane's Raggedy Ann doll. This doll was as tall as I was. As I held her, I carefully walked back down the steep stairs and over to the bookshelf in the living room. I dug out the box of children's cardboard puzzles that we were always allowed to play with when we were here. The adults didn't think I was paying attention to them, but I was well within earshot, my attention lingering on every word they were saying as I lay on the floor while I cuddled the doll and put puzzles together.

"Before the phone rang last night, I knew Mom was there. I felt her presence and could see her figure as if she were standing next to me to tell me goodbye. And then the phone rang. I knew without a doubt that she was gone," Aunt Joyce said, her voice broken up by sobs.

Chills ran down my spine. Aunt Joyce actually *saw* Grandma come to say goodbye? Even though I had pictured Grandma telling me goodbye, I hadn't actually seen her—and I definitely didn't want to see her now that she was dead!

That night, when I was in my bed, fear had me in its clutches and I couldn't get to sleep. I was terrified that Grandma might visit me in her ghost form. I grabbed my teddy bear and held him tight. I lay down and refused to look in the direction of my dark closet. I slept on my belly, scared to turn over or open my eyes in case Grandma appeared before me. (That's when I started sleeping on my belly.)

The next day, there was a viewing of the body in Yuma. "Would you like to see her in the casket?" asked Mom.

"You don't have to," Dad said quickly. "Truthfully, I think it's better for kids not to see people who have died. I was only four years old when my dad died, and I've regretted seeing him like that my entire life."

"I'm scared to see a dead body," I admitted.

"Okay, you can stay outside on the lawn while we go in," Mom said with understanding in her voice.

As we drove to the mortuary, Mom cried softly in the front seat while Dad drove. Lori and I sat quietly and looked out the window, lost in our own thoughts. When we stepped out of the car, Lori took Mom and Dad's hands and walked in to view the body. I sat outside on the grass with Aunt Joyce. Then, Mom and Dad came out to be with me while Aunt Joyce and Uncle Max went in.

Five minutes later, Aunt Joyce and Uncle Max came back outside. Aunt Joyce's eyes were red, and she was crying and talking between breaths.

"I should have known better," she said mournfully. "I reached out to touch her, and she was ice cold and rock hard. It was the most stunning and unloving feeling I've ever felt in my life." Looking at Lori and me and pointing a finger, she said, "Whatever you do, never touch a dead body!"

Lori and I looked at each other, knowing we would remember her warning for the rest of our lives.

On the day of Grandma's funeral, Lori and I stayed at our house to babysit some of Aunt Joann's grandkids, who had traveled far. We played outside on the swing set and jumped on the trampoline, trying to keep our minds off the heaviness of the day. Shortly after the funeral and graveside service, the adults picked us up for the family dinner at the church. Everyone was standing around in small groups, and the downstairs area was jam-packed with several people talking at once.

"Dinner won't be served until noon," Mom said, looking down at her watch. "We still have fifteen minutes, why don't you kids go outside to play?"

"I want to drive out to the cemetery and see if her grave is covered over. Do some of you want to go?" asked Julie, looking at Lori, Janet, and me.

Guilt immediately washed over me. I wondered if perhaps Grandma was upset with me for not wanting to see her at the mortuary.

"I want to go!" I said bravely. I didn't realize that she was in a casket and had already been placed in the ground.

"Okay, you may go with Julie, but hurry back to eat!" said Mom.

At the cemetery, we saw the backhoe throwing dirt over her grave. I remembered Grandma explaining to me that Granddad was buried underground, and I remembered her asking me not to step on him. I now had an unsettling feeling in my stomach, accompanied by the realization that my grandma was now in the dirt too. I hoped she wasn't mad at me for not saying goodbye.

Since the dirt was being pushed in on top of her, Julie drove slowly through the cemetery without even stopping the car before driving straight back to the church.

"You're back already?" said Mom, coming to greet us as we entered the basement where the food was being prepared. "That didn't take long. You can eat now, Dena. I fixed you a plate and got you some tea and sugar."

I sat down at the table and took a few bites before I realized that Uncle Max was sitting behind me talking to some adults. I wasn't very hungry. I left my plate on the table and walked over to where Uncle Max was sitting.

"Hey, Kid!" he said as he reached out and picked me up, sitting me on his lap. I listened to the constant hum of the large crowd talking, which mesmerized me into a state of near-sleep.

Mike came over and disturbed me out of my state. "Hey, Dena, come out and play with us," he begged.

"Yes," agreed Mom, walking toward us. "Everyone is leaving to go to our house, but it's such a nice day out. Why don't all of you kids walk back so the ladies can clean up the church?"

All of the younger cousins formed a group and walked the two blocks back to my house. My mom and her five siblings were already

Dena's mom and her siblings: twins Jean and Joann, Keith, Joyce, Nadine, and Jan.

standing outside, posing and smiling for a picture. Inside, the smell of fresh-cut flowers and plants mingled with the aroma of cigarette smoke.

As a gift to the family, a distant relative had given my mom and her siblings a wooden plaque with lines moving in every direction. That day, it became the topic of all conversations. "Look at this," my mom showed the kids. "Do you see any words when you read this?"

We all stared, then handed it around our semicircle, trying to figure out what the adults were talking about.

"I don't see any words on this," said my cousin Brad.

The adults stood around with smiles on their faces, waiting for us to figure it out, but not wanting to give it away.

"Read between those squiggly lines, not the lines themselves, then tell us what you see," added Aunt Joyce.

"Oh," said Lori, "I got it!"

She took the plaque and traced the inside bare spots with her index finger, running it between the lines. "J-E-S-U-S. Jesus. It spells Jesus," she said with a smile. Now we all could see the mysterious message between the lines. We wondered how on earth we had missed it.

"Like always, Jesus is here with us, whether we believe He is or not," said Uncle Max.

As the evening set in, the adults began to make plans for cleaning out my grandma's house. Uncle Keith had built this house for Grandma after Granddad died, before he and Aunt Dolores had moved back to take over the farm. Our families didn't want to sell this house, but they were hoping they could find someone who would be interested in renting it.

"Let's all take a deep breath for now," said Uncle Keith authoritatively. "Joann will fly back in a couple of weeks, and we'll pick her up at the airport. Then we'll all make plans to go through Mom's house. Tomorrow, before Joann and Earl and their family head home, we'll have a BBQ dinner out at the farm. We'll let the kids ride the new three-wheelers. Let's enjoy each other, then go through the house later. Just like the song we chose at the funeral, it teaches us to take life one day at a time. We'll abide by that and have a great family day tomorrow, then we'll worry about the hard stuff in a couple of weeks."

The next day felt like a celebration. We spent the entire day on the three-wheelers riding all over the farm with Uncle Keith's border collie riding behind us. It was a memorable day of riding through the cornfields and under the sprinklers. I still reflect on those happy memories with our family, which shone brightly in the midst of the sad, gray atmosphere after Grandma's funeral.

A couple of weeks later, Aunt Joann flew back, just as Uncle Keith had planned, and our family had a get-together at Grandma's house.

While the adults and older cousins were clearing out the house, the younger kids played outside. Across the cement walkway we played dodgeball. And on the roof of the garage, we played Annie Annie Over with a small yellow-and-blue ball. That day, my ball flew straight over the garage for the first time.

A tinge of sadness came upon us as we walked into Grandma's house. Aunt Joann and Aunt Nadine were vacuuming the carpets; and Aunt Dolores was cleaning the bathroom; and mom, Aunt Jean, and Aunt Joyce were washing the windows with vinegar water. The bare house smelled fresh and clean, and everything felt brand new. I realized that this would be our last time at Grandma's as a family.

After the house was cleaned, my friend Dusty and her family moved into Grandma's old house. Dusty's mom, Sue, and my cousin Julie were best friends who liked to ride horses together.

One day, Dusty and her siblings, Karen and Troy, invited Lori and me over to swim in their new pool they had just set up. Lori and I walked to their house in our bathing suits. Thoughts of Grandma weren't fully crossing my mind until we walked inside the house; there, by the floor furnace, a brown chair had replaced my grandma's yellow rocking chair. This was a reminder of the change our family had endured.

Chapter 27

Growing up Country

"A righteous man regards the life of his animal, but the tender mercies of the wicked are cruel." —**Proverbs 12:10**

That spring after Grandma died, Lori dealt with her grief by playing the piano. With her weekly lessons and talent for music, it didn't take long before she was playing the same song they had sung at Grandma's funeral. I fondly remember our dad standing behind her singing along as mom marveled over her with love.

I didn't think about Grandma too much throughout the rest of my childhood because something inside me knew that even though Grandma's time on earth was over, she had been sent to heaven to continue there. It made me happy that she would never be tired, hungry, or sick. And according to the grown-ups, she might have even become younger in heaven. Since I knew she was flourishing up there, I felt assured that I didn't need to miss her down here.

Spring was in the air, and Dad began making plans to sell our beloved heifer, Roast Beef. We'd had her for three years, and even though she was a year older than most Holstein heifers who had their first calf, Dad said it was time to get her bred in hopes that a dairy might buy her back for her milk. Uncle Keith invited us to bring her out to his farm, and since Curt had a horse trailer, he volunteered to take her out to the pasture and let her loose.

I was a little emotional, as I knew that once we had her bred, she would be sold. Luckily, my mom's cousin Nedra was married to a guy named Wayne, who was a manager at a dairy farm and had agreed to buy Roast Beef, despite her age. I knew she would be there to give milk, which made me happy and relieved because this meant she wouldn't be slaughtered.

That day, Lori and I watched as Curt chased her through the corrals and up into the trailer. She had only been in a trailer once when she was a baby. She was jumpy and scared when he closed the door behind her. Lori and I hopped into Curt's pickup and headed down the paved road out to the farm.

Through the back window, I caught a glimpse of Roast Beef in the trailer. She wouldn't stand still and was obviously nervous. As we got closer to the farm, I lost sight of her.

"I think she jumped out!" I said to Curt.

"No, she didn't jump out. She wouldn't be able to do that," he said as if my opinion was a silly idea.

"But I don't see her anymore! Do you see her, Lori?" I asked.

Lori looked back. "Yes, she's there, Dena!" she said, but her voice was hesitant.

"I still think she jumped out because I don't see her!"

"Dena, there is no way she could've jumped out. There is a canvas over the trailer, and she can't jump that high! And no way could she fit through that small space between the canvas and the door." Curt sounded annoyed.

I knew that was my cue to quit worrying about something that couldn't possibly happen. This time, I sat in silence.

When we arrived at the pasture, Curt jumped out and opened the electric gate. Then he jumped back into his pickup and we drove to the windmill that was in the center of a hilly, sandy pasture. A windmill is like a wind turbine, except the fan blades are a lot smaller. It has two gears that pull a sucker rod up and down when the wind blows. This turns the gears, which in this case were connected to the pump at the bottom of a water well. This brought the water up the pipe so it flowed out of a spout into the old stock tank. When we arrived at the windmill, several cows were standing around and getting a drink.

Both Lori and I got out with Curt and walked to the back of the trailer. I was sure that Roast Beef would be missing. As Curt opened the back door, his face fell in shock. So did Lori's. As I'd suspected, Roast Beef was gone.

"I told you she jumped out!" I said, more worried about her than happy that I'd been right all along.

"How in the world did she do that? She would've had to climb the wall and bail out," he said, answering his own question. "Oh my, we have to drive back and look for her!"

Not much traffic was on the paved road out to the farm, which was mostly driven by local farmers and ranchers. About five miles down the road, we found her grazing in a ditch. She looked up with sad eyes.

Curt stopped in the middle of the road and put on his hazard lights. Then he walked out into the ditch and stood behind her, checking to see how hurt she was from jumping out while the trailer was still moving.

"She's bleeding a little under her tail," he said. "But I don't think she broke anything. Lori, you open up the door to the trailer, and I'll try to run her in."

Lori opened the door, then we both stood behind the door as Curt ran Roast Beef back in. This time she went right in without any trouble.

As we drove back to our house, Curt was still in a state of silent shock. When we arrived, my parents, Aunt Joyce, and Uncle Max were outside drinking sun tea on our backyard patio.

"You'll never guess what!" I yelled as I hurried through the front door and ran straight through to the back door. "Roast Beef jumped out of the trailer on the way out to Uncle Keith's!"

"Did she really, or are you just joking?" Mom asked, glancing up at Curt to see if I was kidding or not. When she saw the serious look on Curt's face, her face fell in disbelief.

"No, I'm not joking. What's more, I knew she jumped out, but no one believed me until we opened up the trailer and she was gone!" I said, still worried about Roast Beef.

"My stars! How did she do that?" asked Aunt Joyce, shaking her head in shock.

"Did you find her? Was she dead?" questioned Dad.

"No, she was okay, just a little banged up about five miles back. I thought I would have trouble getting her back inside the trailer, but she actually went right in. I think we should call the vet and maybe take her to be checked out," suggested Curt.

We followed Mom into the house, where she opened the phone book and found the vet's number. We watched her with rapt attention as she explained the situation.

She was silent for several moments. "Yes, she is standing up. Okay, we'll send someone to pick up some medicine."

After Mom hung up the phone, she smiled at us. "He says if she is too scared to be in a trailer but she's walking on her own, then we should unload her and come to town, and he'll give us some medicine, plus some healing cream to put on her sores."

"Well, let's unload her and unhook the trailer. Then I'll run to town to get the medicine," said Curt.

We all walked out to the pasture and unloaded her back into her pen, where she was safe and sound. I patted her down and did my best to simply give her love and attention. Curt drove to town to get Roast Beef's medicine. We kept her for another three weeks while she recovered, then Curt loaded her back into his trailer and hauled her out to Uncle Keith's farm. This time, she'd learned her lesson and didn't try to jump out.

When Curt let her out, she backed away from the other cattle and the bull that was standing there to greet her. She had never seen another cow in her life, except when she was little. As tame as she was, she truly believed she was human. Tears streamed out of my eyes as we drove out of the pasture and left her alone to figure out her true identity as a heifer.

Mason's cattle.

A couple of months later, she had a baby in her tummy and was going to be sold straight to the dairy.

That night, my mom had a serious talk with my dad. "We should use the money we receive from Roast Beef on the kids. The Sears store has their above-ground pools on sale during the fall. I think we should buy a nice oval one for them. After all, we both grew up swimming in stock tanks, and I think a swimming pool would be a great family investment."

"Well, if that's what you think would be best, then sure!" Dad agreed.

Both Lori and I gave each other a high five and began making plans for pool parties over the next summer, but that felt like a lifetime away. "I wish we could get it this summer," I whined.

"Next summer will be here before you know it," said Dad.

As luck would have it, Roast Beef became one of the dairy's best milkers, and we received enough money to buy our pool! We were grateful to Mom, who'd always been very generous and fair. We were also grateful to Curt—after all, he'd brought this calf home for us in the first place.

One day, Mom bought a thank-you card at the store and put money inside to thank Curt for buying us our calf. "Now, when we get to Curt and Barb's house tonight, don't say a word about why he is getting this money!" she warned us. "I want it to be a surprise for them."

As we'd anticipated, Curt was totally shocked. "What's this for?" he asked in disbelief as money fell out of the card.

"It's for you and Barb!" Mom said with a huge smile on her face.

"But I don't understand what it's for," he said, utterly confused.

"It's because you bought Roast Beef for us. And this is some of the money we received for selling her back to the dairy," I explained.

"No!" he insisted. "I can't take this. I didn't pay this much for her, and Lord knows you put the feed inside her. That wasn't cheap!"

"But Curt, you helped the girls by teaching her how to lead. Plus, you did the branding, hauled her to and from the pastures, and helped take care of her when she got hurt. Trust me, you deserve this, and you *will* take it."

"Thank you. But I have to admit I feel awful for taking it."

"Well, don't!" said Mom, patting him on the back and giving Barb a hug. "You and Barb can use it for something special just for the two of you. You gave my girls a memory that will last a lifetime!"

Watching this unfold, I actually choked up as I attempted to hold in my tears. For the first time in my life, I understood the meaning of the old saying, "It's better to give than to receive."

A couple of months after we sold Roast Beef to the dairy, Wayne gave us the pen number and Roast Beef's ear tag number to check up on her. Mom drove me to her pen, but there were so many dairy cows standing around that we couldn't find her. I stood on the other side for a very long time, looking for her and hollering her name.

"We have to leave, Dena. Maybe we can try to find her another day," suggested Mom.

I walked closer to the fence in one more attempt. I noticed that many of the cows were eating in a long feed bunk. They were startled by how close I was coming to them. This time, in unison, they began to quickly back away from me. But one of them stopped in her tracks and stared straight at me after hearing my voice. She wasn't close enough for me to pet, and she didn't come to me after I called her name. But for a moment, we stared straight into each other's eyes with love. My heart melted.

"Mom, there she is, there she is!" I exclaimed quietly so I wouldn't scare Roast Beef with loudness or any sudden movement. Tears of love fell down my cheeks as our eyes locked.

"We have to go now," said Mom softly, taking my hand and leading me back to the car. I turned my head and kept my eyes on Roast Beef until we were too far to see her.

On the way home, bitter sweetness came over me. I was glad she wasn't really turning into roast beef and that she was giving milk instead of meat, at least for now.

That was the last time I ever saw her.

But other things quickly entered my life, meaning I didn't dwell too long on the loss of my beloved heifer. Turning the calendar over to the month of May meant that the elementary school's all-day track meet was coming up.

Chapter 28

Scrumptious Homemade Noodles on Track Meet Day!

"Therefore, as we have opportunity, let us do good to all, especially to those who are of the household of faith."
—Galatians 6:10

One day, while Dusty was playing at our house, we discussed the matter of our all-day track meet.

"I hate track meet day. I never win. I'm never fast at running," I complained.

"Me too," she sympathized.

"Hey, I wonder if our moms would let us skip out on that day?"

"Let's ask them," she suggested.

As Dusty's mom, Sue, walked in to pick her up, we ran up to her and smiled in anticipation.

"Mom," said Dusty, "can Dena and I stay home on track day and hang out together instead of going to school?"

"Yeah, Mom, can we, *please*?" I looked at my mom with my best puppy-dog eyes.

"Well, let me think about it," said Sue, glancing up at my mom to see what her reaction was. "But right now, we need to get home!"

"I'll think about it, too, Dena," Mom promised.

The night before the track meet, Mom came to me with some great news. "Dena, instead of going to school tomorrow, you are getting up early to go with Sue and Julie. You girls are going on a long trail ride out to Gardner's Farm. It's about an eight-mile round trip, so you'll leave early."

"Really?" I asked, astounded that she'd actually agreed *and* that I was getting a trail ride out of it!

"Yes, I thought about it, and it feels right."

"Yes! I'm so excited. Does Dusty know yet?" I asked.

"Sue's going to let her know tonight."

The next morning, Mom came into my room to wake me. I hopped straight out of bed and ran to the kitchen for breakfast. Then Mom took me down to Julie's house to get Chiefer saddled.

"Hi, Dena," said Julie. "You can help me saddle Chiefer."

After Chiefer was saddled, I felt a little scared to get on. I hadn't ridden Chiefer since the last time I fell off, about two years ago.

"Don't be scared," Julie reassured me. "He'll do fine with all of us riding. I promise!"

"Come on, Dena, I'll help you on," said Mom as she gave me a boost. Sitting in the saddle, I felt a little unsteady and scared. Mom took the reins and led me around the yard while Julie saddled her other horse, Sally.

"You'll be fine. You need to get back into riding, Dena," Mom said.

When Julie was ready to go, we took off and met Sue and Dusty on the other side of the railroad tracks, where they were sitting on their horses and waiting for us.

"Hi, Dena Bob, how are you this morning?" asked Sue. "Are you ready to ride?"

"Yes," I said with a big smile, remembering that Dusty and I had gotten out of going to the track meet. Dusty and I put our horses beside each other and rode behind Julie and Sue. The longer we rode, the more I relaxed.

We were on a dirt road west of town called Whisky Road.

"I sure hope we don't see any snakes," I said to Dusty.

"You know we will," she replied, her eyes wide. "There are always snakes and turtles on this road."

The ride out to the farm was starting to feel long and tiring, but I wasn't about to complain. When we finally arrived at our destination, Hazel came out to greet us. She was the local 4-H leader and also a teacher at our Bible school. She always had a smile on her face and was happy to see all the kids around town, hoping she could recruit them into 4-H.

One time, Dusty and I came out to Hazel and Merle's farm with Sue. We came out to help with the butchering of their hundreds of chickens. There were so many adults and kids out here to help. The kids would run wild, chasing the chickens and handing them over to the adults, who would hang them upside down, on a clothesline, with their head through a milk jug to kill them. Then the kids would run wild again, chasing after the chickens with their heads cut off, to take them to the next station to get plucked and cut up into meat. For dinner that day, Hazel's famous homemade chicken noodle soup was the scrumptious meal of the day.

"How was your ride out here, cowgirls?" she asked, clapping her hands together and smiling at us.

"It was fun, but we're hot and thirsty," I said, speaking for all of us. I jumped off Chiefer, anticipating a cold drink waiting nearby.

"Well, take this bucket of water and offer a drink to your horses, then tie them up over here on the post for some shade. Make sure you loosen their saddles, then come in the house for some iced tea," she said.

We walked into the house, where glasses of ice were already waiting for us. "I have iced tea, or if you want, you can have a pop," said Hazel. Dusty and I both decided on a Pepsi.

"If you're careful not to spill, you can go sit in the living room," Hazel suggested. Julie and Sue sat down at the kitchen table to catch up on what was going on at the farm. Dusty and I walked into the living room and sat down on the couch, where we could feel the cool breeze coming straight at us from the swamp cooler. Both of us were surprised at how tired we were. For dinner, Hazel fed us some of her homemade chicken and noodles, topped with mashed potatoes and a salad. It was just as delicious as the day we helped with the chickens, and we gobbled it right down, even taking a second helping.

After a while, we were ready to ride back home. Hazel walked out to see us off. Julie tightened Chiefer's cinch and told me to climb on. Then she handed me the reins, and just like that, we were riding back home. By the end of the day, we had spent several miles riding. The sun beat down, and we didn't realize that our arms and faces were sunburnt. Once we got off to unsaddle, I realized that I was a little stiff and sore, and it hurt to move. But I didn't complain. I loved riding so much, and this day was more fun than any old track meet would ever be. Thankfully, we never ended up seeing any snakes.

After the horses were unsaddled and fed, Julie looked at me with a smile.

"I'll take you home, but at the barn, I have a surprise to show you. I bought a new baby colt, a quarter pony that I named T. J., which stands for Tiny Joe," said Julie. "He's super tiny and cute. You're gonna love him. I'm going to keep him up at my mom's place so you can play with him. He's too little to ride right now, but he's leading well. You and Lori can get him out every once in a while so he gets used to people; that way, when he's two years old, he'll be easier to train to ride."

"Wow!" I said, thrilled at the idea, "I can't wait to meet him."

When we walked into the barn, my eyes danced with delight at the cuteness standing before us. "Dena, meet T. J.," said Julie.

"Oh, he's so cute! I'm in love," I said as I oohed and aahed over how adorable he was. I was glad to have another animal inside the barn. Since we'd sold Roast Beef and Cinnamon, both Julie and Curt had moved their horses to their own houses, and the barn had been sitting empty for some time.

Julie put a halter on T. J., and the two of us led him down the trail between Aunt Joyce's house and ours, then into our backyard. "Julie, will you hold him so I can get Lori and my mom?" I asked.

"Sure!" said Julie.

My mom was surprised to see me. "You're home from your ride. How was it?" she asked with excitement.

"It was so much fun and I can't wait to go riding again. But Mom, you and Lori *have* to come see! Julie bought the cutest little pony, and his name is T. J.!"

"You and Julie brought him over here to the yard?" she asked. "Lori and I were with Aunt Joyce this morning, and we've already seen him. But of course, we'll come out and see him again."

I spent the next full week leading T. J. around our yard and petting and brushing him down after I came home from school in the evenings. These moments with T. J. would end up being some of the happiest and most formative times of my life. Eventually, they'd blossom into what would turn out to be a lifelong passion.

Chapter 29

Home on the Range

"For every beast of the Forest it is Mine, and the cattle on a thousand hills." —**Psalm 50:10**

A couple of weeks later school was out for the summer, and Aunt Nadine invited us out to her house for a family cousin day. When we arrived, she also had a surprise. "Come out by the grazing horses," she ordered us excitedly.

We stood by the horses that were being hobbled by the barn. You hobble a horse by tying their front legs together. This way, they can only take short strides instead of running. This gives them more freedom to move and graze instead of being tied to a post when they're out of their pens, but they can't run away. It's also a way to tame them and teach them patience so they don't get scared when a rope gets wrapped around their legs. This was very important for Aunt Nadine and Uncle David, who used their horses for roping cattle.

"Well?" said Aunt Nadine with a grin on her face as she waited for us to figure out her surprise.

"I don't see what the surprise is," said Mom. "All I see are the horses."

"Well, darn it! Look more closely at these horses, and tell me what you see!" Aunt Nadine said impatiently.

Looking closely, my mom studied each of the five horses that were grazing by the barn. Then she covered her mouth, almost in tears.

"Oh! Really?" said Mom, suddenly realizing what Aunt Nadine was referring to. "Where did you get her?" Her voice was filled with astonishment.

"Dena and Lori, come here," Aunt Nadine commanded, not wanting to answer my mom for fear of giving the surprise away before Lori and I had a chance to see it too. As we stepped closer to Aunt Nadine, she put her hands on our backs, leading us to one particular horse. "Pet this horse," she told us.

As we reached out to pet her, I also realized what the surprise was. Vonie's old horse, whom we'd sold about a year ago, was standing right in front of us. "It's Cinnamon!" I said, jumping up and down. Lori also began smiling ear to ear.

"Boy, I never thought I'd see you again!" I said, enfolding Cinnamon in a giant hug.

"We were at the sale barn when she came through the other day, and we saved her from the kill pen," said Aunt Nadine. "I told David, 'We're not letting this happen to her. We will bring her home for the kids to ride her when they come over.'"

The rest of the day, Lori and I, along with my cousins Janet, Janeil, and Mike, had five horses saddled. We rode all morning long in Aunt Nadine's arena behind their big red barn. In fact, that was the first day I ever rode Cinnamon by myself; in the past, Vonie and Lori rode her and occasionally gave me rides. Today, it felt great to have Cinnamon all to myself.

Later, Mom came out to get us. "We're going out to where they're branding cattle a couple of miles away. Why don't you all unsaddle and give the horses a break and come with us?"

We rode our horses to the front of the barn. Janet helped me unsaddle Cinnamon and then handed me a brush to brush her down. I patted her on the neck and gave her a hug and a kiss. "Thanks for the fun ride," I said. "I'll be back to ride you soon!"

Janet, Aunt Nadine, and my mom unsaddled the rest of the horses and put their saddles away in the barn. Then they led the horses back into the pasture and let them loose.

"Jump in the back of the pickup," Aunt Nadine said. "We need to go see how the branding is going." That day, Aunt Nadine and Uncle David had a crew helping them work and brand their calves.

My cousins, Lori, and I jumped into the back of the pickup, while Aunt Nadine, Aunt Jean, Aunt Joyce, and my mom squeezed in the front. Aunt Nadine drove us a couple of miles down a dirt road. When we arrived at our destination, I looked around and saw roughly twenty men and women all on horseback. Behind us, Dad and Uncle Max were following along in another vehicle.

We jumped out of the pickup and quickly climbed the fence to sit on top of the wooden rail for a front-row seat. The cows on one side of the fence were bawling for their calves on the other side of the fence—and the calves were bawling right back to their mamas. It was a low humming sound, like a sad song.

Several cowboys and cowgirls were roping the calves. When one was roped, it was dragged to the fire by a cowboy on a horse, where another cowboy roped his back legs. Three people on the ground worked together in a group. The cowboys on their horses made sure their horse stood tight so there was no slack in the rope. This gave them control over the calf's head and back legs. The calf's body was stretched out while someone had one knee on the calf's neck to help hold it in place. Another person used a sharp blade to cut something from underneath all the boy calves, then threw the contents into a bucket.

"This is called castration. They do this to turn a bull into a steer. That way, it can't make babies," explained Dad.

"And it's also what Rocky Mountain oysters are made of. Yum!" said Uncle Max, rubbing his belly in a circular motion as we watched the cowboy cut off the bloody, stringy balls. "They're really good when you bread them with some cornmeal and flour and deep-fat fry them."

I saw a cowboy throw an oyster to his dog, who was patiently waiting to eat it raw. "Yuck!" I said. "I don't want to *ever* eat that!" Little did I know that I had already eaten them and just didn't know what they were!

Another cowboy took a hot iron from the fire and walked over to where the calf was pinned down. He stuck the hot iron right into the calf's hip bone. He held it there for a good ten seconds. The hot iron against the calf created a scent of smoke and singed fur. The calf began to cry out in pain, but the sound was different from the calves who were bawling out to their mamas.

I hid my teary eyes. I wasn't sure if they were watering because I was sad about watching the calf being burned with an iron, or if it was the dust and the pungent smell of smoke that arose from the branding iron that was burning my eyes. In all honesty, it was probably both.

Dad stood behind me, explaining everything that was being done. I had seen it all before; I remembered when Curt had branded Roast Beef a couple of years ago and how I had cried. Now I loved the excitement and the action of watching how the cowboys used their horses to rope the calves and drag them to the fire, but I felt sad for the calves.

Just then, I saw my cousin Lisa jump on a calf that was being dragged to the fire. She had one knee on the calf and grabbed some skin around its neck as she stuck a needle deep inside.

"That's to keep the calf from getting sick," said Dad.

I saw someone else take another needle and jab it into the calf again, which made me cringe. "It's called immunizations, like when you have to go to the doctor to get your shots." Dad took his index finger and jabbed me in the ribs, making me jump.

"They use a hot iron to brand the calves so they can identify who legally owns them," he continued. "They brand them around the same time each year, when they are small and easier to handle. Then they'll go out to pasture with their moms through the summer and will be sold next fall after they're weaned. Each branding iron has its own identification and has to be registered and licensed under the Colorado State Brand Commissioners. The ear tags are put in when the calves are born. They match the mother's ear tags, so the rancher can tell which calf belongs to which cow."

"You know, out at Uncle Keith's, there's a white-painted V connected P quarter circle on top of the red barn—that was your grandparents' registered brand. It stands for Vonley Probasco, which are the initials of your granddad's name," Uncle Max pointed out.

"I always wondered what that V connected P quarter circle meant. Did Granddad paint it on the barn before he died?" I asked.

"Yes, he sure did," my mom said, happy that I was interested in our family history.

The day was quickly fading. As the sun set, bright orange and blue colors covered the western sky and the dust began to settle. The calves continued to bawl in a sad call-and-response to their mothers. I gave out a big yawn, and my dad carried me to his pickup. I was beginning to understand the ropes of farming and ranching and where our food comes from. I was proud to be a part of such excitement in this Western culture of our beef industry, where farmers and ranchers feed the world.

Chapter 30

Eckley's Old Settlers

"Here is what I have seen: It is good and fitting for one to eat and drink, and to enjoy the good of all his labor in which he toils under the sun all the days of his life which God gives him; for it is his heritage." —**Ecclesiastes 5:18**

The John and Betty Owens family: Jay, Joni, Dave, Brent, Betty, Shelby, Beth, and Roy. Photo by Joni Owens. Used by permission.

Toward the end of that summer, our town's celebration finally came around. Every year, Eckley holds a two-day festival of activities known as the Old Settlers' Picnic. I vividly remember those crisp, cool mornings of Labor Day weekend. As a child, I would feed off the energy to keep warm. People laughing in line at the festival would wait for their first taste of the day. The aroma of bacon, sausage, ham, hash browns, and eggs would sizzle over a hot fire for a chuck wagon breakfast down at the J&B Bar.

This was a time of total freedom for every child in town. Main Street would come alive with friends and family. Clowns with balloons would stroll down the street in a parade of laughter and smiles.

For a couple of years, I rode Chiefer in the parade. One year, Dusty's mom, Sue, made us Indian clothes out of gunnysacks. She painted our faces and made head bands out of construction paper and feathers. We rode down the parade as proud Indians on horseback. The horses' hooves would hit the hard pavement, following the parade line leading to the festivities at the end of Main Street.

The loudspeaker would blare in our ears, sometimes with the sound of my dad's voice announcing that all children ages three and under line up on a white chalked line. Fathers would stand behind their small children, pointing to where their mothers stood, just thirty feet away. In total confusion, the children who could barely walk, let alone run, would sprint across the pavement trying to pick out their mothers from a crowd of what felt like a million. The children were boxed in on all four sides, with a loud roar of people yelling and screaming for them to run faster. Out of fear, they would run as fast as their tiny legs could carry them—with no idea why. With tears in their eyes, they were finally swooped into their mothers' embrace, only to be handed a fifty-cent piece or a soda for no apparent reason. I, too, remember being young, standing there while everyone yelled for me to run. It scared me to death. But when my dad swooped me in his arms and told me to pick out a cold pop from a small stock tank of ice water, it always made the experience worth it in the end.

There were races all morning for every age group, including the grandparents. The competitions became more serious as the group grew older. Running, hopping, gunnysack races, three-legged races, skinned-up-bloody-knees-on-the-concrete races, and bike races. And then there were the egg toss and kick-your-shoe competitions, which were always accompanied by giddy laughter and bright-yellow egg yolks running down your shirts.

The last race of the morning was something everyone had been preparing for. Standing in a big circle of chalk, people would crowd together. They stood, screaming at the top of their lungs, jumping up and down, patiently waiting for the Orton Weaver turtle race to begin. Yes, everyone in a hundred-mile radius had been collecting turtles for weeks. Judges marked a number on their backs with tan duct tape; the number was then written in a notebook with the name of the turtle's owner next to it. The turtles were surely pumped, given the last two weeks of grasshoppers, flies, and hamburger that made up their diet!

White chalk marked the three circles. The small circle was the starting point where twenty to thirty turtles would be placed in a bottomless box. The adults who were in charge would reach in and turn some of these turtles over, as they had accidentally been turned upside down in the commotion. When the box was removed, the turtles were off to the races. Some would shy away and hide in their shells. Others would take off, slow and steady. Still others would see the crowd and head back to the center. The three turtles that crossed the second line first were held back for the final race. Those were usually the turtles that wouldn't hesitate to bite you. The third line was meant to warn the crowd never to cross it. Sometimes there were more than four hundred turtles in those races. If your turtle won the final race, you would win a trophy, five dollars, and get your picture in the local newspaper. This was the most exciting race of the day.

Before the turtle races ended, adults would form a long line to the fire hall, anxiously awaiting the free BBQ that the firemen and their wives scurried around to serve. Hot beef on the bun, straight from the BBQ pit in the ground, was the most delicious meal of the day—along with baked beans, potato chips, and fresh watermelon from the farms just outside of town. The homegrown taste always melted in my mouth.

The firemen's children bypassed the long, hot line. They could be seen sneaking to the back and grabbing a plate. This scheme worked well, until they reached the age where it backfired and all the kids were recruited to help serve.

After the firemen finished serving the crowd, they took out a list of people who were elderly or might not have been here for the festivities because of an illness. They would fill their plates and drive to their houses to leave a delicious free meal.

After lunch, the older generation would head over to the gym for the talent show. Many of the local 4-H kids would sing, dance, read poetry, and model older dresses from the late 1800s and early 1900s. Once, I was asked to model my Aunt Dolores's wedding gown, which her mother had sewn by hand. It was laced all in white with long sleeves and a high neck. I remember feeling both nervous and beautiful as I walked across the stage while someone talked about how it had been made.

The remaining festivities of the day were moved down to the local arena. Water fights and tug-of-war into the mud hole were cheap entertainment for the parents and grandparents, who sat on the bleachers gossiping and cheering for their children. Down at the J&B Bar, horseshoe tournaments were played. For the young adults and teenagers, mud volleyball and beer keg water-fight tournaments were held. For the younger kids, the grease pig and grease pole contest were among the more exciting events of the day. If you caught the pig, you could take it home to raise it for the meat, or receive money for it. Many children cried when their parents made them take the money home instead of the pig. If you climbed the grease pole, a five-dollar bill was waiting at the top.

In the hot sun, Uncle David and Aunt Nadine would back their white Ford pickup next to the concession stand; the bed of the pickup was full of their famous homegrown watermelons. My cousin Mike and I would sit on the tailgate, advertising and selling them to the people who walked by as the biggest and sweetest watermelons in the country and on the vine.

In the evening, children would gather for sleepovers with friends. Older siblings were always left in charge while the adults were over at the gym for a night of supporting our local volunteer fireman and dancing to many local and live bands, such as Gary Stroup and the El Gee Jays Country and Western Dance Band.

On Sunday morning, the families of the firemen would meet over at the gym to pick up all the trash that was left behind at the dance. Then we would gather for an outdoor church service, sitting on small square hay bales under the town's water tower. Once again, people would meet at the arena, where baseball games and gymkhanas were the entertainment of the day. Children would spend their day on horseback, racing around barrels, poles, and flags, and tying down goats.

But on that particular occasion, I received a special surprise. My cousin Lisa woke at the crack of dawn, saddled up Cinnamon and Smoky, and brought them both for us to ride in the Eckley gymkhana.

When we first arrived, we rode into the arena, warming up our horses for the day. I was still a little scared to get into a full lope, so I trotted around the arena, while other horses flew past me.

"Come on," urged Lisa, riding next to me on her horse. The next thing I knew, my cousins Julie, Janet, Lisa, and I were loping around the arena beside each other. With all of them surrounding me, it felt as if we were flying free.

When the competitions started, my uncle David was handing out the tiny hand-held flags to the kids who were ready to run. "Now run fast," he instructed me. I put Cinnamon into a trot, and when we got to the first barrel, I pulled on the reins to stop her and place the flag in the bucket of grain that was sitting on top. Cinnamon stuck her nose in for a taste. I took her nose out by pulling back on her reins. I backed her up, leaned clear over my saddle, and placed the flag inside the bucket with the grain. Then I placed myself back in the saddle and kicked her again to go pick up the next flag that was sitting on top of the next barrel. Grabbing the flag *out* of the bucket was much easier than placing the flag *in* the bucket! Finally, I trotted her back home. My cousins could do this race at full speed, never slowing down, even to place the flag in the bucket or to take the next flag out.

The next event was tying the goat's tail. This seemed like a simple task to me, and I knew I could do it. Out in the middle of the arena, a little white goat was tied to a stake in the ground. I loped my horse out to the goat and jumped off as fast as I could, then I ran to the goat that stood perfectly still. I held a red string in my hand while I straddled the goat backward and tied the string around his tail, then I threw my arms up in the air to indicate I was done. The only thing I worried about was getting back on my horse after my competition. The stirrups were high on Cinnamon, so I could actually reach them while I was riding her. But she was a taller horse than Chiefer. I was scared I wouldn't be able to climb back on her, but I had nothing to fear. Uncle David was there to hold the horses for the kids when they jumped off. And as soon as I got close enough to jump back onto Cinnamon, my uncle picked me up and threw me in the center of the saddle. "Good job," he said, winking at me. "You were fast."

I smiled and loped Cinnamon back out of the arena. This was the one event where I actually placed first in my intermediate age group, and my name was even in the local newspaper. I was relieved that I was still young enough that I didn't have to flip the goat over and tie his three feet together like my other cousins had to.

Throughout the day, I ran the cloverleaf pattern of the barrels and the figure-eight patterns of the poles, smiling ear to ear as Cinnamon was gentle and only went the speed I was comfortable with.

That evening, after all of us kids were finished with the gymkhanas, my friend J.P. and I rode our horses all around outside the arena, watching as the adults roped cattle in a timed event with their horses. It was way past midnight before the roping competitions were finished, and I almost fell asleep while sitting on top of Cinnamon. Aunt Nadine came to me and told me to ride Cinnamon back to our house with Julie.

Since the barn by our house was close and it was super late, Julie and I rode our horses back to our place for the night. Only the moonlight and stars were out to guide us, along with an occasional streetlight along the way. Julie quickly unsaddled the horses and turned them loose in the pasture under the stars. It was a beautiful sight to see them roaming free in the night after a long and tiring day.

My mom met us right there and thanked Julie for helping me throughout the day. Mom took my hand and led me back to the house—tired, sunburned, and dusty. She pulled off my boots, changed me into my pajamas, and tucked me into bed. As I fell asleep, it felt as if I were still in a rocking motion on top of Cinnamon. That day stood out as one of my best days of my childhood.

We kept Cinnamon for about a month. Lori and I rode her every night after school until she went back to Aunt Nadine's for the winter. After that, I never saw her again. Sadly, she died of old age later that winter.

I remember riding my bike down Main Street weeks after the celebration. Turtles remained in town until the middle of September. Over the next several days, the white chalk faded into the blacktop.

Old Settlers' Picnic had been around longer than my mom had been alive. It was a tradition she could remember as a child, and the festivities still continue to this day. It's a celebration of family and friends in a small-town atmosphere, where everyone comes together in harmony and enjoys the same activities that their forebears probably did. I frequently think back to those days—to the love of family, the fun of friends, the smell of horses and sandbox turtles. These memories are treasured and will always dance upon my heart.

Inside the new building of the Eckley Bar & Grill: the old Eckley Tigers school mascot sits in the mirror. Photo courtesy of the Eckley Bar & Grill.

The original building of the J&B Bar.

Chapter 31

Cowgirl Tough

"He heals the brokenhearted and binds up their wounds."
—Psalms 147:3

One day, Dusty called me on the phone. "Dena, I talked Julie and my mom into saddling horses and going riding today! Julie will meet you out at the barn with Chiefer. Then Mom and I will meet you at the arena," she said excitedly.

"Okay!" I covered the receiver with my hand and turned to Mom, whispering, "Julie, Sue, and Dusty want me to go riding with them. May I?"

"Oh, great!" said Mom. "Go get your boots."

"Mom said it was okay," I informed Dusty. "I'll see you in a jiffy." I hung up the phone and ran to my room.

I had been riding Chiefer a little bit through the last winter at Uncle Keith's farm. It had been a while since I had been back in the saddle, but I felt confident. The horses were eager to be out of the barn and trotted along the path that led to the arena. Julie and I arrived before Sue and Dusty. I took off to practice the barrel pattern in a trot as Julie began galloping in big circles on her horse, Sally.

Chiefer was not trained to trot the barrel pattern. As he came around the last barrel, he charged home full speed ahead. The next thing I knew, I was once again eating dirt. I lay there for quite some time until Julie came and sat me back up.

"Are you all right?" she asked.

My left arm began to throb, and it wouldn't let up.

"I feel like I broke my arm!" I cried out.

"It doesn't look swollen! But maybe we'd better check it out," she said. "Look, here come Dusty and Sue on their horses. Let's get you back on Chiefer and take you to Mom's to look at it."

Dusty yelled out, "What are you doing on the ground? Push-ups?"

"I'm not doing push-ups. I fell off Chiefer," I said unhappily, seeing no humor in my predicament.

Dusty felt bad. She'd really thought I was on the ground exercising. Sue jumped off her horse, and she and Julie helped boost me back onto Chiefer. We rode back to Aunt Joyce's, where she and my mom were watching their favorite soap opera, *The Young and the Restless*. Seeing us ride up to the front yard, both of them turned away from the drama on the screen and immediately came out to greet us.

"Dena, why are you crying? Did you fall off again?" said Mom, rushing over to me.

"Yes," I said through my sniffles and tears. "And I think I hurt my arm."

"Well, let's look at it," she replied as she helped me off of Chiefer. "It doesn't look swollen, so I'm sure you can get back on and go for a ride."

"Here, Dena! Take some Tylenol for the pain and then you can go back out," said Aunt Joyce, agreeing with my mom.

I was encouraged by their optimism. I wanted to go for a ride, and I definitely didn't want falling off to stop me from having a good day. But my arm really *did* hurt. And my fear of horses was beginning to take over, despite my simultaneous love for them. It didn't help that this was the second big fall I'd had on Chiefer.

Mom helped me back on. We rode around a dirt road, and Chiefer was good as gold and followed right along. I tucked my left arm in against my chest and put my hand under my right armpit. I held the reins in my right hand, and we rode for another hour. I didn't say two words to anyone. I just closed my eyes and tried to block out the pain in my arm. Julie kept asking me if I was okay, and I lied and nodded yes. I didn't want to quit riding. I wanted to be a tough cowgirl and get back on like I'd always been taught to do before.

When we finished riding, Mom met us at the barn. Julie unsaddled and brushed down the horses, and Mom took my right hand and led me home. I didn't feel like eating that night. I just sat on the couch holding my arm until Mom came over to me.

"Dena, you need to get to bed!"

"But my arm hurts too bad to get ready for bed," I cried.

My mom helped me out of my clothes and into my pajamas. As I lifted my arm, a new rush of pain brought tears to my eyes, and I screamed out. "That hurts!"

"Here, take some more Tylenol to sleep," she said reassuringly, taking another pillow and tucking it under my left arm.

In the next room, I heard my dad talking. "I think she's faking it. She'll be better by morning, so don't worry about it," he told Mom. This made me feel that maybe it didn't hurt as bad as I thought. Maybe I really *was* just being a baby.

The next morning, Mom came to wake me up for school. "Rise and shine!" she said cheerily.

I sat up cautiously.

"You're still not moving it, are you?" she said, frowning.

I looked straight up at her and began to cry. "I'm not faking it, Mom. It really hurts!"

"Okay," she said, folding me into a hug. "I'll help you get dressed, and we'll go to the doctor instead of going to school."

When we arrived at the doctor's office, he promptly ordered an X-ray. "You sprained your arm pretty hard, and even your wrist was hurt pretty badly. I'm going to put you in a wrist brace and a sling for a couple of months. You're not allowed to play sports, go out for PE, or get back on your horse for at least a couple of months. I'll also write you a note for school," he said.

I never knew until I fell off Chiefer that very first time that something you loved with all your heart could hurt you—not once, but multiple times. People say you never get over your first love, which I believe to be true. And even though I vowed to never ride again, my heart was broken because of the confusing love/fear relationship I had with horses.

Chapter 32

From Swimming Suits to Cowboy Boots

"I can do all things through Christ who strengthens me."
—Philippians 4:13

Time passed, and my longing to ride cropped up once more. Whenever I came home from school that spring, I watched Julie from our backyard as she worked T. J. This was the same colt that Lori and I had led around like a puppy, back when he was a baby. He was a small gray dappled quarter pony about twelve hands tall, still a little smaller than Chiefer. As I watched her work him, I thought that just maybe I could ride again. It wouldn't be long until school was out for the summer, so I'd have more time on my hands.

One day, Julie came over and talked to my mom. "James is here this summer and visiting his dad. I would like to get the kids into a schedule and have them ride every night at 6:00 p.m. down at the arena. I've been working T. J., and I feel Dena will get along with him. He's dog gentle and will do whatever he's asked. What do you say?"

"Sure," said Mom. "I'll have her over at the barn tonight."

Walking over to the barn, I was both excited and nervous. I hadn't ridden since I sprained my arm and wrist. Julie already had T. J. saddled and handed the reins to Mom to help me up. When I went to get on him, I immediately felt a wave of fear and panic rise inside me, even though I had led him all over our yard multiple times when he was a baby.

"T. J. is just beginning his training, so he doesn't neck-rein very well. You have to reach down and pull his head to the side when you want him to turn, and then he'll go!" said Julie, who was also showing James how to saddle Chiefer.

All of a sudden, I didn't want to get on at all. Fear engulfed me. I wanted a horse that I could neck-rein. An *easy* horse! I didn't want him to get scared and run away with me, or not know what I was asking and not turn, or simply not stop for me.

"I don't want to ride," I cried to Mom and Julie. "I think I'll just stay home tonight. Maybe I'll try tomorrow night instead?"

Julie walked over and stood beside us. As if sensing my fear, she said, "Dena, this horse is as gentle as they come. I promise you, you'll get along."

"No! I don't want to fall off and get hurt again," I said, slightly embarrassed that I was now crying like a baby.

"Come on, Dena, you *need* to do this. If you do, you'll fall in love with this horse, and you will be happy. You won't regret it," Mom said. "Now, I'll hold him while you get on, and then I will follow you on my bike down to the arena and lead you around in there. You'll be fine—you'll see."

I mustered the courage to climb onto T. J. and let him follow the other two horses down to the arena, while my Mom followed slowly on her bike behind us.

At the arena, Mom took a hold of the reins and led me in. She circled the arena a couple of times while Julie and James rode on Sally and Chiefer.

"Now it's your turn to go out by yourself. I'll be right here, but I'm sure you'll be fine," Mom said, smiling at me as she walked out of the arena.

With a great big sigh, I gave a small kick, turned T. J. toward the north, and began walking all the way around the arena. When James passed me on Chiefer, I just knew T. J. would bolt out and throw me, but he kept his steady walk as if nothing had happened.

"Come on, Dena, let's get into a lope," said Julie, coming around right beside me on Sally. The next thing I knew, I was in a gentle lope, but I was still a little scared.

The whole first night was nerve-racking for me, and by the time we arrived home, the street lamps were on and it was dark. Back at the barn, the bug catcher was buzzing and snapping, and T. J. never flenched even at the loud noise. Julie helped me take off the bridle and hang it up on the saddle horn; then she put on his halter, which had been tied to the tree before we left earlier that day.

"This time I'll show you how to unsaddle and where to put it in the shed. Tomorrow, you'll learn to saddle him," said Julie encouragingly.

That night, I took pride in learning how to unsaddle a horse and put away the saddle myself. I took a bucket of grain and let T. J. eat while I brushed him down. Then I wrapped my arms around him and gave him a great big hug and kiss for giving me such a wonderful ride. The warmth of his touch, as well as the strong smell of fly spray mixed with the sweet smell of dust and horse sweat, melted into my soul. At that moment, I had never experienced a stronger feeling of love for an animal, not even Roast Beef, whom I'd been utterly devoted to.

We led the horses to the pasture in the dark and let them go, then we carried our halters back to the shed to hang them up. "We'll see you tomorrow night at 6:00 p.m.," said Julie and James. I turned to wave to them, then skipped back home under the stars. I couldn't wait until tomorrow night.

With school completely out and the summer just beginning, we had a family get-together to finally set up our long-awaited pool. At the beginning of May, my dad had brought in a dump truck full of sand and emptied it just south of our house, close to the trail that led to Aunt Joyce's. Our mom took a rake and spent hours leveling out the dirt.

That day, Mom fixed hamburgers and hot dogs with all the trimmings for dinner. Then Uncle Max, Aunt Joyce, Tom, Vonie, and my parents spent all afternoon trying to assemble the pool, attempting to follow the directions from the big book. Mom and Vonie spent an hour just separating the screws and bolts and laying them out on our trampoline. Then we took the liner and spread it across the yard. It took up a lot of space; we were just beginning to see how big this pool would actually be. Lori's and my anticipation grew. When we finally unrolled the tin siding, we were in awe of not only how long it was, but how tall it was! Four feet!

It took all day and a lot of hands to hold up the sides. Dad, Uncle Max, and Tom screwed in the nuts and bolts to the pool to support the railing that held the pool up. It was a lot of trial and error. Lori and I were recruited to stand there in the hot sun and help hold up the sides while they were bolted down.

Lori and I grew tired of holding up the sides and began to whine. Being the youngest at the age of ten, I escaped the work pretty easily.

When the pool was finally set up, I couldn't believe the size. The outside was brown, and the inside liner was a beautiful blue. Mom attached two hoses to the water hydrants outside, and turned on the water. Lori and I climbed up and over the ladder that led down into the pool. The walls were so high, I could barely see over them.

We each grabbed a hose and began spraying each other before sitting in the puddles of water that were beginning to form around the pool. Before long, the liner began to stretch out and the water began covering our toes. The two of us were soaked down to our underwear. After a while, Mom hollered at us from the kitchen window: "It's time to come in and eat supper, then you girls need to get ready for bed!"

We climbed the ladder and ran inside to change into dry clothes, before we ate our supper. We went outside once more to check how far the water level had come up. It was taking a long time. Around 10:00 p.m., it was only a quarter of the way full. Mom finally turned off the water. "I'll come out at five in the morning and turn it back on. Now, you girls get to bed."

As I was climbing into bed, it dawned on me that I hadn't gone out to ride T. J. with Julie and James. I was crushed. I jumped out of bed and ran into my parents' room. "Mom, I didn't ride tonight, even though I said I would!"

"I know. I told Julie you were busy today, so you can go tomorrow night."

I breathed a sigh of relief. I didn't want Julie mad at me or think I didn't want to ride anymore.

Around 1:00 p.m. the next day, the pool was a beautiful crystal-blue color. And it was finally full! As we went to step in, Mom was a little cautious. "I want to make sure you're tall enough that it's not over your head," she said as she held on to me from the ladder. Stepping bravely into the sharp, cold water, I let Mom gently guide me until I was touching the bottom with my flat feet. The water came up to my shoulders.

"I can touch!" I said with a smile as I dove to the very bottom and swam halfway across the pool, just like Julie had taught me to do in the big stock tank at Uncle Keith's house.

After a couple of hours swimming, Lori and I came in for some snacks. We shivered in our wet bathing suits, since the inside of our house was cold and air-conditioned.

"Wow, you got some sun!" said Mom, looking at our shoulders. "You had better stay out of the pool for the rest of the day, and from now on, both of you will wear a T-shirt over your suit to protect your shoulders."

Around 5:45 p.m. I remembered what I was supposed to do. "I have to go riding!" I said, dropping everything and rushing back to my room to change from my wet bathing suit into my jeans and boots.

Mom met me at the door with a ham sandwich. "You need to eat something nutritious before you go, young lady," she said, handing it to me as I ran out the door.

This time, Julie gave me a lesson on saddling T. J. "It'll take a couple more tries to get it right, but you're doing a good job," she said.

Tonight, with more confidence than before, I jumped right onto T. J., and we rode down to the arena. Julie worked with her horse, loping big circles, and then she suggested that I do the same. I didn't see the point in it, because being in a tighter circle felt scary, and also a little boring. I wanted to go somewhere, not just in a circle. But before long, James and I were galloping all around the big arena.

Throughout the summer, James and I took turns riding each other's horses. I was okay to get on Chiefer, as long as we stayed away from the barrels.

One night, James began to make fun of T. J. "Your horse is always pooping and he stinks," he said, laughing at me.

It didn't bother me any—T. J. was a horse, of course—but it did seem that T. J. pooped a lot. In fact, any time we would trade horses, Chiefer would poop as soon as I got on. James laughed at me every time.

But I soon realized that the horses released gas before they pooped. James hadn't figured that out yet.

"Hey, James, let's trade horses," I said one day, just in the nick of time. Then I watched for T. J. to poop while James was on him, and it was my turn to laugh. "The horse you're on stinks, but now that he's done pooping, I want him back!" I declared.

On those hot summer nights, we would ride until the arena lights shone above us, and then some. I began introducing T. J. to the barrel pattern, trotting, and eventually loping around them. Around 10:00 p.m., we'd ride home in the dark and unsaddle with just the summer stars leading us home.

Chapter 33

Painting a Picture of Memories

"Therefore, as the elect of God, holy and beloved, put on tender mercies, kindness, humility, meekness, long suffering; bearing with one another, and forgiving one another, if anyone has a complaint against another; even as Christ forgave you, so you also must forgive."
—Colossians 3:12–13

That summer, there was more fun in store for us. Over the last winter, Aunt Joyce had become addicted to painting ceramics. She stumbled across a big shop in Denver and came home with all sorts of ceramics and paints in different colors. Then she signed up for classes in a nearby town and brought her knowledge back to her sisters. Before long, my whole family was hooked.

With Curt and Julie grown and out of the house, she turned a spare bedroom into an art room, with shelves for the ceramics lining the walls. Luckily for her, someone was going out of business and was selling a kiln. She bought the kiln and placed it in her garage. Then she charged a small fee and opened up her house to some neighbors, but mostly her sisters, for an all-day Wednesday paint day, right in her own little dining room.

Every Wednesday that summer we would head over to Aunt Joyce's around 9:00 a.m. My cousins Mike and Janeil would show up around that same time, and so would James. We all sat down and painted together. Some of the projects I created that summer included ashtrays, a tic-tac-toe board game, and green salt and pepper shakers. Lori painted a beautiful little girl standing next to a pony and gave it to me for my birthday. It was a treasure.

Typically, we painted for an hour or so, then we'd lose interest, which was fine for the adults, who wanted us outside anyway.

One day Mike said, "I got these firecrackers with two strings that you pull to make them pop. See?" He demonstrated how it was done. "Here, each of you try one. It doesn't hurt you. It basically just makes a popping sound!"

I couldn't bring myself to pull the strings because the popping sound startled me and made me feel jumpy. Lori, Janeil, and James weren't afraid to try. The initial sound made us jump, which caused us all to erupt in nervous laughter.

"Let's play a joke on the grown-ups," said Mike. "We'll tie the firecrackers to their cigarette cases, with the firecracker down and closed inside the case. When they pull open their case, it'll pop and scare them!"

We all giggled, imagining how fun that was going to be.

"All right, now would be the time to do it, since they're painting and not paying attention to what's going on. Dena and James, you go in and get the cases and bring them outside," said Janeil.

We walked inside and up to the cases, which were lying together on the end of the bar. James and I both grabbed them and walked outside. No one even looked up from their painting. Outside, we lay the cases on the picnic table and went to work, tying them across the opening and sticking the fireworks down inside the cases before closing the top.

"Okay, now you and James take them in, but don't say a thing. Come right back outside before that guilty look on your faces blows our cover," instructed Janeil.

James and I walked in and sat them down, and as we turned to walk out, I put my hands on his shoulders, basically pushing him outside. "Hurry, James," I ordered.

Janeil, Mike, and Lori were standing in a semicircle just outside the door, almost holding their breaths as they waited for our return.

"Did you get caught?" Lori asked excitedly.

"No, I don't think so," we both said.

"Let's get our minds off of it now. We'll definitely know when it happens because we'll hear the bangs," said Mike. We all burst into laughter again.

Soon, we heard a loud pop—and then another, and another! We froze in our tracks as we stared at each other with worried expressions. We heard Aunt Joyce, then Aunt Jean, and then Mom—and even Julie, Vonie, and Barb—start screaming.

"Those little shits! They're in big trouble now!" I heard Mom shriek.

We all ran to the end of Aunt Joyce's yard when Aunt Jean stepped out the back door and began yelling at the top of her lungs.

"All of you kids, get your butts back in this house right now! What the heck do you think you're doing, trying to scare us like that?" she said, her eyes wide with anger.

"You may think it's funny, but it's not funny at all. All of you, get into the living room and sit there and think about what you just did!" yelled Mom.

We all had our heads down as we came back into the house, and I had tears in my eyes. I was thinking about what might have happened if the firecracker really blew up and hurt someone.

Aunt Joyce shook her finger at us and asked the same question I was just thinking: "What if you had seriously hurt someone? Just think about that!" she said.

As we walked through the kitchen and straight to the living room, we all sat together on the couch with our heads down, scared about what our punishment would be. We slowly began to look up at one another, stunned as we heard the adults in the kitchen laughing among themselves. I glanced over at Janeil, and a smile came over her face. I still didn't see anything funny about it. However, when Janeil started smiling, it had a domino effect. Lori smiled, then Mike began to laugh, then Janeil began to laugh, then Lori began to giggle hysterically, and so did James. Then I began to giggle between my tears. We were all rolling with laughter as the adults began to laugh even louder.

Mom came back in, trying to keep a straight face. "Okay, kids, go outside to play. And this time, *stay out of trouble!*"

The tension lifted immediately. We all relaxed, stood up, and walked quickly through the kitchen and back outside with our heads down. Then, in the clear, everyone began to laugh again.

Slip 'N Slides were the entertainment of the 1980s, and Aunt Joyce had bought one, just for us, for painting day. We ran and slid the day away, while burgers and hot dogs sizzled on the grill. That was our life every Wednesday for the month of June. But one day, Aunt Joyce called us with some bad news.

"I know the kids love the Slip 'N Slide, and I hate to be the bad aunt, but it's killing my grass. I just don't think I'm going to let them use it any longer," she said sadly.

"That's okay," said Mom. "I think Janeil and Lori are old enough to watch the kids at our house while they all go swimming. They can just hang out over here when they get bored."

The next Wednesday, after eating delicious hamburgers and hot dogs, supplemented with fresh cucumbers, radishes, and onions from our garden, the five of us walked over to our house in our bathing suits. Janeil and Lori took off the solar cover that was on top of the pool and lay it down on the ground. To make our pool even more luxurious, Tom had built a nice big deck on the west end. We would lie up there on a towel, working on our beautiful tans. We spent the rest of the day swimming and jumping on our trampoline, doing flying flips and daunting tricks until we were exhausted. Then we walked into our house, totally wet, covered up with our already-wet towels, and turned off the air conditioner. We turned on the TV to jam out to Michael Jackson and Madonna videos on MTV while eating ice cream cones with fun names carved into each cone. We began to call each other by our carved names. Sometimes we were Darla or Sarah or even Ethan, which had us all rolling with laughter.

Before long, Mom, Aunt Joyce, and Aunt Jean came over to check on us.

Mom angrily walked straight to the TV and turned off our very loud music. "I shouldn't have to yell over the TV for you to hear me. You all know you're not allowed to sit around on my furniture in wet swimming suits. And who didn't put away the ice cream that's melting all over my bar? And who gave you permission to turn off the air conditioner when I'm trying to keep it cool in here? Now everyone, stop watching these loud music videos and get back out there in that pool this instant! I need you to make me a whirlpool so the debris and dirt will go to the center of the pool and I can sweep it up easier."

"But we're finally dry now! We don't want to get back in!" we all protested.

"If you want to swim again, you'll do as I say," she said, hands on her hips.

We all lined up like dogs with our tails between our legs and followed our mothers and Aunt Joyce back out to the pool. Getting back into the water felt better than we had anticipated. Swimming in a clockwise motion around the pool, we formed a whirlpool. It felt so refreshing that we didn't want to get back out, so we spent over an hour just swimming in a circular motion, playing tag while our moms, Aunt Joyce, Julie, Vonie, and Barb sat under the shade tree drinking sun tea. In the meantime, we tried to swim against the current to get it heading the other way.

When we finished, the water settled and everything fell to the center, just as Mom said it would. She took out the water sweeper, hooked it to the filter, and walked along the edge of the pool, vacuuming it out. It was crystal clear and sparkling blue when she was finished.

The fun of the day soon gave way to something different. That night, as we were riding down to the arena, Julie rode beside me and told me some devastating news. "Dena, I'm trying to sell T. J. Tonight, there will be a lady down at the arena who wants to watch you ride him."

I felt my face and my heart fall. "You're selling him?" I asked in disbelief as the lump in my throat swelled up and I tried to fight back tears. I had developed a deeply trusting relationship with T. J. throughout the summer. Our communication had become so strong that all I had to do was look to where I wanted to go and T. J. could literally feel which way I was looking—and he'd let me know by following my eyes. When I sat back in my saddle, he came to a stop; when I squeezed with my legs, he sped up into a lope. When I took the pressure off my legs, he slowed down. I learned to use my entire body language to develop complete communication with T. J. I knew without a doubt that I could have ridden him without a bridle simply by using my body to tell him where I needed him to go.

That night, there was a softball game next to the arena, and after the game, a lady walked out to us. "Dena, come here," said Julie.

"This lady is interested in buying T. J. and would like to watch you ride him. Can you get him into a lope for me?"

Holding back tears, I took off in a lope. As I came back to the lady, I saw her shake her head. "I don't think this horse would be good for my four-year-old son. You're much older, and I think T. J. has too much energy."

"Oh no!" said Julie. "I can assure you that he'll go at whatever speed you want, and he doesn't take advantage of beginner riders."

"I just don't think he's what we want for our little boy, but I'll think about it," the woman said.

That night, I told Mom how happy I'd been that the woman didn't end up buying T. J. after all. Mom worried that I'd done something to stop the sale, so she had me go and apologize to Julie. Julie reassured us that I didn't do anything to stop her from selling T. J. But I felt guilty all the same. Still, I couldn't bear the thought of losing the horse I'd developed such a deep bond with. That's when I got the idea to ask my dad to buy T. J. for *me*!

"We don't have the money to buy you a horse, Dena, and that's the end of it," he said. I cried myself to sleep several nights in a row.

About a week before James flew back to his mom's house for school, the sale barn had a sale. I knew T. J. would be sold. James had the privilege of riding him through the sale barn because everyone knew it would be too hard on me and that I would end up crying.

That morning, I woke up early and took one last ride with T. J. by myself before Julie came with the horse trailer to load him. Mom took some pictures and a video of me giving him a hug with tears in my eyes.

When he went through the sale barn, I was later told that Aunt Joyce tried to buy him back, but she only had a little money on her. She, too, had tears in her eyes just thinking about my broken heart. I found out that T. J. went to a family north of town who had bought him for their grandkids. I didn't know this family, but I couldn't help but feel jealous of them. I was also upset with Julie for selling him.

Years later, I ran across this picture of T. J. and me. As a result, this poem flowed onto the paper.

The horse T. J., James, and Dena. Photo by Jan Ekberg.

"Hoofprints of the Heart"

The summer I turned ten
Is the summer I'll never forget.
My cousin had three horses
One had given me a fit.

I rode him all that winter
All around the family farm.
But the day we did the barrels
Was the day he sprained my arm.

I spent all winter in a sling.
I spent it all inside.
I wanted to continue riding
But behind my fear, I'd hide.

My cousin's stepson was visiting
The same age as me.
And because my cousin had three horses
There were enough for me.

She put me on a smaller one
A younger one too.
I started out in fear
I started out in tears.

I wanted to do this
I wanted it so bad.
But fear overwhelmed me
And I felt so sad.

My mother stood beside me
Tears ran down my face.
"You'll be okay," she promised
And led me to the gate.

"Take it slow and easy
I promise, you'll get along.
You'll be best friends before you know it
It won't take too long!"

It started out so innocently.
It started out so fun.
We raced each other's barrels.
We were always on the run.

Every single night
And every single day
We'd saddle up three horses
And ride to the arena to play.

I fell in love that summer.
We would gallop with the wind.

He became a part of me
And I a part of him.

And just as summer was about to end
And school was about to start
My cousin's stepson flew back home
My horse and I had to part.

He was sold at a sale.
He was sold from under me.
For I was living proof
That a kid horse he could be.

I knew this horse would break me
I knew it from the start.
I will forever have his hoofprints
Stamped across my heart.

Chapter 34

Behind the Summer Smile

"Now no chastening seems to be joyful for the present, but painful; nevertheless, afterward it yields the peaceable fruit of righteousness to those who have been trained by it."
—Hebrews 12:11

I missed not being able to ride every day, and I missed T. J. terribly. But as an adult, I realize what I really missed was riding with Julie and James. It was an incredible bonding time and so much fun to just be with them, doing something we all loved.

The next few years of my life flew by in a blur. Julie took Chiefer and Sally back to her house, and our pasture sat empty. I found other ways to occupy my time. Between school and homework, I kept busy with my friends playing kickball at the old schoolhouse after we got off the bus in the evenings. But when summer finally rolled around, it was time to be a kid again. I had just finished sixth grade and was twelve years old. I found myself riding my bike all over town, carrying my big boom box with me as I rode so I could listen to my music.

I became so good on my new bike, which I'd received the previous Christmas, that I learned to ride without using the handlebars. I could even start out pedaling and turn a full circle on Main Street without ever touching. To this day, I look back on those fond memories, wishing I could go back to that carefree twelve-year-old girl who could balance herself perfectly on her bike and do full flying flips on our small trampoline.

All the kids from Eckley rode our bikes up and down Main Street on a daily basis. The best place to ride was the big hill at the end of Main Street, which led to the train tracks at the bottom. Coasting down the paved road, we would fly faster and faster until we got to the end of the hill.

Just before we hit the train tracks, we would slam on our brakes like we were sliding into home plate at a baseball game. Sometimes, when we knew it was clear, we would coast straight across the bumpy railroad tracks and around the winding paved road. The sound of our wheels turning on the pavement was smooth as glass. But we got our exercise while pedaling back up the hill to do it all over again. No one ever thought about how dangerous that hill could have been if you couldn't stop and a train was coming.

One morning, a couple of my friends and I were riding our bikes down Main Street when we found our way to the town hall. Aunt Joyce had been working there as the town clerk for quite a few years. My friends, Dusty and Julie Z, and I stopped and parked our bikes on the west side of the building, while Julie Z's dogs, Copper and Susie, sat under the shade tree as we went inside.

Eckley Town Hall, 2021.

Uncle Max and Aunt Joyce were inside and were surprised to see us walk in. "Hello there, Kid, what are you kids up to?" asked Uncle Max, a smile on his face.

"We came to say hi," I said, speaking for Dusty and Julie Z, who were beside me.

"Well, you must come inside to the garage and see the old fire truck that sits in here," he suggested.

Lori and I had been in here and played on the fire truck before. When we were younger, Aunt Joyce would sometimes bring Lori and me to work with her. She would always give each of us a dollar to walk next door to the pool hall to buy a pop and a stick of beef jerky; then we would come back to play on the fire truck the rest of the morning while Aunt Joyce continued working.

Today, my friends and I eagerly followed Uncle Max into the garage, where the old red fire truck proudly sat. I climbed on up into the driver's seat. Right above me was a big bell with a string to pull, and behind me was a long, white fire hose, all folded up nicely in the truck bed.

2018 Old Settlers Parade, Eckley, CO. Left to right: Jake Hagemeier, Ethan Gonzales, Dolores Probasco, Rylan Hagemeier, and Andy Hagemeier. Picture by Richard Bianie. Used by permission.

"You have probably all seen this fire truck in the Eckley Parade. They drive it down Main Street every year," said Uncle Max. "Oh, and come over here and check out this old jail. When people get in trouble with the law, they bring you in here. See, there's even a pull-out bunk bed." He grinned mischievously.

Following him straight into the jail, I knew we were in for it. Sure enough, as we walked in and all three of us sat our behinds directly on the old and dusty bed to see how comfy it was, Uncle Max walked out and promptly locked the door behind us. All three of us were now in the town's jail.

Julie Z looked a little scared, but Dusty and I began to laugh. Dusty had been around Uncle Max long enough to know what a joker he was.

"Aunt Joyce, come rescue us. We didn't do anything wrong! Weirdo should be in jail, not us," I hollered, laughing hysterically.

Aunt Joyce came in with her Polaroid camera and took a picture of Uncle Max pretending to lock the door again as we grabbed hold of the bars, yelling for someone to let us out.

"Don't let them out until I get three pictures taken. Then everyone can take home an instant picture," she said, laughing.

It took a while to get three pictures taken, and we continued to pretend being terrified and panicky while Aunt Joyce messed with her camera.

"She's done taking pictures now! You can let us out, Weirdo!" I instructed.

"Oh, all right! Since it's getting hot in here, I guess I'll let the three of you out!" he said with fake reluctance. "But just know you have to be good or you'll end up right back in here."

Aunt Joyce handed each of us a picture of ourselves that was still developing. "This is such a cool camera—to think we can instantly see the picture you just took," I remarked as it slowly began to develop into a clear photograph over the course of a few minutes.

We then said our goodbyes and headed out.

"Let's go over to the school and see if we can get a game of kickball going," suggested Julie Z. "But first, let's ride by my house and stop to get my soccer ball."

Julie Z lived four blocks down the same dirt road as me. She and I would meet at the old schoolhouse a lot, and when we walked to meet each other, we whistled to let the other know we were on our way. She could always whistle louder than I could.

Today at the school, there were ten of us ready to play kickball. The large tree close to the wooden fence was home base. At the end of the wooden fence, where it curved around the cement and was broken, was first base. Second base was where another tall shade tree stood, and third base was where a tree had been cut down and only a stump remained. In the center of the schoolyard was another tree that had been cut down where another stump remained; that's where the person pitching would toss the ball on the ground.

"I'll be the ball thrower," said Julie Z, who was the most athletic one in Eckley and she knew it.

After she threw the ball to me, I kicked it as hard as I could. It went straight into the air, and she caught it.

"Out!" She laughed.

Aside from being the fastest, Julie Z also had good aim and could throw the ball and usually hit whoever was running. I always played second base. I rarely caught the ball and never hit anyone who ran past me. But it was always a fun way to spend the afternoon.

As time went by, we became hot and tired. The kids took off to their homes, one by one.

"Let's climb this tree," said Julie Z. She was able to pull herself up to the first branch, but I wasn't that strong. I promptly steadied my bike against the trunk of the tree and climbed up on the seat of my bike, where I stood up and swung my leg over. This was where people sat as the bark on both sides of the tree was gone.

We sat up there for a long time that day, talking about how cute the new boy in town, David, was. His dark hair and complexion, dark blue eyes, freckles, and cute smile had us giggling. I knew he probably liked Julie Z better because she was prettier and better at sports than me. But I had never had such a big crush on anyone before, and thinking and talking about him always made me blush.

"He is *sooo* cute! Let's ride our bikes by his house and see if he's outside," I suggested.

Close to his house on Main Street, we rode big circles on our bikes right outside his yard, not at all thinking we were being obvious. Before long, David's sister yelled at him and told him to come out because we wanted to talk to him.

When he came outside, not one of us had anything to say. I was so shy that I couldn't even look at him, so I kicked a rock back and forth between my feet.

Finally, Julie Z spoke up. "Ah . . . we played kickball today, and tonight we're planning on going to the softball field to play. If you want, you can join us around 6 p.m."

"We're playing tonight, down at the softball field?" I piped up. This plan was new to me. "Are you sure we can? What if they have practice and we can't?"

Julie Z looked at me with her big eyes and bit her lip. I realized I'd probably said something I shouldn't have.

"Sure, we can play down there, as long as we're done by 7 p.m.," she quickly replied.

"Okay!" said David. "I'll ask my mom if I can come."

"Great, we'll see you then," said Julie Z, cool as a cucumber.

We both jumped on our bikes and began pedaling faster and faster toward my house.

"I didn't know we were supposed to go to the softball field to play tonight," I said.

"I didn't either, until I asked him. I had to say *something*! Now we've got to go find people to come down and play with us!" she responded.

Instead of heading home, we took a right down another dirt road and went door to door to all the kids who had played kickball with us that day. We invited them to come and play softball at 6 p.m., and everyone thought it was a great idea.

"Why don't you see if you can spend the night with me at our house tonight, Julie Z? After we finish playing baseball, the two of us can sleep outside under the stars on our trampoline and we can go night swimming," I suggested.

"Okay, let's ask your mom first and make sure that's fine. Then, if it is, we'll ride back to my house and get my clothes and talk my mom into letting me stay."

As we walked into the house, my mom greeted us with a smile. "You two look a little suspicious. What are you up to?"

"Can Julie Z spend the night? And then can we go night swimming in the pool?" I asked.

"I suppose so," said Mom.

Back at Julie Z's house, her mom also agreed. "Fine, but you girls be good," she warned.

"We will," we promised.

At 5:30 p.m., as Mom was fixing pork chops on the grill, I ran to her with the news. "Mom, Julie Z and I are going to go play softball down at the ball field at 6 p.m."

"Wait a minute—you never asked me if you could do that! Besides, they have softball practice at 7 p.m. You won't have time."

"But Mom, that's why we're going early. We'll be done before seven. A whole bunch of kids are meeting down there, and we'll be back before long."

"Fine, but come straight home when you're done playing,"

I grabbed my baseball mitt, and Julie Z and I jumped onto our bikes. Down at the baseball field, we quickly picked teams and played softball until Vonie and Tom showed up with all of their teammates and promptly kicked us out of the ball diamond.

We stood at the bleachers talking with all the kids while watching the adults play. Julie Z and I had completely forgotten about our curfew until an hour and a half later, when the adults' practice was finished.

"Dena, you'd better get yourself home! It's completely dark out, and unless things have changed since I lived there, you should have been home an hour ago," warned Vonie.

Julie Z and I looked at each other, quickly said goodbye to all the other kids, and jumped on our bikes, pedaling home as fast as we could.

When we walked into the house at 9:00 p.m., my mom was furious. "Where have the two of you been? You were supposed to be home between 7:00 and 7:30. It's 9 p.m. now, and dark! Your dad was ready to drive down to the ball field and find you. You had better watch it, Dena. You're going to be grounded from your bike and the pool if you keep being late."

Poor Julie Z didn't know what to do about us being in trouble. She was almost in tears.

"I'm sorry, Mom! I won't be late anymore," I said, looking down at the ground.

"Well, the two of you can still go swimming if you want, at least for a while. I have pork chops you can throw in the microwave if you're hungry. But you need to be out of the pool in an hour—is that understood? The cover is already off, and Lori and a couple of her friends are swimming now. They have been waiting for the two of you to come home so they can play Marco Polo in the pool. They even turned off the yard light to make it dark out there."

"Okay," I said, still feeling bad for getting Julie Z and myself in trouble.

Julie Z and I hurried and changed into our bathing suits. Then we went outside in the dark and jumped into the pool. The initial cold was a shock, but I had learned a trick: if you jumped straight into the water, climbed back out, counted to three, and jumped back in, the water actually felt warm.

It was so dark out, we couldn't see anyone when they went under the water, which made our game of Marco Polo super fun. Around 10:30, Mom hollered at us to get out. Julie Z and I rushed inside to change into our warm clothes so we could sleep outside. We put on long-sleeved shirts and a pair of sweats and socks, and used my sister's blow dryer to dry our wet hair. Then, we grabbed the two sleeping bags and two pillows my mom had laid out by the back door.

Sitting on the trampoline, we were comforted by the sounds of our small town as we lay on our backs. The yard light was still off, which made the night darker than usual, and we could see the stars shining brightly.

"How many are up there?" asked Julie Z.

"I don't know, but in Bible school, they say God made each star and only He knows how many there are."

My mom's collie, Casey, lay under the trampoline chewing a bone. We could hear the traffic from the highway, and in the distance, the low hum of cattle and the buzzing sound of wheat being cut. I felt safe and secure as I drifted off to sleep.

Early the next morning, someone landed between us on the trampoline and began to jump. Julie Z and I were immediately startled awake.

"Wake up, you sleepyheads, the day is burning!" Uncle Max and Aunt Joyce had come over for a hot cup of coffee. Uncle Max jumped off, and Julie Z and I looked at each other and began laughing.

One thing about sleeping outside was that the summer sun was hot enough to make our sleeping bags feel like a furnace. It wasn't long before we grabbed our bags and pillows, dropped them off in the utility room, and went to my bedroom to fall back to sleep until around 10 a.m.

Julie Z woke me up. "I'm going to ride my bike home and take a shower. But later, let's go back down to the softball field and see if we can get another game going. We'll stop by again and see if David can go with us."

Both of us started giggling.

"Yes," I said. "Let's see if *David* can go!"

After Julie Z left, my mom immediately laid into me. "Dena, you are losing privileges. This summer has been nothing but you running around all day long, not telling us where you are, and coming home whenever you feel like it. Last week, I told you to be home around 2 p.m., and you walked in the door around 4 p.m. I think you need to stay home today."

Dad agreed. "She's right—but there is plenty to do around the house. Today, you will mow the lawn. You are also grounded from the pool and the TV. There's also some wood out by the wood pile, so you can stack that too."

"But!"

"Dena, no buts!"

"But, Julie Z—"

"No buts!"

"Ugh! But Julie Z and I were going—"

"Quiet!" yelled my dad, putting an end to my attempts at explanation.

Tears were streaming down my face. Julie Z was going to be so mad at me for not being able to go out and play ball.

"Can I call Julie Z to tell her I can't go out today? At least to let her know?" I asked, crying.

"You may call her later and tell her you're busy today," said Mom.

I walked outside and grudgingly mowed the front and the backyard as the sun beat down on me. When I was done, Mom came out to see how I was doing. "You did a good job. Come in for a glass of tea. After that, you're going over to Joyce's, and you are to mow her yard as well."

"Seriously?" I asked in disbelief.

"Yes," she said nonchalantly.

I bit my tongue and silently agreed. I figured that I had to earn back my mom's trust, so protesting (even though it was totally unfair) wasn't a good idea.

After I finished all the mowing, Aunt Joyce came out with a pop. "I fixed a ham-and-cheese sandwich for you and your mom," she said. As I walked inside, it didn't feel like a punishment anymore. Sitting and having lunch with my mom and Aunt Joyce was actually a treat. When we finished eating, both Mom and Aunt Joyce walked over with me in the hot summer sun and helped me stack the wood. With their help, it didn't take long at all.

After we finished stacking the wood, we walked back into our house for a cool drink of water. I heard someone knocking on the front door. It was Julie Z.

Opening the door, I greeted her with a sad look. "Mom said I can't go out today, but maybe we can get together tomorrow," I suggested.

"Okay," she said with a questioning look.

"I'll tell you about it tomorrow," I said.

As Julie Z walked away, I realized I didn't really feel like playing anymore anyway—not after mowing the lawn and stacking wood.

Mom came up behind me. "You did a good job today, Dena! Aunt Joyce and I are hot, so we decided we want to go swimming. If you promise to start taking a little bit more responsibility, you can go swimming with us."

"I promise," I said, almost in tears.

That day, the three of us played tag and had hand-standing competitions while in the pool. When Lori and I played this game, we would both go down and stand on our hands, but when one of us came up for a breath, the other person went down. Lori and I would play for hours, trying to hide the fact that we were cheating. Today, Mom and Aunt Joyce refused to play the cheating game. But I could beat them both while standing on my hands, hands down.

The next day, things settled down. I knew I needed to try to obey and pay attention to time. Mom, Dad, and I had a talk. "You can play with your friends, but every hour and a half to two hours, you need to check in with us," said Mom. "Today, I want you home by four this afternoon. If you want to go out to play when it gets cooler, we will decide then."

Before I left, Mom pulled out an old blue Snoopy watch she had given me when I was in first grade. "This still works. And I know you can tell time, so you can't use that as an excuse to be late again," she warned.

I called Julie Z, and we promptly made plans to go to the softball field. We met each other at the schoolhouse, picked up our friend Dusty, and rode around town looking for anyone who wanted to play.

It was about 2 p.m. when we began playing softball. I hit a ball that landed in the outfield, and I made it to second base before the ball was thrown in. Next was David's hit, which went flying past me. I ran all the way to home plate and made it in! Then David came sliding in behind me and gave me a high five.

"Good hit!" I said to him, taking a deep breath. I think we were both shocked that we had given each other a high five. And because he was so cute, I never wanted to wash my hand again.

Tired and thirsty, everyone headed their separate ways. I looked down at my trusty watch and realized it was already 4:15.

"Oh no!" I cried out. "Gotta go! I'll probably be grounded from now until I graduate."

I pedaled as fast as I could, silently praying to God, *Please let Mom be out in the garden and not paying attention to the time!*

As I walked through the front door, I hollered, "Mom, I'm home." But no one answered.

"Mom, I'm here!" I yelled again. "Where are you?"

Maybe she's out watering the chickens, I thought. I walked to the backyard and out through the garden and toward the chicken shed. I didn't see her anywhere, not even in the garden. As I walked back into the house, an eerie silence fell over me. I wondered if Mom was out driving around looking for me since I was so late. I walked down the hall, heading to my bedroom. As I walked past my mom's room, I saw her standing by the window, staring outside and holding the phone to her chest.

"Mom, what's wrong?" I asked, a pit of worry growing in my stomach. I was sure that she was going to lay into me for being late, and I tried to ready myself. "I would have been home a little earlier, but I lost track of time. I'm so sorry!" I said.

Mom turned toward me as tears began to fall from her eyes, and she just stared at me.

A wave of guilt washed over me. *I really blew it this time!*

"Mom, what's wrong? Please tell me," I begged. Her silent treatment was making me feel even guiltier.

As the tears began to form in my eyes, I opened my mouth to tell her again how sorry I was for being late, but before any words could come, Mom cried out, "Max has cancer! Max has cancer!"

She's not crying because I'm late; she's crying because she just found out Uncle Max has cancer. But I couldn't process what she meant. Had I actually heard right?

"Oh, honey," she said, walking toward me and giving me a hug. "Uncle Max has cancer."

"Oh no! Oh no!" I cried out.

"Dena, I'm so sorry, but he does!"

Time stopped. This couldn't be real. Ever since I was little, the word *cancer* had been a scary one in our household. And now that I was older, it was beginning to hit home what it could mean for Uncle Max.

Death.

"No, no," I repeated over and over, trying to deny the truth.

By the time 5:30 p.m. had rolled around, my mom gathered herself together, put on some red lipstick, and began to defrost five pounds of hamburger in the microwave. She shaped patties into balls and flattened them out with her hands. I wondered if this was almost a meditative activity for her, taking her mind off the bad news of the day. Dad turned on the grill and began frying hot dogs alongside the hamburgers. Vonie showed up and cut up homegrown tomatoes, cucumbers, onions, radishes, and lettuce. Aunt Joyce brought over her canned pickles. Then, around fifteen to twenty of our closest relatives showed up, including Uncle Max. This was the way our family rolled; anytime something difficult happened, we always came together for support . . . and food.

As most people gathered in the living room while my dad was outside grilling hamburgers, Vonie and my cousin Julie were in the kitchen preparing food and talking in soft whispers among themselves. Walking back to my bedroom, I noticed Aunt Joyce and my mom crying and softly talking in Mom's room. Through the hallway, I could hear their conversation.

"I should have known sooner that something was wrong! All winter, he'd come home and only want soup for supper. He just hasn't acted like himself in a long time. Oh Jan, what am I going to do?" Aunt Joyce asked. The fear in her voice was frightening . . . and heartbreaking.

I wanted to cry, too, but I didn't want anyone to see my tears. *I have to get out of the house*, I thought to myself. Taking a deep breath, I walked straight into my mom's room, completely ignoring the emotional scene and pretending I was oblivious to the crying.

"Mom, you said if I wanted to go back out in the evening to play with some friends, I needed to ask you first. Do you care if I go play kickball at the schoolhouse for a while?"

"Sure, but be back by 7:30," she said, with almost a sigh of relief. I realized that she probably thought I'd be traumatized if I stayed and listened to everyone's sadness around my uncle's prognosis.

I didn't have plans to go and play with anyone. But I jumped on my bike and headed over to the schoolhouse all the same. I wanted to leave the sad scene behind . . . and be able to breathe easy again. When I got to the schoolhouse, I was the only one around. I sat my bike up against the tree trunk and climbed onto the seat so I could scramble up to the center of the tree.

As I sat there, I became a quiet witness to the neighbor lady who lived across from the school. I knew she had recently lost her husband. My mom and Aunt Joyce had taken over a whole fried-chicken dinner for her family, who were here for the funeral. A lot of people were huddled together in small groups, hugging each other and crying.

Now, watching from the safe distance of the tree, I saw a vehicle pull up outside her yard, and I saw the woman who lived there come out to greet a bunch of people with hugs. I could hear their laughter, which felt both close and far away at the same time.

Seeing her interact with these people, it dawned on me that even after a death in the family, people actually went on living. Obviously, she was happy to have company. But even though I heard the laughter, I could also hear the deep sadness in her voice. It was loud and clear, at least to me.

I sat there for a while as I watched the scene unfold. Younger children, probably her grandchildren, began playing with a Frisbee, throwing it back and forth. And after some yelling and laughter, they all followed the lady back into her house.

After a while, the silence engulfed me and I decided I needed to head back home. I was in an emotional state that I'd never experienced before, even after my grandmother had died, and I didn't know what to do about it or how to occupy my time. I felt I had no one to talk to. I think the reason it felt so different this time, compared to when Grandma was diagnosed, was because of my closeness to Uncle Max and the fact that I was older and more aware of what was happening around me.

Climbing down from the tree, I jumped onto my bike and pedaled across the grass back to the road. Before I left, I glanced over at our house to see if we still had company. We did.

When I arrived, I kicked the kickstand down and took a deep breath. Everybody greeted me as I walked inside. "Did you win your kickball game?" Uncle Max asked, smiling at me.

I hung my head low, not wanting to look at him out of fear that I'd start to cry. "Yes," I lied, "but I'm starving" (another lie). "What is there to eat?" I asked as I walked quickly past him into the kitchen, pretending to be on a mission to find food.

Chapter 35

Into the Unknown

"Fear not, for I am with you; be not dismayed, for I am your God. I will strengthen you, yes, I will help you, I will uphold you with My righteous right hand." **—Isaiah 41:10**

The next few days felt normal. My parents pretended nothing had changed, and we went on with our regularly scheduled programming. Life went on as usual.

One afternoon, Aunt Joyce walked through our back door in tears.

"I'm so scared!" she cried out. "Max has surgery in Sterling on Tuesday. They'll be able to tell us if his cancer has spread, then we'll know for sure what we're up against!"

Dad replied, "Tuesday morning is when we take our chickens to Brush to get butchered. After we drop them off, we can head to Sterling and be with you. But we'll have to pick up the chickens after the surgery and get them home in the freezer."

"Well, our camper is on the back of our yellow pickup. Julie and I are driving it to Sterling to sleep in there, so we can stay while Max is in the hospital," Aunt Joyce said. By this time, she was crying and shaking. "I just don't know how we'll get through this. Why is this happening to us? Why? Why? Why? Why? Why?" she repeated over and over, her voice changing emotions from sadness, to disbelief, to anger, to pure fear.

I sat there listening to her desperation, and sure enough, my eyes began to sting and tears began to fall. My emotions carried me into her arms and into her loving embrace. Aunt Joyce played with my hair and rubbed my back as her demeanor changed from worrying about herself to worrying about me.

"Don't you fret about this!" she said, trying to suffice a smile through her tears. "It will be okay, I promise!"

The morning came, and the chickens had to be at the butcher's by 7 a.m. By 4:30 a.m., we were loading 125 chickens to the stock trailer to head to Brush. We used Curt's bumper trailer and Uncle Max's blue pickup with a camper shell attached. In the camper shell was a small two-seater couch. I opened the side windows and rode in the back. I brought my pillow and rested on the way to Brush, listening to the wind coming through the windows as I wondered what this day had in store. When we arrived, we quickly unloaded the chickens into a pen.

"These chickens will be processed and finished by two this afternoon, so bring in a lot of ice to take them home and get them in the freezer by four," instructed the butcher.

"We're going to Sterling for the day, but we'll be back by two," said Dad. Then he unhitched the trailer. I jumped in the back and lay down while we drove another hour to the hospital.

When we walked into the waiting room, we saw Aunt Jean and my cousin Mike, as well as Uncle Keith, Aunt Dolores, Aunt Joyce, Curt, Barb, and Julie. Among the sea of adults, I was happy to see Mike.

"They took him back to surgery about ten minutes ago," Aunt Joyce told us. "You and Mike come here, and I'll fix you some hot chocolate while we wait."

"Since it's only 8:30, why don't we all walk down to the cafeteria for some breakfast?" suggested Dad. We all agreed. I got some bacon, hash browns, eggs, and toast to go along with my hot chocolate.

"If you two are bored, you can go out to the camper and play cards," suggested Julie.

"It's not locked, but make sure you leave the door and the windows open so it doesn't get too hot in there," added Aunt Joyce.

We walked outside to the camper, climbed in, and kept the door open. We sat down at the table, and every so often a cool breeze blew against the curtains next to where we were sitting. After finding the cards in a drawer, Mike shuffled them and handed me part of the deck.

"Pick a card!" he instructed me.

I picked a card from the deck.

"Now, memorize it and don't forget it! I'm going to show you a trick. Put the card back on top of this pile," he said.

I put it on top of the pile, and he threw the other cards on top. "I'm going to go through this deck, one by one, and I will show you which card you picked," he said confidently.

One by one, he went through the cards until he came to the one I'd picked. "This is the one!" he pronounced as he turned over an Ace of Spades.

"How did you do that?" I asked, shocked.

"I'm magic!" he insisted.

"Let's do it again," I said, marveling over the trick. He performed it again two more times, and without fail, he came up with the card I'd picked.

"Oh, come on, Mike, you have to show me how you do that! *Please?*" I begged.

"Oh, all right. It's simple. I shuffle the cards and separate them into two piles. You keep one pile in your hand, and I tell you to pick out a card. Then you lay your pile down on the table. Then, while you're not paying attention, I hurry and count the cards in my hands. I have you lay the card you picked on top of the pile on the table, and I put the cards in my hands on top of the card you laid down. Then I count the cards I had in my hands, and when I reach that number, I know the next card is the one you picked."

"Oh, clever! Now, let me try it on you so I can trick my friends back home," I said.

After I perfected it, we decided to play two games of rummy and one game of Go Fish. We both kept busy enough to pass the morning without worrying too much about Uncle Max's surgery. But before long, we heard a knock at the door. It was my mom and Aunt Jean.

"You two need to come out of the camper for a while. We need to talk to you," said Aunt Jean, a serious look on her face. "Unfortunately, Uncle Max's cancer has spread, and they're giving him around a year to live."

I jumped out of the camper onto the hot asphalt of the parking lot. Aunt Joyce and Julie were walking toward us, holding on to one another. I felt like I'd barely had time to react to the news, but looking at Julie did me in. Her face was in shock, and I could tell she was struggling to hold it together. I ran to Aunt Joyce, and she enfolded me in a giant hug. Then, Julie lost it and began crying really hard. I felt so bad for my cousin. I couldn't even look at her. That day, I cried harder than I had ever cried before.

"Dena, we have to go now," said Dad. "We're going to be late, and all those chickens will spoil if we don't get them on ice and home soon."

"We'll be back later tonight," Mom tearfully said as she hugged my aunt and Julie. I waved to Mike, jumped into the back of the camper shell, and lay back down while dad drove to Brush to get our processed chickens.

We stopped and picked up bags of ice at the 7-Eleven, leaving them completely out of stock. Then we drove to the packing plant and hooked up the trailer. In the back of the trailer was a stock tank into which we dumped the ice and the chickens that were tied up in plastic bags and ready for the freezers. We also put some chickens in the coolers we'd brought. As I looked at them, I felt numb.

I was glad we were in Uncle Max's pickup so I could ride in the back of the camper shell to avoid the spiral of emotions Mom and Dad were going through in the front seat. We drove all the way home and unloaded the chickens into our freezer and dropped some off for other family members.

"Now we're heading back up to Sterling to be with Aunt Joyce, Curt, and Julie. I don't know what time we'll be home, but you can stay here if you'd like," said Mom.

"If you don't mind, I think I will," I said, not wanting to face my family members or see Uncle Max in the hospital.

When they left, I stood in our bathroom and looked in the mirror. My eyes were red from crying. I didn't know what to expect from here on out, and I didn't know how to deal with my emotions. It felt like what my family had been through with Grandma all over again . . . but this time was different. This time, I was feeling *everything*.

Standing alone, gazing at myself in the mirror, I repeated, "Only a year to live. Only a year to live!" A year to a twelve-year-old was like an eternity. Now, all of a sudden a year seemed short—*very* short. Standing there, a feeling I'd never felt before came over me. My face felt as if I'd touched an electric fence, like the ones in Uncle Keith's pasture. It radiated throughout my entire body. I stood there, stunned.

When Lori came home that night, she was also devastated by the news, and we held each other in a long, wordless hug.

It wasn't until I was an adult and lost my mother that I began to understand the different degrees of pain and suffering. My mom always said that all children need animals in their lives because they teach us about responsibility, love, and even loss at an early age. I believe that to be true, but nothing could prepare us for the kind of loss we would be suffering over the next year while we were slowly losing my beloved uncle. I wasn't even feeling the deepest part of that pain yet.

Chapter 36

Saved by Grace

"Put on the whole armor of God, that you may be able to stand against the wiles of the devil. For we do not wrestle against flesh and blood, but against principalities, against powers, against the rulers of the darkness of this age, against spiritual hosts of wickedness in the heavenly places."
—**Ephesians 6:11–12**

The news of Uncle Max having only one year to live made everyone in my family stop to evaluate their own lives. And we took extra time to assist Aunt Joyce and Uncle Max with whatever needed to be done.

Uncle Max was at Sterling Hospital for a while, and after he heard the news of having a year to live, it was time for us to try and cheer him up with our visits.

Uncle Max had always been like a second father to me. He was too close to my heart for me to face the reality of what lay ahead. I couldn't imagine my life without him. But I felt uneasy going to visit him in the hospital.

"Mom, I don't want to go in and see him," I said to her on our way to Sterling.

She sighed. "Dena, it will be alright. We'll go to K-Mart and find something special to give him as a gift. He really likes caramel candy squares, so maybe we could buy him some candy."

The distraction of finding a tangible way to cheer him up appealed to me. As we browsed the store, the perfect gift showed up. Mom spotted a coffee cup with the words, "Favorite Uncle," on it. "Look, Dena! You could put the candy in this cup and give it to him." That sounded like a great idea. We bought a bag of caramel candies, and as Mom drove to the hospital, I filled the cup to the brim.

As I walked into the hospital, I was nervous and shaking a little bit. What would I say to him? When we walked into the room, Uncle Max smiled as I handed over the cup full of candy. Although he looked somewhat small and fragile lying there, he still managed to crack one of his usual jokes. "You brought all this candy for *me*? I don't have to share it with you, do I, Kid?"

Then he glanced down and saw the words on the cup. His face became serious, and he looked at me with emotion in his eyes. "Thanks, Kid."

I didn't miss a beat. "You're welcome, but I still expect you to share your candy. Why do you think I bought it for you in the first place, Dipstick?"

I grabbed one of the square treats and passed the cup to everyone who was standing around his bed. Everyone began to unwrap the sweet treats and popped them in their mouths before tossing the plastic wrappers into the trash can beneath Uncle Max's sink, almost like they were shooting hoops into a basketball net. Uncle Max closed his eyes and drowned out the crowd as he fell into what looked like an unsettling sleep. A couple of minutes later, his body twitched and he awoke with tears in his eyes.

Aunt Joyce was visibly alarmed; she rushed to his side and grabbed his hand. "It'll be okay," she said softly.

He patted her hand and gave her a smile of reassurance. "Just a couple of bad dreams," he replied.

Two days later, Uncle Max felt well enough to come home from the hospital. Now, he was challenged by a brand-new schedule of doctor appointments and chemotherapy, which he had to somehow fit into his busy life. On Mondays he was instructed to have someone drive him an hour and a half each way to Sterling and sit through his chemotherapy treatments. After those treatments, he was too sick and nauseous to drive himself back home. Every Monday, he came home in a state of physical and emotional exhaustion. We never bothered them on those days; instead, we let Uncle Max and Aunt Joyce sleep the day away.

On Tuesdays, he usually felt well enough to head to work. I didn't know exactly how his illness "worked." I believed that he only had to give up one day of the week to be sick and that the rest of the week, everything would be back to normal. To the outside world, he played this part well. He rarely complained about being in pain, and he spent much of his free time in his woodworking shop.

On those hot summer nights, my back bedroom remained hot and stuffy, I slept outside on our trampoline, gazing up at the stars. One morning, Uncle Max and Aunt Joyce came over. He quietly walked to the trampoline and grabbed the springs, shaking me awake.

"The day is burning. Get up, Kid!"

"Dipstick, won't you let me sleep? A girl needs her beauty rest, you know," I hollered back at him. As they walked toward the house for coffee, it dawned on me that the summer was coming to an end and school was about to start. This would be my last summer of being routinely woken up by Uncle Max as I lay sleeping on the trampoline. I felt the stinging return to my eyes and a lump rise in my throat.

Throughout the summer, Uncle Max continued working at Wray Feed, hauling corn on a semi on the days he felt well enough to work. Lori and I marveled at the beauty of his two-toned blue semi, that he parked on the side of the road.

One morning, he asked, "Dena and Lori, would you like to go with me to haul corn to Sterling on Saturday?"

"That sounds fun," we both agreed.

"Well, you will have to wake up early, because I'm leaving at 5:00 a.m."

"You can just take your pillow and blanket and climb in the back and sleep in the sleeper!" suggested Aunt Joyce.

By the time Saturday rolled around, Lori, who was seventeen, had other plans with friends, so I went alone.

It was always fun to ride in the big semis. It made me feel ten feet tall. That morning, I was a little tired, and a little shy. All my life, I'd never had a problem talking to Uncle Max, but now that his condition had worsened and I was trying to hide my emotions (not to mention the embarrassing fact that puberty had set in), I felt more awkward than usual.

I climbed into the back of the sleeper while listening to the hum of eighteen wheels below me and the roar of the diesel engine. The whole ride up to Sterling, my mind was racing with questions, as well as the scary answers that were starting to emerge.

After Uncle Max unloaded the corn, he hollered back at me, "Come sit up front with me, Kid! Aunt Joyce packed us a sandwich." He handed me a bologna sandwich with potato chips mashed in the center and a Pepsi to drink.

"It's just the way she knows you like it," he said with a smile. "I tried to get her to put horseradish, cheese, pickles, mustard, ketchup, and mayonnaise on it, but she wouldn't budge. Why won't you eat any of that good stuff, Kid? You're just weird!"

I laughed. "You're the weirdo, Weirdo!"

The rest of the way home felt as if time had not moved our respective mountains far from each other. Everything was normal, as it should be. The heaviness that lay just under the surface of our conversations was buried by our laughter.

"It sounds like the church is going to open back up. You should consider going on Sundays, Kid. When I talked with your mom and dad about it the other day, they both seemed interested in supporting it," Uncle Max said.

"I suppose I could find the time to go," I said, pretending that my twelve-year-old schedule was super busy.

Eckley Church had been closed for about three years, and around this time, community members held meetings centered around hiring a new pastor to come to town on Sundays. My parents agreed to help support the church. Given that I'd attended Bible school and Sunday school classes, as well as some of the youth group activities, I felt it would be okay to start going to church on a regular basis. Before long, they opened the doors to the church, and we began attending.

"The new pastor is Pastor Sidebottom!" my mom said with a smile as we headed out the door to greet Aunt Joyce and Uncle Max at the corner where our roads met.

"Sidebottom?" asked Lori. "I've never heard that name before!"

"It's a little different, but you would be surprised how many different names there are in this world," said Mom.

As we walked into church, we were greeted by an older pastor and his wife, Beverly, who would be our piano player. During the sermon, I quickly became bored as I sat there not really paying attention to what was being preached.

But when we began to sing hymns out of the songbook, Pastor Sidebottom sang at the top of his lungs, and his singing rang out above the crowd. Lori and I looked at each other with a smile, then we both looked away to keep from giggling out loud. Mom nudged us both in the ribs and gave us a look that shut us up. Then we proudly sang along, completely out of tune, but it was fun—and as Pastor Sidebottom pointed out, it was the glorification of God that really mattered.

Toward the end of the sermon, Pastor Sidebottom ended with four verses from the Bible. As he gazed out at his congregation, I could feel that he was talking to me, so I paid attention. "In Romans 3:23, it reads, 'For all have sinned and fall short of the glory of God.' But if you flip to Romans 6:23, it says, 'For the wages of sin is death, but the gift of God is eternal life in Christ Jesus our Lord.' And turning back to John 3:16–17, it states, 'For God so loved the world.'"

Pastor Sidebottom paused to let that sink in as he glanced around at every single person in the audience. Then he continued, "'That He gave His only begotten Son.'"

He stopped again to let that sink in. "'That whoever believes in Him should not perish but have everlasting life.'" Then he read verse 17: "'For God did not send His Son into the world to condemn the world, but that the world through Him might be saved.'"

The way he announced those words captivated my attention, even though I didn't quite understand. After church ended, we headed home to our Sunday fried-chicken dinner, forgetting all that had been preached that day.

Our new pastor arrived at a time when Uncle Max was sick, but he was still functional when it came to everyday living. On Sundays, we met at the corner of our roads and walked together. This was the beginning of a new family tradition in our lives that felt extremely important now that we knew Uncle Max was dying.

One day, while I was reading a book in my room, I heard Aunt Joyce come into our house in tears.

"It's been so hard lately. Max's cancer is spreading and he's not feeling very well, but you know what? He's been sitting in a chair with the Bible in hand, reading it word for word. I see a renewed strength in him!"

"That's good," said Mom. "He needs something to help him through this emotional time."

"Yes. Pastor Sidebottom has been stopping by our house and praying with us on Sundays. Max is really glad our church has a pastor. He's wondering if you would like to pray with us sometime when Pastor Sidebottom comes over."

Later that night, I heard my mom mention it to my dad. "Joyce came over today and was talking about how Max has been reading the Bible, and he's wondering if we would come over when Pastor Sidebottom stops by next Sunday."

"We can go support him, as long as I don't have to be the one to say a prayer," quipped Dad.

"Yes, praying makes me nervous too!" agreed Mom.

The next Sunday after church, we met with Uncle Max and Aunt Joyce at their home, and Pastor Sidebottom stopped by for a prayer.

"Let's all bow our heads in prayer before I head out," he said. "Dear Heavenly Father, I ask you to put your healing hands on this family and help them accept the things they cannot change. Amen!"

This was the first time we ever prayed together as a family, and it felt a little strange and reassuring at the same time. Later that night, Mom and Dad talked about religion—a topic that rarely came up in my family.

"We never grew up going to church or praying," Mom said with a sigh. "My daddy didn't believe in church. He said you could get to heaven just by being a good person, and you didn't need to go to church. We were never baptized either. Mom always wanted our family to go to church, but Daddy didn't."

"My family grew up in a Christian home, and I grew up attending church. I was also baptized, but I don't like to pray in front of people—and the pastor would look down on me if he saw how much beer was in my fridge," said Dad. "And honestly, after losing my dad at such a young age, it's pretty hard to trust God if he'd let that sort of thing happen to our family when we were so young."

I didn't fully understand how my family felt about church and God, but I figured that if Uncle Max believed and was reading the Bible, and now my parents were supporting the church and didn't prohibit me from attending youth activities, it must mean that they were reconciling with Christianity. As time marched on, I continued with Sunday school and youth group activities. Over time, my dedication to my faith seemed to inspire new possibilities in responsibility and generosity.

Chapter 37

Gifts of the Heart

"And He said to them, 'Go into all the world and preach the gospel to every creature.'" **—Mark 16:15**

As the school year was back in session, Mom had a talk with me. "Dena, I was thinking about all the money you made from mowing lawns for neighbors and babysitting this past summer. You always save it, and you never spend it. What if you were to use it for something special, like buying a gift for Uncle Max and Aunt Joyce? Do you remember when they bought that cement deer for me and sat it out in our yard when you were little? Why don't you use your money for buying them one?"

I thought it was an awesome idea. The next Saturday, my mom and I drove to Haxtun, a town an hour away, where a home business called Kurtzer's had cement molds of many different animals: deer, birds, elephants, and more. But I knew I wanted a deer. After looking at all the deer, I began to feel distressed. I only had one hundred dollars, and everything cost twice as much. I was in tears because I knew I would never be able to afford it.

My mom was sad too. "I didn't realize they cost so much, Dena! I'm sorry."

I was determined not to leave. I kept skimming through the smaller cement lawn ornaments, debating about settling for something less. But the more I searched, the sadder I became. After a while, my mother looked hard at me and said, "If I pay for half of this, you can raise the money and pay me back. Because I clearly see that we can't leave without that large deer in the front of the store."

This was a moment in which words were not needed, and the hug we shared said everything we needed to express.

The people who worked there took my cash as I counted it out to them, and Mom wrote a check for the remaining amount. That night, we secretly placed the deer in Aunt Joyce and Uncle Max's backyard, just as they had done for Mom eight years earlier.

The next morning, the phone rang.

"No," said my mom after picking up the phone. "I have no idea where that deer came from. It must've been an elf!"

I could hear Aunt Joyce on the other line. "Well, it is so beautiful! Thank you from the bottom of my heart. Max and I love it!"

"Well, you had better thank Dena Bob. She was the one who bought it for you, using her own babysitting and lawn-mowing money."

"My stars! Wow! Tell her thank you."

I knew I had wanted to give them something special that demonstrated how much I loved them. Although I couldn't share with him everything that was in my heart, I wanted Uncle Max to know how much I would miss him when he was gone.

The next Saturday, I was out riding my bike and rode to the front of my aunt and uncle's house to say hello. I was shocked to see that the door that was always open was locked. I began to bang on the door, and when no one answered, I cupped my hands and peeked into the window. The room was dark, and Uncle Max was asleep in his recliner. Suddenly, I felt bad for banging on the door and possibly waking him from a nap.

He must be by himself and not feeling well today, I thought to myself. I knew cancer was taking its toll on him, and as I watched from the window, I was seized by the fear that perhaps he had died right there, in his recliner. *What if I am the one to find him dead?* I wondered. At that moment, his eyes popped open and he looked straight at me. I felt silly just standing there, watching him from the window, with those awful thoughts running through my head.

He promptly got up out of his chair and opened the door. "I guess if I can wake you up off the trampoline in the morning, you think you can wake me up from my nap, huh, Kid?" he asked, hitting me over the head with his ball cap. "Come in and have a pop."

He took the saltshaker by his chair and poured some in the palm of his hand. "Do you want some salt too?"

"Sure," I said as he poured some in my hand.

"I sure like the deer you bought for me!" he said.

"Thank you," I replied, suddenly feeling shy about it.

After I drank my pop, I turned to him. "Well, the day is burning, and I'm going to go see if I can find someone to play kickball with me. I just wanted to come by and say hi, but I'll let you finish your nap now."

"You kick that ball hard and win that game," he said with a wink and smile.

As I hopped on my bike, I felt the tears flowing. They stung my face as the wind blew around me. My parents were giving their free time to graciously help my aunt and uncle as he deteriorated before our eyes, but we never really talked about any of it.

"Why talk about the bad things in life? You just deal with them," I had heard my mom say over and over to my dad. "Life is what you make it; you take the good with the bad!"

To me, this felt like a cue to hold my anguish inside, never mentioning it to anyone. But deep down, I was terrified. More than anything, I worried that when Uncle Max was gone, I would forget him. After all, I was so young. What if my memories got covered over by new memories? Would I forget what he looked like? How he sounded? How he teased me? Who he was? I was also afraid at the thought of Aunt Joyce living alone. But I didn't know how to express all this fear to the people around me.

After wiping away my tears, I rode over to Dusty's to see if she wanted to play kickball. Her mother, Sue, saw me ride up in her driveway. "Hi, Dena Bob! How are you?" she asked, walking down the driveway to greet me.

"I'm good. I was wondering if Dusty was around to go play with me at the school?"

"No, she's not home today. She's with her sister in town, but she'll be back later."

"Okay. Well, just have her call me when she gets back. See you later!" I said, turning to walk back to my bike.

"Dena Bob, don't leave yet. Come in and have some tea!"

I felt a little reluctant to hang out with my friend's mother, but I agreed and followed Sue into the kitchen as she pulled out a chair. "Have a seat. How are things going? How are you handling things at home? Are you doing okay? You know . . . with your uncle being sick?" she blurted out.

I felt my face begin to heat up. Mom had always told us we weren't supposed to talk about these kinds of things. A lump was welling up inside my throat. I had to say something, but what could I say? I began to breathe a little harder.

"Yes, I'm doing okay." I began to sniff, and then the tears fell uncontrollably. I cried harder than I ever had before when thinking about Uncle Max's situation.

Sue came behind me and wrapped me in her arms.

"Let it all out," she said, crying along with me. "Just let it all out, dear. This is tough, and I know how close you are to him. It's hard to watch someone you love die. But life will go on, you will see, and you won't forget him, ever. I promise that he will always hold a special place in your heart."

She seemed to be answering all the scary questions I had been worrying about. It felt good for someone to hold me and tell me that I would be okay and that I would remember my uncle. It was a relief to feel what I was feeling without holding it in.

After a while, Sue went to the sink and handed me a wet washcloth to dry my eyes. "Do you feel better now?" she asked.

"I do," I said. "But I need to get home!"

"Okay, but if you need to talk, just know I'm here. You take care of yourself, Dena Bob," she said as she watched me jump back on my bike. "I'll have Dusty call you as soon as she gets home."

I pedaled as fast as I could, and I only stopped when I got to the church. I climbed the stairs and sat on the cement banister. All alone, I cried without shame. It felt like my soul was finally soothed. Only years later would I understand that Sue had helped me to come to terms with accepting his impending death. That small step was a direction in my healing.

Eventually, Uncle Max's health worsened as the treatments became harder and harder. His cancer was beginning to spread throughout his body and affect his liver. His skin and the whites of his eyes began to turn dark yellow. He could no longer sleep comfortably in a regular bed. Aunt Joyce made the decision to have a hospital bed delivered to their house. My parents cleared out the living-room furniture, storing it in the garage; then, a crew brought in the hospital bed and stuck it in the middle of the small living room, where it looked humongous. To make light of the situation, my family began teasing me and telling me that I could be Uncle Max's nurse again.

A couple of days later, we walked over for a visit. Uncle Max just lay there, trying to stay awake for his company. I decided to sit next to him in the yellow rocking chair and began thumbing through the "get well" cards that were placed by his bedside. I began reading them quietly to myself. At the bottom of the pile, I picked up his Bible and opened it up to where a beautiful bookmark had been placed in the center of the book.

Uncle Max was watching me as I began to read the poem on the bookmark quietly to myself. It was called "Footprints in the Sand."

"One night a man had a dream. He dreamed he was walking along the beach with the Lord. Across the sky flashed scenes from his life. For each scene, he noticed two sets of footprints in the sand; one belonged to him, and the other to the Lord."

I read further. "When the last scene of the man's life flashed before him, he looked back at the footprints in the sand. He noticed that many times along the path of his life, there was only one set of footprints. He also noticed that this happened at the very lowest and saddest times in his life."

At this point in the poem, I was questioning why this guy was walking alone and why God would leave him in his most desperate hour, and I felt a little upset and confused by what I was reading. I continued.

"This really bothered him and he questioned the Lord about it. 'Lord, you said that once I decided to follow you, you'd walk with me all the way. But I have noticed that during the most troublesome times in my life, there is only one set of footprints. I don't understand why when I needed you most you would leave me.'"

My thoughts exactly, I thought to myself as I continued reading.

"The Lord replied, 'My precious, precious child, I love you and would never leave you. During your times of trial and suffering, when you see only one set of footprints in the sand, it was then that I carried you.'"

When I read this, my mouth dropped open and I felt shock run through my entire body as the reality of God's love hit me for the first time. I felt tears stream out of my eyes. As Uncle Max watched my reaction, I tried to not make a big deal over what I'd just read. But this was one of those awe-inspiring moments that change your life forever in which you begin to realize that something bigger than you is all around. Maybe, unbeknownst to me, God was holding Uncle Max as he was suffering . . . and just maybe, he was holding me too.

Trying to play it cool, I jumped up and headed to the kitchen, wiping my eyes dry as I walked in, trying not to let my mom and Aunt Joyce see that I'd been crying.

"I'm hungry," I said, digging into the bowl of popcorn sitting beside the stove.

A couple of days later, the phone rang. "Yes, I'll send her right over," I heard Mom say.

Then she turned to me. "Dena, Uncle Max wants you to come over for a while. He has something he wants to give you."

As I opened the back door, I was surprised to see Uncle Max out of his hospital bed and sitting at the table. Aunt Joyce was still hanging onto the phone, talking to my mom.

"She's here now," said Aunt Joyce. "I'll call you later."

"Sit down, Dena. I have something for you," my uncle said, smiling. "Because you bought me that deer with your own money, I wanted to give something special back to you. Joyce and I were in Sterling for a treatment the other day, and we stopped at the Bible Lighthouse store. I found this Bible for you. We had your name engraved on it."

As he handed the beautiful white Bible to me, I felt the essence of this powerful moment engulf me. The tears were unstoppable as I saw my name engraved in golden letters on the bottom of the Bible. *Dena Bob*, with *Kid* under it. It left me speechless. Opening the inside cover, I realized that Uncle Max had signed his name inside.

"This Bible has the answers to everything in life. The more you read it, the more the Holy Spirit will come through to you. You need to understand that God is around you at all times and is always holding you. Now, I got this white Bible for you because on your wedding day; it will match your white dress. I want you to carry it with you when you walk down to marry your future husband, and I want you to know I'll be watching you from heaven. When you choose someone to marry, marry someone who believes wholeheartedly in this book."

Wait a minute! I thought to myself. *I'm only twelve!* I felt myself blushing at the thought of getting married, but it made me feel treasured to know that Uncle Max was actually thinking about my future.

"Now, let's walk outside," he said as he took the Bible out of my hands. I followed him out back under the shade tree where a long white log sat beside the fish pond. The goldfish were swimming, and the water of the pond glistened in the warm spring weather. Aunt Joyce and my mom had recently taken the goldfish out of the stock tanks and put them in their ponds. Sitting on the log, and watching the fish was nice. I didn't have to look at my uncle, especially since I was having trouble holding my tears in.

"The only way to reach heaven is through a relationship with Jesus Christ. You see, Dena, God the Father, sent his only Son, Jesus to be born of the Virgin Mary. He came, as the perfect God, the perfect Son, and as the perfect Holy Spirit to dwell upon this earth in the human flesh. The trinity is God the Father, Jesus the Son, and the Holy Spirit—all separate, yet all one," he said, holding up his two index fingers and thumbs as he made a Triangle. "It's not critical that you or I understand this, but it is critical that you and I believe it. When Jesus became a man, he willingly gave his life for our sins upon the cross. As they beat his bare body with whips and chains, and crushed the crown of thorns deep into his skull, they soon began hammering nails into his hands and feet to hang him upon the wooden cross. The sins of the world were being washed away by the shedding of His blood for all humanity. After His death, He was buried and the Bible says He descended into Hell, and on the third day, He rose again and ascended into heaven, where He is seated at the right hand of the Father. He will come again to judge the living and the dead. If you believe that no human is perfect, except for Jesus, in the flesh, and if you believe that he died for your sins and that God raised him from the dead, you shall be saved. For in John 14:6, we read that Jesus said, 'I am the way, the truth, and the life. No one comes to the Father except through Me.' And Romans 10:13 says, 'Whoever calls on the name of the Lord shall be saved.' And in Ephesians 2:8–9 it reads, 'For by grace you have been saved through faith, and that not of yourselves; it is a gift of God, not of works, lest anyone should boast.'"

Uncle Max took my hands and stared into my eyes to make sure I was following. "This means that once you call on the name of the Lord, you are giving your life to Him, and nothing can ever separate you from God again. Even on your darkest days and the days you feel you're failing, you won't be, because you will be saved by grace."

I hung on to every word my uncle was saying as he continued. "You cannot get to heaven for being a good person. God does not keep score. The Bible tells us that we are all sinners, and we have all fallen short to the glory of God. Eternal life in heaven is a gift. Jesus paid the price at the cross. You can accept it or decline it, just as you can tell me no, you don't want this Bible, or I can tell you no, I don't want the deer. But the choice is yours to make, and only you can decide for yourself."

Holding the Bible up in his hands, he asked, "Will you accept this Bible from me?"

I couldn't bring the words out of my mouth because of the lump that had formed from holding my tears in. I nodded my head yes.

"Then, do you accept the free gift of Jesus Christ at the cross?"

Again, I couldn't speak, nor could I breathe. The lump in my throat exploded in tears, and all that came out of my mouth was, "Yes, I accept the gift of Jesus. I do." As I fell into his skeletal embrace, Aunt Joyce came behind me and wrapped us both in a group hug.

As I pulled away, Uncle Max repeated, "Follow this Bible all your life, and your life will be blessed. This Bible is the living word, and if you read it, you will feel the power of God working in you. When you walk down the aisle carrying this book on your wedding day, just know I'll be watching you from heaven, and your marriage will be blessed by God."

I wanted to get out of there and find a place to absorb all this and cry. But I didn't want to leave this precious moment with my uncle and aunt. When I arrived home, I sat my Bible on the yellow safety mats of our trampoline and began flying back and forth from my stomach to my back as I bounced high. When I stopped and lay down, I opened my Bible and the bookmark of the "Footprints" poem fell out. I read it again, mesmerized by the power of the words: "My precious, precious child, I love you and would never leave you. During your times of trial and suffering, when you see only one set of footprints in the sand, it was then that I carried you."

I smiled as I walked into the house and showed my mom my gift. "Dipstick gave me a Bible with my name on it!" I said proudly, but not looking at her for fear she'd see the tears in my eyes.

"That's very precious! Let me take a look at it." She was impressed as she turned it over in her hands. "Wow, you will have to take care of this one!"

"Yes, I know! He told me I had to carry it down the aisle when I get married, but I don't know that I will ever get married," I said, feeling my cheeks turn red at the very idea.

"That's pretty special! Let's buy a cover for it," she suggested. I treasured that Bible, and as time passed, I held its significance even closer to my heart.

Chapter 38

Death: A Part of Life

"Trust in the Lord *with all your heart, and lean not on your own understanding. In all your ways acknowledge Him, and He shall direct your paths."* —**Proverbs 3:5–6**

Soon, it was summer. It had almost been a full year since we'd received the news of Uncle Max's impending death. Although I'd come to terms with my emotions, I'd learned to avoid the conversation at all costs. I simply soaked in the scene like a sponge as I watched his rapid decline.

James was back for the summer, and as we were jumping on the trampoline, we began talking. "This summer, I bought a suit coat and a nice pair of slacks because last summer I didn't have any nice clothes to wear during a wedding," he said.

As soon as he said that, our thoughts crossed paths, wordlessly, as we realized it would be a funeral this year instead of a wedding. An eerie silence lingered between us.

"Let's go get an ice cream cone," I suggested, to break the uncomfortable moment.

During this troublesome time, my parents began spending the night with Aunt Joyce to help her through the night terrors that my uncle was enduring. One night, he couldn't sleep and complained of constant pain. The only decision left was to send him to the hospital so he could spend his last moments with some relief.

Our family basically moved to the hospital during the days to follow, but I couldn't bear to watch my uncle suffer so much. Mike, James, and I spent most of our time outside playing on the grass. That evening, as I ran outside on the front lawn with Mike and James, the sirens began to ring. As they approached the hospital, they became extremely loud. The sirens announced that an emergency was afoot in this small town. Simply hearing the sirens made my heart stop with worry, and it took me back to that day in the schoolyard so many years ago, when the siren had announced Uncle Max's fall.

In the next half hour, Tom came outside to where my mom was sitting and watching us play. He explained that there had been a car wreck outside of town, and a child had been lost. The news felt strange to take in. Children weren't supposed to die, and certainly not from such horrible incidents.

Mike and James went into the hospital to buy a pop as I sat on the front steps with my hands propping up my face. I was lost in thought when a group of people walked up behind me, crying. It was a desperate cry I'd never heard before.

My mom came and took my arm and led me back into the hospital. She softly said, "Dena, they just lost a child in a car wreck. We need to leave them alone."

Dad sadly said, "I'm sure it's hard for him to look at you, given that they just lost a child."

This made me feel worse for having been there in the first place. I wished I had gone into the hospital when Mike and James went inside. The realization that death doesn't discriminate with respect to age or circumstance was becoming a scary reality.

"Aunt Jean is taking the kids to the Pizza Factory for supper, and we will pick you up on our way home tonight," Mom said, giving me a little squeeze of assurance.

At the Pizza Factory, we ordered a Canadian bacon pizza with homemade curly Q fries and full pitchers of Mountain Dew and Pepsi. The curly Qs were the Pizza Factory's specialty and were so good to eat. Before long, we were laughing and having a good time, singing along to "Jack and Diane" on the loud jukebox that Janeil and Lori had fed quarters to.

A little later, Mom and Dad came in. "Lori and Dena, we're ready to go home. Aunt Joyce is in the car waiting for us. She's spending the night with us since Uncle Max is in the hospital."

For some reason, I intuitively felt that this would be the night my uncle would die. I was restless in my bed, waiting for that middle-of-the-night phone call—similar to the one we had received when Grandma had died.

Sure enough, around two in the morning the phone rang. My heart practically stopped. I lay there for a moment not even breathing, just frozen as I listened closely to my dad's voice.

"Hello, yes, this is Earle. Yes, Joyce Brown is here with us. Yes, I can give her this news. His death was at 1:45 this morning," Dad solemnly repeated. "Yes, thank you for calling."

Before I realized what was happening, I sat straight up in bed and found myself out in the hallway outside my parents' room as Aunt Joyce met me in her dark-red robe. I ran to her, and she engulfed me in a hug. She didn't say a word. We both cried for a long time, and Mom and Dad fell behind us. We all clung together for a long moment. Dad walked out to the kitchen and turned on the bright, blinding lights as Mom picked up the phone and began to call our family members for the devastating, and yet relieving, news of Uncle Max's passing.

He was gone. I had watched him suffer long enough, and although the mourning was deep, I felt relieved that he was in heaven now. But unlike Grandma's death, this time a great sadness also fell over me.

Before 3:00 a.m., family members began showing up on our doorstep with hugs, tears, and—true to my uncle's spirit—laughter. "His suffering is over," I heard someone say.

Tom remarked, "I have to remind myself to eat, and nothing seems to taste very good."

I began to evaluate my own eating habits of late. It seemed as if I had been eating a lot lately, even more than usual.

Maybe I'm kidding myself and I'm not that sad, I thought. *Maybe I had better stop eating or people will think I'm not actually upset about Uncle Max.*

By 8:00 a.m., people began showing up with all kinds of food—from fresh fruit, to bacon and eggs, to donuts and even muffins. I noticed that even Aunt Joyce was eating a donut, so I grabbed one and sat right beside her. I was beginning to understand that people mourn in all different ways.

A whirlwind of activity ensued around us. Aunt Joyce, Julie, and Curt went home to find some nice clothes to take up to the mortuary. Mom and Dad went with them, and the teenagers stayed at our house to swim in the pool all afternoon. The next day, James and I were asked if we would like to go and see the body. At age thirteen, I had never seen a body or been to a funeral—not even my own grandma's. This time, I was ready. I decided I wanted to go.

As we walked into the mortuary, Aunt Joyce took my hand in one of hers and James's hand in the other. I also grabbed Lori's hand. "Now, when we go in, just remember that you don't want to touch him. He's been in a freezer, and he is ice cold. It's a feeling you never want to remember. So just stand back and look," she instructed. I recalled her warning to Lori and me when my grandma died.

Lori and I walked by the casket in our blue dresses, and James was in his suit and nice slacks. It felt strange to see Uncle Max lying there. He'd always been so much larger than life, and yet he now appeared so small and frail. A huge smile was stretched across his face, which had a deep yellow tinge to it. He looked peaceful. I held my breath and wondered how long a person could go without breathing before they, too, would die.

The next day at the funeral, the shock hit me like a freight train. *He is gone. Remember this moment. Remember him! Never forget!*

Pastor Sidebottom conducted the service, which ended with John 3:16, the same verse I was so captivated by when he ended every Sunday sermon.

I still remember the smell of all the beautiful flowers that were sent to the family. One beautiful display had ribbons with words tied to it, explaining who Uncle Max had been: husband, father, uncle, and friend. I remember standing at the cemetery as the American Legion Veterans began shooting guns to honor Uncle Max, who had served in the Navy. I remember them handing Aunt Joyce the folded flag as she sat under the tent next to Curt and Julie. I remember holding hands again with Great-Aunt Olive, as I always had during the Memorial Day service as a small child. This time, not a word was mentioned about being scared of the guns. A moment of connection and sadness passed between us as we both used our free hand to wipe away the tears in our eyes.

By this age, I'd learned that the feelings I couldn't express in conversation with others could be expressed in poetry. Shortly after he passed, I wrote this poem to commemorate all the moments, big and small, that I never wanted to forget:

"Faith in Heaven"

The birds are flying overhead
You wonder where he is.
The sky points to a cloud
You're sure it is his.

The promise and joy of yesterday
Brought sadness and loneliness today.
The secret of tomorrow
Will hold on to its own sorrow.

Hold on to the sweet memories
For that is the key.
Because there is a Heaven
Waiting there for thee.

Chapter 39

A Moment of Truth

"For thus says the Lord God: 'Indeed I Myself will search for My sheep and seek them out.'" —**Ezekiel 34:11**

After the funeral, Aunt Joyce stayed with us for a couple of weeks. When she decided to go back home, she asked if I would stay with her. I was more than happy to keep her company. I couldn't imagine returning home and waking up with the knowledge that Uncle Max would never be coming home. I didn't want her to face this alone.

That first morning, I heard Aunt Joyce wake up and walk to the kitchen to make herself some coffee. I rolled over and fell back to sleep. I had the craziest dream . . . and it felt so real. I saw Uncle Max walk into the bedroom. "Would you like to go for a ride with me in the semi?" he asked, a mischievous smile on his face. "Sure, I would love to!" I said. As he walked out of the room, he went straight through the wall, and within the dream, I realized that he had died.

I was talking to a ghost. I started to follow him and opened a door to the bathroom, where only his face was in the sink, with his tongue sticking out as he laughed at me. I woke up in a panic, my heart racing. The sun shone in through the bedroom window. I was breathing hard and felt totally shaken.

Lying there for a while, I replayed the dream in my head, and it occurred to me that if Uncle Max was going to connect with me, he would do it as a joke—and this made me smile.

As I lay there quietly, I realized that there was company in the kitchen, and I could hear them talking. It was one of our neighbor ladies who lived down the street. I listened closely, and what I heard filled me with wonder.

"Yes, it's been hard coming home, but I have my niece staying with me at night. She's been great company."

"You are blessed to have her here. I'm sure it's comforting not to have to face this completely alone."

"Yes, for now. But she'll be going back to school soon, so I'll be on my own sooner than later!" Aunt Joyce replied.

"You know, I have something to tell you. I hope that it's okay and brings you comfort, but I feel you need to know."

"What is it?" asked Aunt Joyce, a hint of curiosity and alarm in her voice.

"Well, I don't know what you believe in, but I . . . knew that morning that Max had passed away," the neighbor lady said. "I had a dream that night that I was in the hospital watching everything take place, and I saw your mother come and take him to heaven. I know without a doubt it was real, Joyce!"

I heard my aunt gasp. "Oh my stars, I'm sure you're right. I believe in things like this. This is so comforting to me. Thank you for telling me. Life is so full of God's mysterious miracles, and this is one of them."

I wondered just how true this could be, but then I remembered the smile on my uncle's face at the mortuary. It suggested that perhaps he'd seen something before he'd died that gave him comfort. Could it really have been Grandma leading the way to heaven?

As I walked out to the kitchen, I made a coughing sound so they would realize they weren't alone.

"Well, hello, Dena! Did you sleep well last night?" asked Aunt Joyce.

"Yes," I said, deciding I wasn't ready to share my dream.

"Well, I fixed you a Carnation Instant Breakfast," she said, handing me a tall glass of chocolate milk.

For the next couple of weeks, I stayed with Aunt Joyce. I could tell she didn't want me to feel bad for her, and she made every effort not to show her sad emotions. She tried to make our time together fun, sometimes playing tic-tac-toe or rummy before bedtime. For the most part, I was only with her during the evenings and overnight. But I slept right next to her in the same bed, and sometimes at night, I could hear her crying in her sleep.

Before long, the school year was back in session, and I entered eighth grade. I was glad to be back in my own bed, but I felt guilty leaving Aunt Joyce at night, fighting the demons of this tragedy alone in her darkest hours. But I was ready for the new challenges of school and playing basketball. Still, my favorite all-time activity was to ride horses, even though I hadn't been riding much since T. J. was sold a couple of years ago.

One day during fall, Curt called on the phone and my mom answered.

"Oh, hi, Curt. Yes, I think that would be a great idea. She's sitting right here. I'll let you talk to her." She turned to me. "Dena, Curt would like to talk to you."

When I took the phone, my cousin said, "Dena, I have Blaze down at my house, and I haven't had any time to ride him. If I brought him up to Mom's, with his feed, would you be willing to do chores every day and take care of him? I'll bring his saddle up, and you can ride whenever you want!"

"Sure, I would be happy to!" I replied, excited to finally have a horse in our backyard again.

Blaze was a much taller horse than what I was used to, but he was dog gentle. When I would feed him in the evenings, he would follow me with the bucket of grain over to Uncle Max's old, yellow '57 Chevy pickup that sat under the tree. I would toss the bucket on the tailgate, then climb on top of the pickup to jump onto Blaze, bareback and without a halter. While he ate, I would nuzzle against his neck with my arms around him, staying warm against his body as the chilly evening set in.

Some nights I would put a halter and a lead rope on him and then ride him around our small pasture bareback, building my confidence to get into a trot and eventually a lope. Blaze had a tinge of a Tennessee walker breed in him, which meant he had a gait that was as smooth as glass, with a gentle rocking horse lope. Riding felt like healing. As I contemplated our lives and how dramatically my own had changed over the summer, I began to understand the value of this memory.

One Sunday, Julie walked into our house after we had just finished our fried-chicken dinner. "This morning, I brought both Sally and Chiefer up to Mom's, and I thought maybe we could all go riding this afternoon. Lori, you can ride Chiefer. Dena, you can saddle up Blaze."

That Sunday was spent down at the arena riding our afternoon away, which reminded me of the summer three years ago before Uncle Max became sick and before T.J. was sold. It felt good to be riding again, galloping with the wind as if we were flying. That evening, as we unsaddled, I prayed that we would have many more days of carefree riding, which felt like important healing for all three of us.

One winter afternoon, the snow was falling and covering the ground, but the sun was still shining through the glass pane of our bay window.

"Mom, isn't it beautiful how God lets the snow reflect into crystals?"

"Yes, it is!" she said abruptly as she went about her chores. She didn't seem like she was in the mood to talk about God.

"Mom, do you believe Uncle Max went to heaven?" I asked bluntly, taking in the beauty of the moment and not really feeling sad anymore, only curious about heaven. The moment reminded me of the 1977 blizzard we spent with Uncle Max pretending we were the Waltons.

"Honestly, I really don't know what I believe," she said. She stopped folding clothes and looked straight at me.

I stared at her in astonishment. I couldn't believe that my mother didn't know what she believed. "So, you don't know if you believe in heaven and hell?"

"No, I don't," she said brusquely, "and I don't like people who try and push their religion on me."

"But, Mom, we've been going to church for a couple of years. I know I believe! And I'm sure Aunt Joyce believes. Why don't you?"

"Dena, I know you believe. I've watched you go to Bible school and come home excited. I've seen how it affected you when Max gave you a Bible, and that's fine. I will never try to take that away from you." I could tell she was trying to be patient with me, but it was hard for me to hear my mother admit that she didn't share my beliefs.

I earnestly spoke up. "I believe God sent His son to die for us. I also believe there is a heaven and a hell. And if you don't believe, you will go to hell for eternity. You don't want to go to hell, do you?"

The room went quiet, and she studied me for a second.

"Dena, I am a good person, and we have been going to church pretty regularly. If there is a God who is all-loving, then He wouldn't send me to hell. My daddy didn't believe either, but he was the best person I have ever known. You can't push religion on me, Dena. I will make my own choice, as you will too. And if my daddy's in hell, I want to go there, too, just so I can be with him."

I sat with my mouth wide open, stunned and almost in tears. How could she say such a thing? "Even if I'm in heaven, you would still rather go to hell to be with your dad?" I asked as shock ran through my body.

"That's enough talk out of you for one day," she said. I could tell I'd hit a nerve in her that I had never hit before. I vowed in that moment I would never talk to her about my Christian faith again. I was a child who wanted to please my mom under all circumstances. If she told me she didn't want me to mention it, I wouldn't go against her wishes—even though I felt she was dead wrong.

As the months passed, I no longer felt like a child. I was in eighth grade, and feelings of confusion often swept over me. I felt that no one really understood what was going on in my head. Losing Uncle Max had been like losing a second dad. And it seemed like I'd grown up simply by watching my aunt deal with the loss while staying with her at her house.

My uncle's influence lived on within me, and my faith in God was deepening inside me as I watched my aunt lead by example with her own faith in God. I became a strong recruiter for inviting my non-Christian friends to church and youth groups—all thanks to Uncle Max, who gave me the freedom to deeply believe in Christianity no matter what anyone else around me thought.

As the seasons turned into another year and Labor Day weekend came around, the Old Settlers' Picnic was here once again. That year, I rode Blaze in the downtown parade. As I was waiting in the line of horses, Julie was on Sally and stood right beside me, grinning ear to ear.

"Dena," she said excitedly. "You've got to look! You'll never believe it!"

Juiie Marshall's painting for the 100th Old Settlers Picnic.

I glanced at everyone around us on horses, and I finally spotted what she was talking about. Two small children, around seven and eight years old, were on a spotted dappled-gray quarter pony, all dressed up in their cowboy attire with boots, spurs, cowboy hats, and shiny toy guns.

I glanced at Julie, and we both smiled. "I never realized that T. J. was such a small horse when I was riding him," I said, shaking my head in disbelief. My heart was jumping with joy.

After the parade, I climbed off Blaze and walked over to the kids.

"Hey," I said, with a smile. "Your horse is a beautiful dappled gray. May I pet him?"

"Sure! His name is Apple, because he likes apples," said the smaller boy, smiling up at me.

Looking into T. J.'s eyes, I could tell he remembered me too. He watched me and even tried to follow as I backed up from him. The boys held him back with their reins.

"Well, he looks like a great little horse," I said to the boys. I gave T. J. a pat on the neck, and with tears in my eyes, I said, "Take care of these kids who love you so much! And you boys take good care of him too."

At that moment, Mom, Aunt Joyce, and Julie came up behind me as the boys' parents greeted them. Aunt Joyce cooed over seeing T. J. "It's our little T. J.!" she cried out, walking over to pet him. "I'm glad to see you have some little boys that love on you. Aren't these boys cute, Dena?" she asked, looking straight at me to see how I was handling this.

"Is this the girl who rode T. J. before we bought him and before we changed his name to Apple?" the boys' mother asked.

I nodded. "Yes, and he's the best little horse in the world!"

"Well you did a great job with him."

"I just rode him! Julie gets the credit for training him," I said.

At that moment, I realized I had finally forgiven Julie for selling T. J. Even though I didn't say so, I hoped she knew. Riding T. J. was not something I was entitled to; it was a gift I had been given, and it ended up offering me the best summer of my life. Nothing could ever take that away from me. In that moment, I felt an enormous amount of love for both Julie and this dappled-gray pony that had stamped his hoofprints right into the center of my heart.

"Come on, Dena," Julie said, grabbing me by the arm. "Tie Blaze up at the horse trailer and come be my partner in the egg contest."

I quickly tied Blaze next to Julie's horse, and we ran to Main Street to stand in line for the egg toss. I loved this game, but I never got far before I dropped the egg and was disqualified.

Julie and I were up against at least fifty or more teams; one by one, they were dropping their eggs like flies, but we held on. I took a step backward each time I caught the egg and before I threw it back to Julie. It came down to three teams, and we were still going strong. In the front of the crowd were Aunt Joyce, my mom, my dad, and Great-Aunt Olive, who were cheering us on with huge smiles on their faces. I was sure this was going to be the year we would win. The lady beside me dropped her egg, and now it was our turn. If we could just hold onto it one more time, the next couple might drop theirs, which would declare us the winner of two brand-new food coolers.

"Ready?" asked Julie.

"Ready!" I said, anticipating that I *would* catch the egg. As she threw it, I caught it in my bare hands, and the yellow yolk fell between my fingers. The whole crowd made a sound of disappointment, and the next couple was declared the winner. Julie and I smiled at each other. Then we met in the middle for a quick, bittersweet hug.

"Good job," we both said to each other, with tears in our eyes and big smiles on our faces. We had just lost, but we were so proud of how far we had come.

After the egg contest, I hopped back onto Blaze and glanced over at my mom and Aunt Joyce, who were getting ready to walk to the street races to watch their grandchildren run. Vonie and Tom now had boys of their own, and Curt and Barb had two little girls who would be competing too. Mom and Aunt Joyce both had smiles on their faces, which made me feel happy. As I rode Blaze back to the barn to unsaddle him; I heard the loudspeaker projecting my dad's voice down Main Street as the kids were ready to race.

I was glad to be by myself with Blaze. Indeed, I felt as if I had come full circle this morning. Seeing T. J. being ridden by those adorable boys made me realize I had outgrown him well before Julie sold him. And sharing this moment with Julie warmed my heart.

While loping Blaze down the dirt road, I knew I wouldn't have him much longer, as Curt's two little girls would soon be learning to ride. I no longer felt sad about losing Blaze; rather, I was happy that my cousins would have the same experience I'd had with T. J.

Kids running a gunny sack race. Used with permission of The Yuma Pioneer.

Although I still wanted to own a horse of my very own, I knew my parents wouldn't let that happen. High school would begin on Tuesday, and so would a new chapter in my life. I was scared and excited all at once.

That day, I took my time unsaddling and brushing down Blaze, creating a precious memory to last a lifetime.

***

Even now, I remember those moments as I rock back and forth on my mom's memorial swing, reminiscing over my childhood. I feel

The memorial wall.

a little disoriented. It feels strange to have sat on this bench for only thirty minutes right in the heartland of where I grew up. So much has changed. But looking to the south, the house I grew up in is still right there, down that long dirt road I rode my bike and horses on so long ago. Today, my mind has traveled through space and time, seeing my old memories painted so vividly before me, like visions in a book. The stories we hold are bred right into us and engraved in our souls. Our creativity in all we do lives in the artwork that's painted on barn walls, our writings we leave behind, and all the evidence of our hard work— the sweat, determination, and blood that we willingly sacrifice on the land upon which we live. Our beliefs and morals leave the legacy that we pass on to our children and grandchildren for generations to come. As I leave, I watch as a family of four strolls through the park pulling their giggling children in a little red wagon. My heart is consoled.

Arriving home, I realize I have a message from Julie: "Mom passed away after you left. I'll call you later with the details of the service."

I sit down and concentrate on just breathing. Today, I have come to terms with my aunt's death. I no longer feel sad, because I know our family is slowly being reunited in heaven. I fully understand now, that life is just a journey to eternity.

Listening closely, I hear our diesel pickup pull into our driveway. Randy and the kids are home from checking the cattle with their grandparents. As they come running in, they engulf me in a hug that feels incredibly safe and uplifting.

"How was your day?" I ask them.

"It was good, but we're starved!"

"Good, because I brought pizza!"

"Yummy! Thanks, Mom!" they say.

The realization that this moment won't last forever invades my soul as I swallow the lump in my throat and wipe a tear before anyone notices.

A couple of days later, we gathered around Uncle Max's gravesite, much the same as we did thirty years ago. This time, we have our own branches of children and grandchildren standing beside us as we say goodbye to Aunt Joyce. It's clear that a whole new generation has joined our circle, and we are temporarily the leaders of a marching band, moving to the rhythm of our own drum.

At the end of the service, Aunt Dolores stands tall with her dark sunglasses. As she strolls by, she gives each of us a squeeze on our hands. I can feel the hurt and love that radiate between our souls. She is the last one standing from my mom's generation.

The next day, we head to a family reunion on my dad's side. Uncle Swede, the last of all my dad's siblings, has an extremely hard time seeing all of his nieces and nephews without our parents. As he embraces me, I hear the echo of my dad's voice crack through his tears. "I love you, Dena!" he cries.

My mind drifts back to a few years ago, when Aunt Jean was dying of cancer. I remember hearing the echo of my mother's voice through her tears. "You be strong and live your life well," she said with pure wisdom.

After coming home, I sit and listen to the beautiful music of our children playing outside. Their laughter echoes through my heart. I quickly grab a pen to preserve the memory. My emotions run through my body and out through my fingertips, spilling my tears on to the paper.

I dedicate this poem to my three beautiful children. I want them to understand that when life throws you curves and you feel that you can no longer stand . . . that, my child, is when the Lord will carry you.

"Family Reunion"

We only have a memory of yesterday
When we were the ones to run and play

A care in the world was not to be
We loved each other, our family

Cousins playing, the best of friends
Who would have thought it would ever end?

Circle of life spinning fast
Gone are the days of our recent past

Parents gone and now we see
We are the ones holding the key

Searching for something that can't be found
In a memory of scrapbooks and stories bound

My heart, it aches, as we say goodbye
The tears begin to form in my eye

A hug from my uncle standing strong
My dad's voice echoes in his song

Watching my aunt struggle with cancer
Like watching a rerun of my mother

Hugging my children tight as can be
Tomorrow, they'll be the ones holding the key

Time just keeps slipping away
We only have a memory of yesterday

But remember, life is what you make it—
and we always have the gift of the presence, today
And the eternity of heaven, tomorrow,
as long as we accept Jesus Christ at the Cross of Calvary

The Probasco cousins.

Discussion Guide Questions

In the first chapter, we get a sense of Dena's closeness with the rest of the family members, especially her Uncle Max. How do you feel this sets the stage for the rest of this book?

Dena's relatives are always gifting her with animals. But her animals are always taken away in some form or another, either through death or her parents selling them. However, there is always a sense of closure, even if it occurs years later. How have you experienced closure in your life?

Dena is carefree in the cemetery and running wild until her grandmother scolds her and tells her she is stepping on the grave of her grandfather. How does this moment carry on to the memory of when her grandmother's grave is being covered over with dirt?

Dena witnesses her mom giving Curt money from selling Roast Beef. Later, Dena begins to understand the meaning of this biblical statement: "It is better to give than to receive." How was this moment significant with respect to later acts of generosity in the book? How is the gift of generosity a part of God's gift to us?

When young Dena is gifted the pony from Uncle Keith, did you understand the connection that her Uncle Keith played Santa Claus when Dena asked Santa for a pony?

When her uncle Max introduced Dena to the owl, and Dena scared the owl away because she was too excited, do you feel that her uncle responded with discipline and love?

When Dena sees the auras of her relatives, she realizes that she is the only one who can perceive them. Do you believe that some people are gifted with spiritual sight? Are kids more prone to this? Why or why not?

Dena's mom asks her if she would like to view her grandmother's body. Her dad speaks up and explains that she shouldn't because of his own experience in losing his dad at such a young age. Do you feel this was the deciding factor for Dena? Why or why not?

When Dena is at the old farmhouse after her grandmother dies, she looks to the trees and imagines her grandparents watching her play. Later, she is the quiet witness to the adults talking. When her aunt says that she felt and saw her mom's presence when she died, this bothers Dena. Why do you think that is?

By witnessing how the adults talked to Dena about death, how did you feel? Do adults ignore the big questions that kids might silently think about? How can this story help adults reach out to kids?

Dena doesn't feel sad when her grandmother dies; instead, she feels guilty. She feels that her grandmother is happy to be in heaven. But later, she is heartbroken when her uncle is dying. Why did her feelings change? Do you believe that younger kids have a sense of heaven that adults may not have? How does this affect the way we deal with painful situations?

Uncle Max secretly pays close attention to how his illness impacts his young niece. We see how Dena gifts him with a cement deer, then he turns and gifts her with a Bible that changes her life. What kind of impact does her uncle leave on her when he advises her to carry the white Bible down the aisle when she gets married?

Do you believe that Uncle Max prayed for his young niece to find a Christian man to marry in her future? Do you believe you can change the world with your gifts and prayers you offer to people? Is this how we become ambassadors for Christ?

Dena's parents grew up on a farm and attended a one-room schoolhouse. During Dena's kindergarten year, she attended a two-room schoolhouse, and her kids today attend Arickaree, an extremely small country school. How has this changed through the years with public schools versus homeschooling?

How is Uncle Max an ambassador for Christ? How does his life and death inspire Dena to follow in his footsteps?

Dena's mom states that she would rather go to hell to be with her dad who didn't believe rather than go to heaven even if Dena would be there. As a side note, Dena believes her mom accepted Christ before she died. That, in itself, is another story.

When Julie tells Dena she is selling T. J., Dena's heart breaks. But later, she realizes that her time riding T. J. was a gift. How can we rise above our heartaches and find the gifts in hard situations?

We see Dena attend Bible school at a young age and catch a glimpse of God's profound love. Do you believe that kids should be introduced to God and His teachings at a young age? Why or why not?

In what ways can this story encourage us to stamp the world with our own footprints that leave an everlasting impression on the heart of this world? What were your biggest takeaways, and how will you apply them to your life?

About the Author

DENA MASON is married to the love of her life, her farmer and rancher Randy. Together they have three beautiful children, Shayna, Jared, and Maranda. They live on a farm in the Eastern Plains of Colorado and proudly raise cattle and wheat alongside Randy's parents, Merrill and Georgia Mason. They live close to Randy's brother, Rodney, and his wife, Bridgett Mason. Their grown children are living in the state of Colorado.

Dena's children proudly attend Arickaree Indians School, a small country school surrounded by wheat fields.

Although Dena refuses to tell you what her worst day of life has been, because she hasn't seen the future, she will tell you her best days have been when she accepted Christ as her personal Savior, when she said "I do" to Randy, and when each one of her three children were born.

Dena stays busy helping her husband on the farm; running to all the activities, including FFA and 4-H, that her children are involved in; babysitting for the local teachers' kids; writing for the weekly newspaper; and raising golden retriever puppies. Her love for horses never waivered, and she still finds time to go riding with her kids.

ABOUT THE AUTHOR

Dena decided to write this book to commemorate her fond childhood memories of her beloved family. She believes she can capture a moment and preserve a memory through her writings and photography. This book was written as a legacy for her family and a gift to her children and future grandchildren with the hopes that they, too, will pass down the love of nature to their families and realize the importance of knowing Christ as their personal Savior.

Visit the author's website at authordenamason.com.

CPSIA information can be obtained
at www.ICGtesting.com
Printed in the USA
FSHW012300111121
86092FS

9 781955 043106